His Name Was Murder

Real Crime Stories from the Prosecutor

Phil LeVota

ISBN-10:0-692-62465-1
ISBN-13:978-0-692-62465-4

Table of Contents

INTRODUCTION

Kansas City, Missouri is a city of more than 470,000 people and is the 37th largest city by population in the nation. It is also the 23rd largest city by area in the country. However, the city itself gets the majority of its nationwide popularity by including the entire metropolitan area in its identity. The *'city proper'* itself expands into three counties and borders the Kansas state line but the *'metro'* area consists of over 25 cities and 5 counties. The *"KC area"* expands about a thirty mile circumference from the city's downtown and it is all full of diehard Chiefs football and Royals baseball fans.

If you are from another part of the country, you may have met someone who said they are from "Kansas City" when actually they lived in Lee's Summit, Missouri or Overland Park, Kansas. There is a great sense of unity in being "from Kansas City" between the suburbs and the city proper when it comes to sports teams, area perception, and Midwest pride. Recently, the Huffington Post said *"Kansas City is the most up-and-coming city in the country."* The site ranked Kansas City as the most exciting "it" city in the United States. The food, Midwestern hospitality, and music were all highlighted as reasons the city is so special.

The entire metropolitan area is what creates this amazing dynamic that puts "Kansas City" on the map and that includes the suburbs. However, the large difference between the folks in Lenexa and Blue Springs with the citizens in the "city" is that they do not share the same problems of violent crime that occur in the inner city of Kansas City, Missouri.

In the United States, the "inner city" of any major city always has the most extensive amount of violent crime compared to other areas of the town or the suburbs. It is in this area which includes the usually older, poorer, and more densely populated central section of a city where crime rates are highest. I'll defer to others more educated and studied in the areas of demographics, economics, and other issues to pontificate on the reasons for why this exists but in Kansas City that is most definitely the case. In relation to dealing with serious crime, it falls upon the Kansas City Missouri Police Department to investigate the crime and the Jackson County Prosecuting Attorney's office to prosecute the offenders. This book involves real life crime stories from the sometimes violent heart of Kansas City from the perspective of a prosecuting attorney with over a decade of representing the citizens of the state of Missouri and victims of violent crime in Jackson County, Missouri.

When you work as a prosecutor, you are routinely asked about cases you are working on because of the compelling interest people have in stories of crime, violence, law enforcement, and the courts. You just have to look to the TV and successful television programs like all the CSI spinoffs, Law and Order, and many others to realize that people love to hear about crime stories. When these are "real" stories and happen in your city, it is even that much more interesting. So in many social settings, a prosecutor will find themselves being asked about their cases, other cases in the news, and other areas of their job.

The best and most rewarding experiences I ever had in talking about my cases in my time as a prosecutor were the times I spent with my grandparents while they were still alive. Every Tuesday evening I would have dinner with my grandfather, Sam LeVota, and then after he passed, with my grandmother, Ruth Provance. My grandparents were both widowed and loved having visitors. And as a young, underpaid government attorney, I loved getting a home cooked meal every week. Over these dinners, we would talk about all kinds of things like current events and family history and I cherished the time. But it never mattered what the topic was we started with, we always got around to what cases I was working on. They would ask me about the cases and we would discuss them.

As much as they enjoyed hearing about their grandson's job, I enjoyed the conversation because I learned a great deal from their questions and comments. Their insight and questions made me realize what issues non-lawyers picked up on and thought were important. This helped me immensely in my trial preparation and presentation to identify issues to jurors without legal background who are just regular people. I chalk up a part of my successes in almost fifty jury trials to those conversations. It were those Tuesday night dinners and the questions: *"What are you working on now?"* that were the inspiration for me to take the time to sit down, organize this book, and get these stories in a printed form to share with others.

These cases are real crimes and are prosecutions that occurred in Jackson County, Missouri. I had a difficult time deciding whether to use everyone's real names or not because they are public records. However, when I thought of victim's families, witnesses, and other individuals, I was concerned that this could bother them. So in moving forward, I substituted some actual names for pseudo names to protect the innocent. However, the stories are real. The following chapters of real crime come from thousands of pages of reports, hundreds of hours of interviews, and days of trial testimony. I took some literary license to get inside of the head of individuals on their thoughts at the time just to tell you a better story, but these are the real stories of crime in Kansas City.

Special thanks to the men and women of the Kansas City Police Department for their professionalism and dedication to law enforcement. Thank you to Charli Craven for your work helping me get the real live cases to printed form. And special thanks to the men and women of the Jackson County Prosecutor's office where, at the time, they employed some of the best trial attorneys, investigators, and support staff in this country. Enjoy.

1

The Robbery Gone Terribly Wrong

Drug dealing in Jackson County is a competitive sport and being good at it takes a lot of expertise and knowledge. However, Dennis Moore had a nose for marketing and a hard-edged personality that kept his clients returning and his business running better than any of his numerous competitors. Moore had a disciplined advertising practice that consisted of a combination of routinely being in the same location for his sales, added with just a little bit of intimidation to his customers. That methodology promoted his product without him ever having to say a word.

Dennis Moore was well known in his Kansas City neighborhood. He was a man easily recognized as he always accessorized himself with red clothing, a flashy car, and his gold grill in the same way a wealthy woman might flash her gaudy diamonds. The ostentatious 24 year old drove a custom 1971 Chevrolet Impala convertible. He was proud of it because it was built the same year he was born and he cruised around town with the sole intention of drawing attention.

However, despite Moore's daunting yet proficient methods, he wasn't the only drug dealer with gang ties in town and other dealers and their gang members didn't take kindly to people cutting in on their market. Gang retaliation was an endless cycle. Moore's in-your-face style worked well for soliciting customers but it put his competition on the defensive and when men like this were defensive, it meant there would be violence.

Moore loved his flashy persona and his peach-colored car with a flawless paint job. His car and expensive wheels were the envy of many young men on the streets and even his other rivals in the drug sales arena. These "envious" guys were not the kind to respect someone's car and be encouraged to start saving their money to go buy something they liked. No, they were more the kind to utilize the practice of taking what they wanted, regardless of the consequences. Unfortunately, this was a commonly practiced sin in the neighborhood. This sort of crime between drug dealers went unreported to the police and violence won the day. Moore knew that, but his displays of grandiosity were selfishly self-promoting the sole agenda of trying to become one of county's biggest independent drug dealers. He didn't care what others thought. He was just focused on his productivity. He was productive because buyers knew that when that flashy car was out and about, Moore was open for business.

Nineteen-year old Johnny Chapple wasn't an official gang member but he hung with men that were deeply involved in the gang culture. Even though Dennis Moore wore the 'opposite' color than the guys that Johnny typically associated with, Johnny's alliance with the color *blue* faded whenever Moore came around. As a customer of Dennis Moore, Johnny became friends with the drug dealer with the flamboyant car. The gang stuff didn't matter to Johnny and he was more concerned about hanging with Dennis and making money than he was worried about what color he wore.

In the last summer weekend of 1995, with the convertible top down, Johnny rode in the passenger's seat of Moore's car. It was over 90 degrees in a very hot Kansas City August. The heat index was just over 100 but the air felt cool as it rushed passed the two men in the car on that sunny day. Johnny smiled and hung his arm outside the window and tapped the side of the car door to a loud beat of the 2Pac's *"California Love:"*

"Now let me welcome everybody to the wild, wild west
A state that's untouchable like Elliot Ness
The track hits ya eardrum like a slug to ya chest
Pack a vest for your Jimmy in the city of sex
We in that sunshine state with a bomb ass hemp beat
The state where ya never find a dance floor empty
And pimps be on a mission for them greens
Lean mean money-making-machines serving fiends
I been in the game for ten years making rap tunes
Ever since honeys was wearing Sassoon
Now it's '95 and they clock me and watch me
Diamonds shining looking like I robbed Liberace!"

Moore and Chapple drove through their neighborhood and, like always, the neighborhood saw and heard them and knew they were looking to make a deal. As if the metallic painted vehicle was the feature attraction of an on-going car show, it always had its spectators. It was a holiday weekend and the "lookers" and shoppers were even more numerous because they were looking for a better summer 'high' and more entertainment than just barbeque and beer. In the similar way children wait for the ice cream truck, people gathered in the streets and waited for the *'Dennis Moore vehicle'* selling a product not-so-similar to ice cream. To the crowd, it was a typical and average afternoon. Everyone was socializing. Some were drinking and some doing drugs. Some were doing both. However, one of the onlookers wasn't pleased with the car or the crowd around the car. One man didn't care for everything that this "Dennis Moore Show" was all about and that man was 19 year old Calvin Miller.

Calvin Miller was without a doubt the most violent gang member inside the circle that Johnny Chapple hung out with. Calvin Miller had little patience for the opposing gang and even less patience for any of them who crossed over into conflicting territory. Everyone has heard of the phrase "turf wars." Well it wouldn't be surprising if that phrase was coined right here in this KC neighborhood. Gang members felt very strongly about the boundaries of their area or their turf and did not like it when the other gangs infringed upon their streets. Gangs felt disrespected when others did this and these disputes weren't settled by a mediator in a court room. These "disses" were settled by guns and violence.

Calvin was irritated by Dennis Moore and also pissed off that his friend Johnny Chapple was with him. However, that particular weekend, Calvin should have been happy instead of mad because he had just been released from the Jackson County Jail. He had just bailed out on an assault case and Calvin was free for the time being. Calvin was angry at the men, but his irritation and bad attitude was mostly motivated because he was broke, in legal trouble, and desperate for funds.

Calvin Miller had a terrible reputation and seemed to lack the standard collection of emotions and rational insight that most people have; nonetheless, he maintained a prolific repertoire of job titles. He also had an accomplished membership with a highly recognizable organization that kept him busy and respected by his colleagues. However, his employment choices and societal affiliation were less than legitimate. Some of his emotionally detached occupations were "'robber of drug dealers" and "murderer of rivals" to name a few. Those closest to him described him as 'deranged' and 'trigger happy.' It were those traits, along with his gun, that gained him a lot of what he thought was respect. But since he was so quick tempered and unstable, the respect he thought he had earned from others was probably more accurately defined as fear.

On September 6, 1995, Marc Powell, a stocky, 23-three-year-old, small-time drug dealer, picked up his roommate, 22 year-old Mathew Gulley, from the bus stop and drove to their buddy Trevor Wilson's house on Florence Avenue. Trevor seemed to be hosting a little get together but not the kind of "get together" that most people reading this book will be thinking about. It was more like several young men, with maliciousness in their eyes, hanging out at someone's house. Not just some friends spending time together but a group of young men who were involved in criminal enterprise. Not particularly planning on a specific crime, but always ready to get into some sort of wrongdoing.

Either way, Wilson, Powell, and Gulley were gathered around the side of Wilson's house and were smoking PCP and pot when two other gang members, Calvin Miller and Johnny Chapple showed up. The five young men who all had some kind of learned criminal background talked about what had been going on in the street. They didn't just talk about criminal behavior but talked about all sorts of topics. They talked about television, drugs, girls, fights, and other things as they hung out in the summer heat.

In that alley, the topic of conversation of the group turned to Dennis Moore and his way of driving around flashing his "shit" and their shared dislike for it. It was guys making fun of another and in a somewhat light hearted mood with each man taking his verbal jabs at Moore's physical demeanor and his car. As they smoked and drank beer, the topics went on to girls and sports but the topic soon returned to Dennis Moore and his disrespecting the gang on more than one occasion. At some point, Calvin Miller's tone changed from jovial to outright aggressive as he led the conversation expressing his dislike of Moore. But then Calvin's tone became even more than anger about Moore, Miller told the group he had a very serious problem with Johnny Chapple's interactions with Moore.

Everyone knew about Moore being a Blood gang member but Calvin made sure to tell the other men about their buddy Johnny Chapple hanging around with and running with Moore. It was clear that Miller adamantly felt that Johnny's actions were nothing less than a gang betrayal to them. It might not have just been Johnny's actions alone that had Calvin in such a violent mood. Calvin's current financial status had him more worked up than usual and calling Johnny out as a defector only added fuel to his already intolerant flame. Calvin's anger went on as he explained he just maybe had found a way to use the betrayal to his advantage and his "friend" Johnny became the collateral Calvin needed to pad his empty pockets. As the conversation was going, Johnny's brother, Ronald Chapple showed up and joined in.

In this narrow alleyway between two houses, Johnny continued to defend his relationship with Dennis Moore as just business and raised his voice to Calvin. The two men screamed at each other until everyone could see Calvin hit his breaking point. Calvin abruptly pushed Johnny in the chest with both hands and Johnny fell back against the brick wall of the outside of the house. Calvin grabbed Johnny by his shirt, pulled it up against his neck and, out of nowhere, pulled a gun.

16

Calvin now had the end of his Glock 9 pressed into Johnny's neck and the right side of his face as the gun clicked. Calvin kept screaming and was nose-to-nose with him. Johnny felt the tiny stings of Calvin's spit on his face and the cold steel pressing very hard against his neck. The rest of the men didn't dream of getting between Calvin's gun and whoever he was mad at and even Johnny's own brother watched helplessly. It's not that twenty-one-year-old Ronald Chapple didn't feel scared and concerned for his little brother but he just watched nonetheless. Ronald didn't want to challenge Calvin. He knew it was a challenge he couldn't win.

As Calvin pressed the gun to Johnny's neck, he offered Johnny one way to make things right. Calvin told Johnny that the only way he could prove his loyalty to them was to help them rob Dennis Moore. Johnny's first reaction was to say "no." He quickly rejected that idea because he knew how trigger happy Calvin was so he reluctantly agreed. Calvin wouldn't have responded well to Johnny saying no and he told Johnny not only would he help the gang rob Dennis Moore, Johnny was going to be happy about it. Calvin said there was not going to be any of this sad crap about them taking down a rival gang member. He said to Johnny, *"Oh you're going to help us rob that boy and you are going to smile the whole time."*

Another one of the onlookers to the Calvin and Johnny fight and development of the robbery plan was Marc Powell. Marc Powell and Calvin Miller had been friends since childhood and just like Calvin, Powell similarly appeared deficient in his ability to adhere to conventional social values. To Powell, committing crimes was more than lining his pockets and increasing his social status, it was a predatory sport. Like most hunters, the pursuit was where he took the most pleasure so when Calvin suggested they rob one of their rivals, Powell accepted the challenge.

17

Powell had his eye on Moore's high profile Impala since the first day Dennis Moore had paraded it down the neighborhood streets. Powell believed Calvin had a great plan to take Moore's stash of cash. Plus stealing his money would resolve all of their immediate money issues. With a history of violence and seemingly no fear, Powell and Calvin were in harmony that summer day as they started talking about and plotting a scheme to ensure they made some summer cash. The benefactor of their summer windfall would be Dennis Moore.

With a little help from their friends, Powell and Calvin anticipated that filling their wallets would be as easy as withdrawing money from an ATM. Calvin dropped an ultimatum on Johnny and gave him his marching orders. The other three men were drafted into service into the impeding profitable adventure and Powell strategized a trip to Moore's residence on Indiana Avenue. They all said they would meet back at the same place in three hours.

They all surely thought they had a great idea but the plan, outlined by Calvin mostly consisted of, *"We are going to go in there and take his shit and that mother fucker better not even think about not giving it up or he's fucked."* Calvin went on to say, *"You mother fuckers aren't going to have to do a thing. I got this. You can just watch to see how this shit is done."* The plan was more bravado than substance but the men left thinking they had some sort of advanced, strategic military operation in the planning.

The saying goes that "idle hands are the devil's workshop" and that alleyway at Trevor Wilson's house was that workshop. Six men were about to embark on an evening that would change not only their lives, but other lives forever. To keep the story straight, the players in this devilish production were Calvin Miller, Johnny Chapple, Ronald Chapple, Marc Powell, Matthew Gulley, and Trevor Wilson. This story is complicated trying to keep track of all the different names with so many guys, but hang in there, it gets even more complex.

Later that night, six young men piled inside two cars and headed in the direction of Dennis Moore's house. In a yellow Cadillac that was just as showy as Moore's car, the two Chapple brothers led the way. They were followed by Trevor Wilson, Calvin Miller, Marc Powell, and Matthew Gulley in Trevor Wilson's Orange Caprice Classic. Although Calvin and Powell were the planners of the robbery, the other four were not particularly unwilling participants in the pending robbery about to take place. Everyone knew what was going down and they did not go in with clean hands. All six males, still high from a full day of partying, each had a gun and pulled up to Moore's house with the plan to take whatever they could from Dennis Moore.

Maybe it was Dennis Moore's profitable drug dealing history or maybe it was the nice car, but somehow he ended up with a longtime girlfriend named Natasha Morgan. Twenty-four-year-old Natasha Morgan, like her boyfriend, had a flare for overdressing and bright red lipstick painted her full lips on any given day. She wore a thick layer of eye shadow, large hoop earrings, and even though she was unemployed, her attire demonstrated just the opposite. Raised in a wealthy neighborhood by upper middleclass parents, Natasha was once setup for a very different life. However, as some kids often do, she strayed into a darker lifestyle and a more complicated type of living. Natasha was looking for something more exciting. In doing so, she foolishly followed the wrong crowd, bypassed a life with a secure financial connection, and accepted one filled with drug addiction and illegitimate ways.

People who make poor choices inevitably find themselves in undesirable situations and Natasha was no different. By the time she was twenty-one, she was pregnant and had no permanent residence to live with her soon to be baby boy. She was in a bad way but was smart enough to be able to find a way to survive. Despite her personal choice to migrate to a less resourceful habitat than Blue Springs, Missouri, she found her own way to endure and instinctively learned that scheming was a great survival tactic. Natasha's best tool for successful schemes was to use her small child as she found that everyone's heart was always softer when a baby was involved.

As Natasha's parents struggled through many years of disappointing attempts to bring their daughter back to the other side, they eventually turned to self-preservation. After tears of emotional distress and thousands of dollars spent on their efforts to help their daughter, mom and dad reluctantly disengaged themselves from Natasha's toxic decisions. They backed completely away from Natasha and her destructive behavior. From afar, they monitored Natasha but continued to stay uninvolved even as they watched their daughter move herself and her baby boy in with Dennis Moore who even they knew was a drug dealer and thought to be a member of the "Bloods" gang. They believed it was another terrible decision but they knew any efforts to convince her to do anything different would prove fruitless.

Natasha had always been a very bright young girl but was presently in this relationship even though she knew it wasn't good for her. But it was her drug addiction that kept her from making the best choices. She needed to be close to her drug connections for free access to the poison. As far as relationships go, Natasha clung to a false notion that being with someone was better than being alone. Dennis Moore and his money were the closest match to Natasha's previous lifestyle and with fistfuls of cash whenever she needed it, the choice to move in with him was guaranteed security and freedom from loneliness. However, in the end, her parents were correct in their assumptions. Natasha and her baby boy unfortunately gained neither security nor the freedom from loneliness.

At the beginning of the summer, after knowing each other for only a short time, Natasha and her son, J.D. moved into Moore's house on Indiana Avenue in Kansas City. With the exception of their different upbringings, she and Moore shared common interests and personalities. Although Natasha's flashiness was more subtle than her boyfriend's was, it did not go unnoticed by Moore. It was the familiarity of her showy and brash character that initially attracted him to her.

It was Wednesday and it was a hot summer afternoon. Natasha, dressed in a sleeveless, pink dress and heels, felt a trickle of perspiration slide down her back as she pulled up to the Indiana Street home after a trip to the Happy Foods grocery store. She hoisted J.D., her two-year-old son, up the front steps with her left hand while managing an armload of grocery store bags with the other. The toddler held his mother's acrylic-nailed hand as she helped him up the few concrete steps that led into the home she shared with Moore. Still too short to raise his chunky legs high enough to reach the steps on his own, J.D. willingly accepted his mom's assistance as they took the small journey toward the front door.

Contrary to the perfect state in which Moore kept his flashy car, that was not the case for his house. Natasha released her son's hand as they entered this almost uninhabitable environment. With the exception of a large, solid wood piece of furniture that sat flush up against the wall to the right of the entryway, Moore's residence was cluttered and dirty. Toys, trash, and clothes covered most every available space inside the Kansas City home. Now free from his mother's grip, J.D. took to playing amongst the filth anyway. Like most children, the boy adapted to his surroundings and held an advantage over adults because he did not fully comprehend the unhealthy living conditions which he lived.

Natasha had only small intervals of time and very little personal space between her little one's demands and the constant traffic of people coming and going for drugs throughout most evenings. As a supplement to her minuscule amount of freedom, she gave the boy free reign inside the messy residence. However, despite his endless reservoir of curiosity, the busy toddler always stayed close to his mother's side. The child did well at occupying himself but always attempted to incorporate his mother into his imaginative play. His requests for interaction were often unrequited and J.D., starved for attention, accepted it whenever he could get it.

J.D. was a little boy full of life that was always smiling and happy and he had quite a history of attempting to entertain the steady flow of guests coming through his house. Not unlike the two adults he lived with, his boldness did not go unnoticed and although J.D.'s efforts were frequently uninvited, he charmed even the most incompatible of visitors. It was Natasha's combination of exhaustion and chasing her own self-interest that exaggerated her poor parenting skills. With the exception of the drug customers that visited the house, her baby boy played mostly alone.

From people with a heavy drug problem to those just wanting to indulge during the last days of summer, many people were interested in what Dennis Moore was selling. This week in particular, Moore's dealings proved very profitable for him. Cash dropped into Moore's hands from the good and bad alike and by the end of the long weekend, he had no more product left to sell. Like any good salesperson, just as quickly as he had sold out, he reinvested in a new supply. However, resupplying your items for sale is not like any other purchasable and an immediate pick up of more product was not an option. So just like his clientele, Moore had to wait for the deliveryman to come by.

The previous extended weekend was demanding and eventful. A continuous stream of customers kept Natasha and Dennis busy and sleep deprived through Tuesday. By Wednesday, Natasha was exhausted and hoped for a quiet night on the couch. Dennis could use the night off also as he was still recuperating from an injury to his foot from three weeks ago where he got caught in the line of fire in a drive by shooting. The bullet was not meant for him but he got jammed up in the shots anyway. As he settled into his chair that night, he mentioned to Natasha that he thought he was finally walking without a limp for the first time since the shooting. Dennis Moore was feeling pretty good that summer night. Natasha sort of listened to what Dennis was saying but she was already in the other room changing out of her dress and into a comfortable pair of jeans and t- shirt. Throughout the rest of the night, they watched TV and zoned in and out of consciousness and Natasha only got up once to remove a penny from her son's sticky mouth.

Natasha always wanted Moore to sit with her on the couch but he always chose his chair over her. So just like every night, he sat in his over-stuffed leather chair watching TV with his gun tucked in between the cushion and the side of the chair. With his foot bandaged and propped up on his coffee table, he and Natasha sat in the dark and watched a movie on his big-screen TV.

In his custom made entertainment center were high-end VCRs, receivers, and speakers that took up every inch of the glass-enclosed shelves. Voices and sounds from the TV boomed from the Bose surround-sound speakers that could even be heard from outside the home. In observing the quality and cost of his home entertainment center, it was obvious where Moore spent a large portion of profits. The flashy technology-filled piece of furniture was just one of his bragging rights to his successful business practices.

People buying drugs from Dennis Moore knew when he was ready to sell. If Moore had his front porch light on at his Indiana home, it held the same significance as the traveling Impala. It told any would be customers that the product was available. However, on the very late hours of September 6, there was no lit path for his customers and Moore had the light turned off. He was out of product and he wasn't expecting any company. Unlike those he did business with on the street, Moore was more particular about the ones he let inside his home. In addition, the darkened doorstep was as much of a clever marketing strategy as it was a way to filter his guests. No light, nothing for sale. Pretty simple.

With the light off and nothing to sell, Moore didn't think he would be working tonight. Moore rarely opened his door to uninvited people anyway and would just let them knock and go away after no one answered, if he didn't want to engage with them. So on this night, with no light on, he had checked out for the night and was getting lost in his movie.

It was very dark and very late when the two cars carrying the six men pulled up a few houses down from Dennis Moore's home. They all got out as quiet as they could. The plan was simple. They knew Dennis Moore would not open the door for anyone but surely he would open it up for his buddy, Johnny Chapple. Then when Moore made that mistake of opening that door for his "friend," they would all rush in the house with guns drawn. The great plan was that when Moore saw he was out gunned, he would give up the money and drugs. They would take it and be gone. It would be real easy.

Johnny Chapple bound up the steps leading to Moore's gated front door two at a time unlike the trouble little J.D. had getting up the same steps earlier in the day. Dennis's famous Impala was nowhere in sight but there was a small garage under the house. Johnny could hear the TV booming through the walls and even though the light was out, he accepted it as a good sign that Moore was home. Johnny slid his hands between the iron bars of the gate that protected the entryway and knocked hard on an equally protective heavy metal door. Like cats ready to pounce, the other five men, wearing symbolic blue bandanas over their faces, carefully maneuvered themselves out of sight. They could not be seen but they were all close to the front door and waiting for that well secured entry way to open.

Moore had nothing to sell and his recent gunshot injury had him moving slowly, so he was in no hurry to get out of his comfortable leather chair. He tried to ignore the unwelcome knocks. Nevertheless, the thumping continued. So, barefoot and with sleepy annoyance, Dennis pushed himself up and out of the chair. In the dark, he groggily limped his way to his front door. In the few steps it took to reach the doorknob, Moore stepped on two piles of J.D's plastic toys. He lifted his left foot up to his knee and cursed as he removed a miniature soldier stuck to his foot. He flipped on the porch light and peered through the peephole. He was surprised to see his friend Johnny on the opposite side. Moore quickly turned the light back off and, as he naively unlocked the first of three deadbolts for the familiar face of his friend, the rest of the group prepared themselves for ambush.

It was very uncharacteristic for Moore to open the door this late at night even for a friendly face. Maybe it was that he was tired or maybe it was because he already had the light off so it wouldn't be anyone wanting drugs, but either way, it was the wrong move. As that door opened and Moore smiled at his friend, Johnny immediately stepped aside. As was Calvin's plan, with

Johnny out of the way, the doorway was free for the men to rush in.

The locked door was now open and Powell, Calvin, and their posse now had full access to the entrance of the home and they took it. The men yelled and hollered as they rushed into the doorway and the sound startled Dennis more than anything. The once simple irritation Moore felt about having to answer the door quickly cycled to rage then fear when Moore saw the others appear before him. Shocked, outnumbered, and terrified, Moore stepped back and limped backwards. Like a SWAT team, the armed men swarmed the residence with weapons raised.

With his 20 gauge shotgun extended, Calvin took the lead and backed Moore into the kitchen, just to the right of the doorway. Within seconds of entering the residence, Calvin had complete physical control over Moore and immediately demanded all his cash and valuables. Calvin pushed Moore against the white ceramic kitchen sink and its ledge dug into Moore's back. Calvin withheld nothing and just like he had handled Johnny earlier, he pushed the nose of his shotgun into Moore's forehead. The men all scattered to the corners of the room and waited for Calvin's orders. Instead of turning the volume down, someone smashed the TV so it would be quiet in the house. Johnny Chapple finally came in last and shut the door behind him.

Despite the weapon being glued to his head, Moore denied having anything for them to take. He also was now pissed that these masked men had entered his home and he wasn't having any of this gun to his head business. Moore had caught his breath from being scared and was now in survival mode. Moore made a quick sweep of his arm and he knocked the shotgun from Calvin's grip. The shotgun flew out of Calvin's hand and slid across the dirty linoleum floor. Moore charged his opponent and for a split second, he was a free man. Moore dove across the

26

kitchen floor toward the shotgun that now rested underneath a white wooden microwave table near the kitchen's entrance. However, despite Moore's fast and clever thinking, his bad foot made him slower than usual and Calvin got to the shotgun first.

The communities of the east side of Kansas City are tight and it was almost sad to realize that at that instant, everyone inside the residence on Indiana Avenue knew each other. This wasn't a random robbery but actually seven men that had actually socialized with each other on a friendly basis at some point in their lives. However, it was just this knowledge about each other and their business that encouraged the men to take advantage of this opportunity to betray Moore's trust and rob him. But on that night, there were two things that neither Calvin nor Powell anticipated in their brilliant plan. They didn't plan for the extra people inside Moore's home and those were J.D. and Natasha. Nonetheless, Natasha's existence did not dilute their main goal. The expectations of additional profit loomed in their selfish minds. The only problem was that every time Moore and Natasha responded that they had no money, it only fueled the violence and energized the hostile takeover.

It was almost two o'clock in the morning as the situation was unfolding. J.D. was dressed in a short pair of fringed cowboy pajamas but appeared nowhere ready for bed and he seemed not to be phased by what was going on. He sat on his knees, played with a pile of plastic army men on the floor, and did not even feel the evil that filled the room. As screams and threats filled the house, J.D. got up and offered one of his plastic soldiers to Johnny Chapple who was standing closest to him. With his sweet demeanor, J.D. had never known a stranger and tugged on Johnny's loose pant leg. As an offering to play, J.D. held up a wet, green army man he had been chewing on. At first, Johnny was preoccupied with the real war going on and he ignored the toddler's gesture, but then, as a possible remedy to satisfy J.D., Johnny took the toy from the chubby outreached hand.

The adults in J.D.'s life, who were morally bound to protect him, had completely disregarded his tender age with their lifestyle. Unfortunately, the sight of guns and sound of raised voices were both a constant accessory to both Moore and the guests he entertained. In a weird way, their terrible parenting of allowing exposure to this routine actually proved beneficial on that night to keep J.D. calm. The mere presentation of the guns or the masked men might be devastating to other two year-olds, but to J.D, he was not alarmed. At least for a while, he remained content and satisfied in spite of the conflict around him.

Although her baby was quiet, Natasha feared the commotion of a crying child would overstress the already horrible situation, so contrary to her customary standard, Natasha focused hard on her small child in an attempt to keep him calm. As she sat with a gun pointed at her, Natasha started talking to J.D. with uncomplicated chatter as he innocently occupied himself on the floor.

While Calvin terrorized Moore with his shotgun in the kitchen, Powell's AK47 kept Natasha hostage on the couch. Natasha stared at her son and pretended to ignore Powell; however, Powell enjoyed her reluctance and accepted her unwillingness to cooperate as a challenge. Taking full advantage of the assault weapon's persuasiveness, Powell unleashed the evil that had been building inside him since he and Calvin devised their plan. Powell enjoyed this power trip over his hostage and with a firm hand on the polished brown pistol grip, he guided the barrel towards Natasha's face and forcefully redirected her attention back to him.

Natasha's normal pride-filled attitude kicked into full gear and she temporarily refused to give in to his scare tactics. But as the steel dug into the side of her mouth and into her gums, Natasha's focus was turned back toward her gunman. Natasha attempted to use her son as a bargaining tool and begged that her life be preserved for his sake. That plea held no weight with her assailant.   Natasha, like many faced with life-or-death situations, chose to err on the side of caution and as a possible life-saving technique, she surrendered to Powell's demands.

Natasha found that her talent for conniving was of no use to her current circumstance and accepted she was no match for her predator.   Powell's enthusiasm in preying on her was short-lived and he found himself unsatisfied with her lack of any willingness to fight.   But Powell wanted to extend the thrill of terrorizing Natasha and ordered her into an area where he knew she would fight back.   For Powell, Natasha was no different than her toddler's toys, and in the same way J.D. played with his toys, Powell toyed with Natasha.

The Chapple brothers, as well as Gulley and Wilson, were all there to help rob Dennis Moore of his cash and drugs as instructed by Calvin.   They were certainly prepared to keep Moore at bay while others ransacked the house looking for money but the menial responsibilities for which they had been assigned had now turned out to be far more involved than what they had anticipated. What these four men had thought to be a simple robbery unexpectedly turned violent and instead of moving to their designated posts, Calvin and Powell's four helpers stood shocked inside the front entrance and attempted to absorb and understand the unplanned viciousness.

When Dennis said he had no money, Calvin didn't believe him. Calvin barked at the other men to start looking for money. Someone mentioned that if he didn't have money they could take Moore's car and sell it for cash.   So regardless of their initial hesitation, the four men dispersed themselves into different parts of the house.   Gulley and Ronald went in search of drugs, money, and Moore's car keys. Johnny stood near the door and kept watch. Trevor Wilson took a position near Powell and waited for further instruction.

29

Back in the kitchen, Calvin was trying to regain control of the situation after Moore fought back. With the butt-end of his gun, Calvin pummeled Moore in the forehead. The blunt force temporarily stunned Moore and once again, Calvin had complete control over his victim. In his confused condition, Moore fell to his knees and in one quick move, Calvin repositioned his gun in his left hand, grabbed the neck of Moore's long-sleeved black t-shirt, and dragged him into the same room where Powell kept Natasha.

In his short journey from the kitchen into the living room, the thin cotton material dug into Moore's throat and choked him. Moore grabbed at his collar and pulled it away from his neck. Calvin released him and with a thump his head hit the debris-covered, carpeted floor. Moore knew his ordeal was not over but was relieved to catch his breath. He looked his masked enemy up and down and tried to identify him but before he could find anything remarkable, Calvin stepped over him and straddled the drug dealer.

For the second time Calvin pointed the barrel of his 20-gauge in Moore's face. Powerless, Moore instinctively covered his face and turned away from his predator. Moore felt the sandy grit of the rarely vacuumed floor on his face and he breathed in the sour smell from the soiled rug. Knowing that this was a matter of life or death, Moore kept screaming he had no money and pleaded with Calvin. Moore swore to the man with the gun that he would be able to get him a bunch of money and promised the masked man that he would give him all the drugs that were to be delivered if only he would spare his life.

Calvin didn't seem satisfied with the promise but he also realized that none of his crew had found any cash anywhere. Calvin was interested in the specifics of this drug delivery Moore spoke of. With Moore lying face-up and between his legs, Calvin seemed to become conscious of his own susceptibility to violence to possibly shoot Moore too soon and quickly stepped backward a couple of steps and contemplated his next move. Calvin seemed to realize that even though he had Moore compliant with a gun in his face, maybe his goals could be better carried out if his hostage were restrained.

Calvin slid his size twelve foot under Moore's shirt and ordered his already vulnerable victim to take off his clothes. Calvin took a few more steps back and allowed Moore the room he needed to remove his jeans and shirt. As Moore took off his clothes, Calvin searched the clothes for drugs or money and with the exception of a set of Chevrolet car keys, he came up empty-handed. Calvin then tied Moore's feet together with his shirt. Calvin ripped an extension cord from the wall to tie his hands. But before tying his hands together, he placed them inopportunely and uncomfortably behind his head. With one more inference of power, Calvin rolled Moore onto his stomach.

Calvin didn't believe Moore when he kept saying he had no drugs or money and was certain he had a stash hidden somewhere inside the house. He was also confident he would find it with or without Moore's help. Regardless of Moore's pleas for his life, Calvin's selfish tendencies and flawed personality disqualified him from feeling sympathy for Moore. The evil ingrained within him helped Calvin remain focused on his goal.

The six robbers had smoked a lot of marijuana that day and the usual sedative-like effect of the marijuana did not get in anyone's way. Instead, their marijuana had an additional ingredient of PCP, so rage and aggression took the forefront of the other men's behavior. Calvin and Powell handled the residents as the rest of the crew ransacked the home.

With one goal in mind, Ronald and Gulley paired up to plunder the house and headed down the long hall that led to four doors. The two doors on the left were the entrances to a makeshift child's bedroom and the other to a dirty bathroom.

J.D.'s room was a crude combination of household storage and basic children's furniture. A blue metal toddler's bed and a red, three-tiered bin combination, that housed both J.D.'s toys and clothes, appeared lost among the full, black garbage bags and cardboard boxes that filled the rest of the room. The bathroom was messy, smelled of urine and dirty diapers, and clumps of long black hair stuck to the ancient blue, ceramic sink. Centered at the end of the hallway, was the third door that appeared to be the master bedroom, but it was also bare of traditional contents. A frameless mattress and box springs covered by a white sheet sat directly on the floor and a TV sat on top of the only dresser at the foot of the bed. Ronald and Gulley kicked holes in the walls, opened drawers and cabinets. After rummaging through the contents, they dumped them on the floor. They did exactly as instructed and searched all the rooms, but despite their thoroughness, they came up empty-handed.

Gulley followed Ronald to the fourth door that unknowingly led them downstairs and into the garage. It was dark and Ronald went down first. He felt the wall and found the light switch and the two climbed down an unstable and uncarpeted wooden staircase. A pungent smell of motor oil filled the enclosed space and met the young men as they rounded the corner at the end of the stairwell. Metal shelves filled with unopened sandwich bag boxes and semi-organized bins of tools, car parts, and building hardware lined two walls of the spacious room.

The downstairs garage was neat and orderly, unlike the messy upstairs and the star of that downstairs basement was Dennis Moore's famous Chevy Impala. The men simultaneously took off the masks that covered their identities, stuffed them in their back pockets, and walked across an oil-stained, concrete floor towards the Chevy. Ronald attempted to open the driver's side at the same time Gulley tried the passenger's side door but the doors were locked. Dennis Moore kept his vehicle secured, even in his own garage.

32

As Ronald dumped out bins looking for a screwdriver or some tool to open the car, Gulley scoped out the resource filled room for a more efficient way inside the car since they had no keys. His eyes scanned the entire room multiple times before he spotted a metal door flush against the back wall. Initially, Gulley thought it was a door to a circuit breaker box; nonetheless, he took the time to investigate the contents. Gulley's efficient thinking paid off, as inside the metal housing was a pegboard full of keys.

Back upstairs, Trevor Wilson was sweating profusely. Yes he was a gang member with a history of violence and a lack of remorse but despite his own sociopathic tendencies, he stood away from Powell with his back directly in front of J.D. as he attempted to block the sight of his mother's suffering from the little boy. Wilson watched as Powell made Natasha take off her clothes just as Calvin made Moore do. It was a terrible sight for the little boy to see and Wilson must have taken pity on the child, because he then removed his bandana. Wilson carried J.D. and a handful of toys down the hall into the back bedroom. Wilson kicked an overturned laundry basket off on to the floor, turned on the TV, and placed the child on the bed. Wilson turned to go back into the living area and J.D. screamed and held his hands out for Wilson to pick him back up but Wilson ignored the child's pleas, left the room, and shut the door behind him.

When Wilson returned to his post, things had changed. Powell and Calvin had removed their masks and Moore and Natasha were now face-to-face with their captors. Wilson stopped in front of the coffee table that separated himself from Powell and his victim and silently waited for instructions. Up until that point, he had been a mere spectator to the activities but Powell soon put him to work and ordered him to grab Natasha's feet. Natasha kicked and flailed her legs but despite the intense struggle, her efforts were fruitless. Wilson fastened his hands around her ankles and propped her legs on the table. With the

33

strength behind his young hands, Wilson kept a tight grip on Natasha, and just as Powell instructed, he locked her exposed legs into a fixed, spread position.

Powell's immoral objectives became crystal clear and he assumed a new position and sat beside Natasha on the sofa. Natasha's worst nightmare became a reality and she shivered and cried quietly as Powell traced a rose tattoo on her naked right shoulder with his rough fingers. He wrapped his left arm around the back of her neck and firmly gripped her left bare shoulder. He ran the end of his gun between her exposed breasts and down her stomach. Before he could touch anything else, Natasha realized she had nothing to lose and fought hard against the man about to rape her.

Calvin found himself fascinated and energized by the events taking place on the sofa and he and his gun temporarily stepped away from Moore to join Powell and Wilson in their depraved exploits against Natasha. Ironically, the only thing that separated Moore and Natasha was Moore's favorite chair but he found getting to her was an insurmountable obstacle. Dennis Moore remained imprisoned in his restrained position on the floor. Although Moore could not see his girlfriend, he knew what was about to happen and he was in no position to retrieve his pistol hidden in his chair. Nevertheless, he aggressively squirmed on the floor and attempted to free himself. Calvin, on the other hand, was not about to let what he thought was his path towards financial gain reclaim the upper hand and quickly returned to assure that Moore did not escape.

Calvin put the gun to the back of Moore's head but even in the face of his own impending death, Moore again emphatically denied having access to any tangible money or drugs. Calvin suspected Moore had more resources than he admitted and had no intention of giving up his quest. Calvin screamed at Moore that if he didn't come up with something right then, he was going to kill him. Then Calvin remembered that Moore had a brother that he did business with. With that knowledge, Calvin presented Moore with one last opportunity to get him some money and save his own life.

With one hand, Calvin kept the gun aimed at Moore as he stretched and leaned to grab a cordless phone off a dusty end table between the couch and Moore's chair. In his getting the phone, Calvin got more than he bargained for, as he noticed Dennis Moore's 9mm Luger tucked in his favorite chair. Calvin grabbed both the weapon and the phone with one hand and juggled them carefully. He turned and shot an evil smile at Moore as if to say, *"Too bad.....I just found your last chance to live."* Calvin then tucked the phone under his chin and secured Moore's weapon in the back of his pants.

Calvin cradled the phone in his left hand and ordered Moore to give him his brother's number. Calvin was very explicit and carefully laid out clear instructions when he told Moore what to tell his brother when he answered. Dennis was to tell his brother, Walter Moore, to bring money and drugs to his house, immediately. Calvin asked, *"Do you got it?"* and struck Moore across the face. Moore nodded his head in acknowledgement and slowly called out the numbers for him to dial. When Calvin heard the phone ringing on the other end, he held the phone down to Moore's face. However when Dennis's brother Walter answered, Dennis did not stay true to the specifics of what he was supposed to say but instead talked to his brother in some sort of coded speech that Calvin couldn't understand.

Even the most self-centered of parents rise above their selfishness when their child is hurt or in danger and Natasha couldn't bear the sounds of her baby crying down the hall. She had no idea what the men were doing or had done to her boy. With that fear, Natasha's "mother bear" instincts kicked in. She didn't care what it took, she was going to free herself to rescue her child. As she was enduring a violent rape at the hands of a psychopath, it was a level of sheer terror that most people will never be able to comprehend but she decided to fight for her life and for her son. In one quick motion, Natasha grabbed at Powell's face with her hard painted nails and dug them deep into his skin on his cheek. Immediately, she created long open wounds that gushed red. Blood streamed down the left side of Powell's face. He instinctively covered his injury with the palm of his free hand and just as quickly, he retaliated with a hard punch to her face.

Natasha's act of bravery in the face of impending death only energized Powell and he increased his aggressive touching and mauling her naked body. Even after such a hard blow to the head, Natasha still squirmed to free herself as Powell placed an open hand on her chest which he used as leverage and pushed himself off the couch. The blood that spilled out of her mouth and the path of red marks that trailed down her chest were only a small example of Powell's heartlessness. The full measure of his cruelty had not yet been unleashed.

With his face bleeding from her claw marks, Powell laughed and moved down and straddled himself across Natasha's legs. As Powell faced his victim with her legs now secured by his partner, the wickedness increased as Powell moved his weapon towards her. Then in an act of sheer evil, Powell sodomized Natasha with his gun. Natasha sobbed in the terror. Natasha wasn't able to get to her baby.

Gulley and Ronald pulled every car key off that basement pegboard. But despite the curious amount of keys, not one fit the door to the locked car. Other than the fear of punishment from upstairs, the two had no other investment in the vehicle but they continued their diligence in finding a way into the driver's seat without defacing it. They did know that the flawlessness of the car was the main reason it had any value.

Whether it was the drugs or simple immaturity, the two were overdue in figuring out the obvious. It was not until they exhausted all their options downstairs, did they decide to go directly to the main source for a solution. While Gulley stayed downstairs and tinkered with the locks, with renewed optimism, Ronald climbed back up the stairs to check in with Calvin for the keys. But before Ronald made it back up to the main floor, a familiar noise filled his ears. More than a noise but an explosion. It was the explosion from a shotgun that he knew too well. A shot had been fired upstairs. Then he could hear a chaotic combination of screaming and pathetic cries from the terrified child. Ronald cautiously made his way up the rest of the stairs. As he entered the living area, Ronald purposely avoided the activities taking place on the couch with Natasha and focused on Dennis Moore who lay bleeding on the floor.

Unlike Ronald and Gulley, it didn't take that long for Calvin to figure out the obvious. When Moore called his brother, he was trying to warn his brother by using words that only he and his brother understood. Calvin had told Dennis to tell his brother to come over with money or drugs and Dennis had disobeyed by probably telling his brother in a secret code about the robbery. Calvin was infuriated that Dennis Moore was trying to trick him and that Moore had disobeyed his orders. His rage, his violent temper, and his empty soul took over and he shoved the shotgun into the back of Dennis Moore's head.

There didn't seem to be any hesitation as the shotgun was inches from Moore's head and Calvin Miller pulled the trigger on the shotgun. The sound was deafening in the small room. The power behind the blast of the rifle caused Moore's body to flip awkwardly from the facedown position to face-up position. Calvin was amused by the phenomenon and laughed at Moore.

Calvin was sure that Moore was dead, but the blow to the back of his head did not kill him and Moore was still alive. Dennis Moore's nightmare wasn't over and he was still breathing. However most of the blast that Calvin directed toward the back of Moore's head had actually been taken by Moore's hands. Calvin had tied Moore's hands in an awkward way behind his head and his hands suffered most of the blow from the gunshot blast meant for his head.

From the time the group had arrived, Johnny Chapple stayed and guarded the front door. However, when Powell's violation of Natasha started, Johnny turned and got out of the house. Johnny was the reason they got into the house and created all of the mayhem, but now he had actually split the scene even before the first gunshot was fired. Johnny ran to get away from the crime and he left his brother in the midst of chaos just minutes before Calvin shot Dennis Moore. Ironically, if he had not left, he would have been clearly covered in the by-product of the crime. Two of Moore's fingers were blown off of his left hand in the gunshot and blood spattered the exact area where Johnny Chapple was standing just minutes earlier.

Ronald silently took in the seriousness of the injuries to Dennis Moore as Calvin was still laughing at Moore. Ronald was surprised and stood silent and noticed it all. Ronald found it odd that a penny had adhered itself to Moore's bare thigh but was stunned by Moore's blood stained face. He was shocked by the amount of blood now soaking into the carpet underneath his head. Calvin was still enjoying and commenting about the flopping of the body and did not notice that Dennis Moore was still alive. To inform Calvin that he shouldn't be laughing just yet, Ronald said to Calvin, "*Big boy's still breathing.*" To which Calvin replied, "*Well Mother Fucker!*" as he pointed the shotgun directly at Dennis Moore's still beating heart and fired again. Blood splattered across the room and sprayed them both. Ronald startled at the sound and the sight again stood silent. Then without any further thought of what had just happened, Calvin, nonchalantly, tossed a set of car keys at Ronald. The keys hit Ronald in the chest and fell to the floor as he was still too shocked to catch them. Ronald then picked up the keys and looked surprisingly at Calvin as if he had read his mind of why Ronald had returned from the basement in the first place.

After committing a brutal murder, Calvin then moved towards the sofa as if there was a party with Natasha and Powell that was waiting for him to attend. Calvin quickly moved to join in. Clearly not at the same deviant level as the others and shocked by Dennis Moore's murder, Ronald took pity on the young mother and nervously intervened. Ronald said they ought to get the hell out of there and convinced the men to let her go by saying they should leave now. Powell, Calvin, and Wilson moved away from Natasha. Calvin bent down, gathered Natasha's clothes, which lay in a small pile at the end of the couch, and threw them at her.

With great relief, Ronald thought he had significantly lessened the damage about to take place and just like his brother, Ronald had ideas of leaving. However, as followers often do, Ronald feared his recent intervention, regardless of its value, would cause strain upon his relationship with the gang leaders. Despite his own dirty hands, Ronald knew that Calvin and Powell were capable of far worse behavior than he had imagined. He felt an immediate need to mitigate any possible damages he might have started by interfering with their actions. Ronald decided that appeasing Calvin and Powell was his only chance for redemption. With self-preservation in mind and the keys in his hand, Ronald headed back downstairs to collect the vehicle to get something productive from their visit to Dennis's home.

With the exception of her shoes, Natasha was now fully clothed and in the same black jeans and white shirt she originally had on. Natasha stumbled down the hall towards her son. With

39

one goal in mind, she opened the bedroom door and gathered her crying baby in her arms. Their joyful reconnection was extremely short as Calvin and Powell had an alternative goal in mind. Unknowingly to Natasha, the two men had followed her into the bedroom.

Natasha was clearly distraught by Dennis's murder but relieved that her and her son were still alive. But now she turned around and came face-to-face with the two men in the bedroom. With their guns drawn, they backed her towards the bed. As the back of her legs met the mattress, Natasha lost her balance and with her boy still in her arms, she fell into a sitting position onto the bed. She swung her legs over and with her one available hand, she scooted herself and J.D. closer to the head of the bed. In an instinctual effort to protect her son, Natasha pushed the boy off to the side as far away from the men as she could.

Ronald came back down the steps to the basement where the car was parked and he was extremely out of breath. The combination of stress, fear, and running up and down the stairs had Ronald dripping in sweat. He pulled his bandana out of his pocket, wiped his face, and handed the keys to Gulley as he briefed him on the events taking place upstairs. They both gave each other a look that they realized the evening has gotten way out of hand and they needed to get the car out of this garage.

Ronald unlocked the passenger side of the car and jumped in. But before they both could even close the doors, they heard the explosion of the shotgun once again. With morbid curiosity, Ronald got out of the car and sped back up to the main floor as the last and final gunshot rang out. But in the driver's side of the car, Gulley decided to not go back upstairs and he nervously fumbled with the keys to get the key into the Impala's ignition.

"Cold blooded killer" is a phrase that is used but rarely understood. The fact that one human being can be so callous and violent to another is incomprehensible to most. But in that house that night, there was the purest example of "cold blood." After Calvin had freed Natasha and allowed her to put on her clothes, he released her to check on her son. But he had never really planned to set her free and he had always planned on this being her last day alive. With no compassion for another's life, Calvin manhandled Natasha on to her stomach and ordered Powell to put a pillow over the back of her head. He told her to count to 100 before she got up so they had time to leave. He also told her not to tell the police who they were.

When Natasha muffled out an agreement with her face in the mattress and a pillow over the back of her head, Calvin placed the shotgun against that pillow. Calvin smirked at Powell and then pulled the trigger. He had fired the shotgun into the pillow and Natasha's head. The blast was even louder in the smaller bedroom. Unlike her boyfriend's hands, the pillow that covered Natasha's head did not spare her life and she was dead as soon as the gun went off. The blast nearly blew Natasha's entire head off of her body but with the pillow covering her, no one could tell.

Calvin killed the young mother with even more detached and unemotional malevolence as when he shot her boyfriend. Powell thought that maybe Calvin possibly used the pillow in a delusional attempt to protect the baby from the horror he was about to observe. Maybe Calvin had a tiny bit of pity for the toddler? Probably not.

The sound of the thundering blast frightened the child so much that he jumped away. But his next instinct was to go right back to his natural protector, his mother. J.D. jumped on his mother and was crying hysterically. The child could not

41

comprehend what had happened but he was scared. Calvin and Powell knew they needed to get out of there. Even though they tried as they might even their lost and evil souls were touched by J.D's pitiful attempts to wake his dead mother. So in one more example of depravity of conscience by a somewhat diluted act of civility, Calvin and Powell tried to console the child and took him out of the room.

There is no record of whose idea it was, but somehow the men thought maybe getting the little boy a snack might help ease his emotions or maybe they were just hungry. The men searched through the kitchen and then decided to pop some popcorn. They gave the microwave popcorn to the little boy and they ran out of the house. J.D. sat in the kitchen of the death house eating popcorn and crying.

Unlike, Ronald and Gulley who were down in the garage, Trevor Wilson remained upstairs and was aware of everything that took place that evening. While he did not participate in the actual murders, he did nothing to stop them. Contrary to the small amount of pity he showed for the child in the beginning, Wilson acted unconcerned and emotionally detached as he loaded all of Moore's electronic equipment into his trunk while Calvin and Powell killed Natasha in the same bedroom he once placed the child in for protection.

From the basement/garage, Gulley backed Moore's car out of the garage as Ronald was heading up the steps to make one final appearance upstairs when he heard the final shot. Ronald quickly found that the death toll had doubled and he saw the three men moving frantically about the house. With no respect for the dead, Calvin stumbled over Moore's body as Powell helped Wilson carry out the rest of Moore's electronic equipment. Ronald followed them out the door but remained on the front porch and waited for Calvin. Ronald watched as J.D.

42

walked down the hall from the kitchen to the bedroom where his mother lay.

Ronald then ran out the door. He watched as Gulley pulled up in the Impala behind the Caprice. Wilson and Powell climbed safely inside of the Caprice. However, both cars tore away before Ronald and Calvin could get inside. When they saw high beams from another car approaching them this late at night, they knew the person was looking for them. Wilson raced away in his car with Powell in the passenger seat and then Gulley sped away driving Dennis Moore's car. These two very highly recognizable vehicles took off and left two of their crew and an extremely graphic scene behind them. Ronald and Calvin had no choice and sprinted off on foot in pursuit of safety with their accomplices.

Even though Calvin Miller couldn't understand the code Dennis was speaking into the phone, his brother did. Walter Moore did understand his brother's message and after the call, he grabbed his gun. Walter jumped in his car and headed south towards Indiana Avenue. Although Walter arrived much too late to save his brother, he was just in time to see the responsible parties leaving the residence and heading down Indiana. Walter knew they were involved in something terrible with his brother so he gave chase. The men fleeing the murder scene knew the person chasing them was out to get them. At one point, Powell hung out the passenger window and shot at Walter. Walter shot back many times. Walter kept shooting as Trevor Wilson's Caprice pulled over to hide from him a few blocks away.

As Wilson stopped it gave Calvin and Ronald time to catch up by foot. But by then Walter had doubled back around the block and saw them. Dodging bullets from both ends, Calvin and Ronald jumped safely into Wilson's car and raced away. Walter lost the chase somewhere on a highway on ramp and couldn't

43

see which way they went. Both vehicles with the men disappeared into the dark Kansas City streets after spraying gunfire into the night air.

So much for Calvin's brilliant plan to easily go rob Dennis Moore. The simple 'would be' robbery ended in a double homicide where two lives were ended and a young life would be forever changed and it was all for nothing. Calvin did not line his pockets with the drugs and cash that were the goals of his plan. Even though the men were able to pull the car out of that garage after such a brutal murder, it could never be driven. It was quickly sold and dismantled for parts for a few hundred bucks a few days later.

But back on that warm September morning on an unmade bed, a crying two-year-old snuggled close to his mother for protection and comfort. Despite the warm temperature outside and the closeness of the two bodies, he shivered as tears dried on his cheeks and blood collected in the crevices of the sheets where his small legs rested. He found no relief from the encroaching cold as his mother's body cooled and the comfort he sought was lost. The baby fought for his breath as his chest heaved from uncontrollable sobs wanting consolation his mother could never again give.

By the end of the same year, Calvin Miller was under the supervision of the Missouri Department of Corrections but not for his actions at Dennis Moore's house. Calvin was convicted in December of a different murder and he was sentenced to two life prison terms. As Calvin went off to prison for another murder, the homicides of Dennis Moore and Natasha were never solved by the Kansas City Police Department as there were no witnesses other than the little boy who police officers found snuggled up to his dead mother's body in that horrible crime scene on Indiana Street.

And it wasn't for lack of trying because the Kansas City Police Department threw all of its resources at solving those homicides. Crime Scene Investigators went through the house with a fine tooth comb. Officers went door to door asking questions. Detectives followed every lead. But in the end, they found no suspects and no leads to any suspects. The only people that could identify the six men that went in that house were dead. Word on the street was that Dennis Moore was killed in a drug deal gone badly but there was not even a rumor as to who was involved.

Two of the Kansas City police department's best detectives were assigned to the case. Detective Robert Delameter and Detective Marcus Regan worked tireless analyzing evidence collected at the scene and following up on lead after lead but nothing ever panned out as any sort of suspect name. As a detective, it is frustrating to not be able to solve a homicide but when it is a double homicide with a little boy left at the scene, it seemed the case was even more exasperating. It was even much more of an emotional drain when there were no resolution to the crime.

So many years passed and the case received as much investigation as this nationally recognized police department could muster. The case found itself unsolved and transferred to the Cold Case Unit. This detective unit was specially trained to pick up these old cases on a schedule, give it a fresh look, and utilize any new technology that had progressed since the last investigation. Even though the Cold Case Unit periodically reviewed the case and followed up any and all leads over the years, the case remained unsolved.

Fast forward to eight years after the murders. Calvin was still in prison and ironically Trevor Wilson had been murdered in an incident not unlike the one he participated in years before. As for

45

the other men, the Chapple brothers, Marc Powell, and Mathew Gulley remained free and undetected. The men never spoke of that night and it seemed that they had actually gotten away with murder. For such a violent double homicide that left a two year old boy huddled over his dead mother's body to remain un-talked about was amazing. It was a horrific crime that usually leads people to say something about it to someone.

But one thing for sure is that criminals talk. Maybe they confess to loved ones about the crime or maybe they brag about it to friends. Maybe they slip up and by accident mention something or maybe the grief overtakes them to speak about it to a friend. When they do that, criminals always think that whoever they are talking to would never tell anyone. But they do. Current girlfriends become former girlfriends and talk about things they heard. Friends of criminals like to gossip to others about things they were told.

One way or another when you have six men involved in such a heinous crime, someone talks. It just always happens that way. Well, except for this time. This was the exception to that rule. For eight years, no one talked and if they did, the story didn't get out far enough to get on law enforcement's radar. The longer the time from when the murder happened passed, the harder and more improbable that the case would ever be solved. Eight long years with no activity usually meant that it would remain that way. Eight long years with no action usually meant someone got away with murder

It is just a fact that these horrific homicides would have remained unsolved and these men would have gotten away with murder except for one thing. That one thing was the greediness of Calvin Miller. Calvin had a lot of time to sit and think as he had been in prison for the last eight years. Of course, he was the same charming person behind bars as he was outside and in such, he had earned the nickname of "Cheesy Rat." His need and his greed got him wanting for things while he was in prison. He saw other inmates that were able to make their incarceration a little more bearable because of money to buy things and he wanted some.

One might think that prisons provide for all the essentials for a convict so why would an inmate need money. But the fact is that an inmate doesn't "need" extra money but having money to spend on items makes prison more bearable. The prison provides the 'essentials' like soap, shampoo, toothpaste, etc., but they are usually the cheap, low-cost, low-quality items. Further, no inmate has ever said that prison food is wonderful. Also, prisons do not provide books, stamps, envelopes, snacks, electronics, illegal drugs, magazines, money for phone calls, electric razors, cigarettes, medications, but an inmate can buy all of these things at a high price at the prison canteen. So basically an inmate doesn't 'need' money but if he has cash he can buy some things that can his time behind bars more comfortable.

And of course, Cheesy Rat needed money in prison and to get some money he once again came up with a great plan. Since the six men had gotten away with murder, he was sure that they were all still worried about it ever coming out who was involved. There is no statute of limitations on murder and if any new evidence was to come to light, the men could all still be charged. Calvin had another great plan and decided he would reach out to his accomplices and threaten to expose them for the crime unless they sent him cash or "put money on his books" in the penitentiary. Since Trevor Wilson was dead, Calvin's brilliant new strategy was to blackmail his four remaining partners in crime.

Just as much as Calvin Miller lacked in social skills, he was equally deficient in his intellect and insight. Calvin mailed letters and threatened to expose his accomplices. In each letter he demanded money from them in exchange for his silence.

However, in as much as the men were afraid of him on the outside, they were less afraid of him behind prison bars. Maybe the men didn't think Calvin would follow through or they didn't realize the seriousness of the threat but none of them responded. So after close to a decade, Calvin's attempts to reel his former buddies back into his ploys were not successful. None of the men even responded to the threats and Cheesy Rat remained broke in his prison cell.

An inmate has a lot of time to think and dwell and get mad. That's what Calvin did. He was mad. One of his foolproof plans had failed once again. So with his endeavor to pad his prison account having been futile, Calvin thought of a new plot. He would just go ahead and do what he threatened to do. It was no big deal to him. Calvin was serving two life sentences so he figured he had nothing to lose.

Calvin's now revised idea was that if he shared his information about the homicide with the authorities, it might lead to him being able to shave off some time of his current sentence. So, just as he threatened his cohorts he would do, Calvin called the police ready to tell all. Calvin found it was not easy to just call the cops from the Missouri Department of Corrections to give them information but he was persistent and finally got the right person he needed to talk with.

From the high security prison where he was serving two life sentences, Calvin Miller called the Kansas City Police Department Detective's Unit and told them he had some information they needed to find the offenders in two unsolved eight-year-old homicides. As it was an unsolved case, the call was forwarded to the cold case unit. Sometimes luck falls into the laps of the very unsuspecting and that's what happened to Detective Anthony Cooper on October 23, 2003 when he received a collect call from Calvin Miller. Calvin Miller talked and talked and Detective Cooper listened and listened. After Cooper found that there actually might be some merit to the story, Cooper's next call was to Assistant Prosecuting Attorney Phil LeVota.

Phil LeVota was the Assistant Jackson County prosecutor that was currently acting as the Trial Team Leader of the Community Justice Unit of the Jackson County Prosecutor's office. LeVota had been hired while in law school by then prosecutor Claire McCaskill. McCaskill had brought LeVota in to her office seven years earlier and he was now a trial veteran in prosecution. In his position at that time in the Community Justice Unit, LeVota was responsible for supervising a team of trial attorneys who worked directly with the police department handling cases from homicides and robberies to working with the police and neighborhood associations. The unit was created by McCaskill in the mid 1990's to establish a direct link between the prosecutor's office and each patrol unit of the Kansas City, Missouri Police Department. Each of the attorneys LeVota supervised had an office in the prosecutor's office's elite 10th floor in the Jackson County Courthouse as well as an office in their respective KCPD patrol divisions.

LeVota listened to Cooper's recanting of Cheesy Rat's telephone conversation and thought it was worth a follow up. LeVota and Assistant Prosecutor Michael Hunt met with the Cold Case Unit to discuss the case and they all decided that this story was definitely worth a trip from Detective Cooper to visit Calvin Miller in his cell. Cooper and other detectives visited Calvin several times in prison and relayed that his story did match the specifics of the homicides. After those prison visits and more follow up interviews and detective work, the case was presented to the prosecutor's office and charges were finally filed in the homicides of Dennis Moore and Natasha Morgan. Can you guess who else was charged in the murders? None other than Cheesy Rat himself, Calvin Miller. His plan had backfired. Calvin thought he

49

had another great scheme but he was now a defendant in a double homicide case.

The young boy left clinging to his mother's dead body was now eleven years old when the police arrested four of the five remaining people who acted together to murder his mother and Dennis Moore. After all of the interviews and detective work, none of the men could consistently say that Matthew Gulley was in the house when the shots were fired and all said certainly he was not upstairs. Some of the men didn't even remember if he was there or not. So in evaluating the evidence against Matthew Gulley, the prosecutors found that even though he may have been with the men, there simply wasn't enough evidence to prove Matthew Gulley guilty beyond a reasonable doubt and he was not charged but he would be called as a witness in the cases.

The multiple defendants that faced homicide counts were charged under the legal theory of "acting in concert" which means they didn't have to be the actual shooter but if they helped the crime in any way, they were guilty of murder even if they didn't pull the trigger. However, there still wasn't any physical evidence that linked anyone to the crime and the only way to get a conviction was for the men to testify about who was involved.

In sorting through the cases and the different defense attorneys representing the different defendants, deals had to be offered to entice the men to testify in the other cases. Calvin Miller and the Chapple brothers all pled guilty to two counts of second-degree murder, two counts of armed criminal action and first-degree burglary in exchange for their truthful testimony in trial if needed. Marc Powell was offered the same opportunity that the other three were offered but Powell and his public defender wouldn't take the offer. Powell had a right to trial and many other rights under the constitution and it was the burden of the state to find him guilty. Powell did not have to prove himself innocent. Powell and his attorney knew the case against him consisted of testimony from other criminals so they decided to take their chances and opted for a jury trial.

Prosecutor Phil LeVota often told his juries in the jury selection process that unfortunately the people that are witnesses to murders are not always trustworthy people like boy scouts or clergy members but are more often less credible people themselves. However that's what you have to deal with in a homicide trial. That was what Public Defender Tom Symson was banking on. He knew that the State's witnesses were all dirtball, drug dealing thugs that the jury wouldn't like anyway so he just had to poke some holes in their testimony and Marc Powell could be acquitted. However, this was a gamble with Marc Powell's life and as LeVota said, *"It's harder to get 12 people to agree on where to have lunch let alone see the evidence the same and come to the unanimous verdict needed."* So both sides had a battle ahead. Marc Powell's deal remained on the table as the prosecutors worked up the case for pre-trial meetings with the witnesses and preparing the case for trial. Marc Powell never accepted the offer so jury selection began.

As well as his supervisory responsibilities and community outreach, LeVota's other duties as a prosecutor were to carry his own homicide trial docket as well as providing the management and trial training for his attorney group. His team of young prosecutors consisted of the best and brightest young prosecutors in the office. Their unit was a close-knit group of ambitious lawyers. LeVota realized the potential of his team and worked hard to attain good quality cases for them. His goal was to help them become outstanding trial lawyers as well as neighborhood and community problem solvers. LeVota boasts that from his unit of young prosecutors, three of those former prosecutors, Kevin Harrell, Kenny Garrett, and Jennifer Phillips, were all appointed by Governor Jay Nixon as Jackson County Circuit Judges. The governor cited that some of their best qualifications to be appointed to the bench came from their time with LeVota on the 10th floor.

One of LeVota's other duties as a supervising attorney was to supervise the DART unit prosecutor. DART stands for Drug Abatement Response Team. DART is a collaborative, multi-jurisdictional team created to provide assistance to the community by using all legal means to eliminate illegal drug houses in Jackson County neighborhoods. The team consists of the Kansas City Police Department, the Fire Marshall, Department of Family Services, the Water Department and the KCPD Street Narcotics Unit.

The DART team is led by a Jackson County assistant prosecutor and the team identifies and investigates drug activity in residential properties. With this information, the DART unit coordinates the enforcement of all applicable city codes and state laws, and holds property owners and managers accountable for the ill effect their property has on the surrounding area. These functions of the DART unit serve to displace drug dealers and penalize the owners who allow drug activity to continue in and around their property. The DART unit utilizes such legal actions as nuisance, forfeiture and expedited evictions to address drug activity in Jackson County. DART is funded by COMBAT and the State of Missouri Department of Public Safety.

For those not familiar with the COMBAT tax in Jackson County, Missouri, it is important to take a little time to educate you on this one of a kind success. From the County's website: Jackson County voters first approved a tax to "combat" drug use and drug-related crime in 1989. Later dubbed "COMBAT" -- for the Community Backed Anti-Drug Tax -- the tax has permitted

Jackson County to approach the impact of drugs on individuals and entire communities as both a legal issue and public health crisis. The four pillars of the COMBAT program are Prevention, Treatment, Law Enforcement and Anti-Violence.

The theory is that if authorities can prevent a person from ever trying drugs, the person won't ever become an addict. Therefore, many COMBAT-support programs are geared toward children and adolescents, trying to convince them to never have "first taste" of drugs. COMBAT also funds treatment programs that literally save lives, helping drug abusers confront their addiction, "get clean" and stay clean as productive members of our society. COMBAT plays a vital role in law enforcement efforts to shutdown illegal production, with an emphasis on targeting drug traffickers and the dealers. COMBAT has been an unqualified success for more than two decades. Other communities from across the nation and even from around globe have attempted to duplicate what Jackson County has done to "combat" drug abuse and crime.

The Community Backed Anti-Drug Tax (COMBAT) is supported by a renewable county-wide sales tax, at the rate of one-quarter of one percent for a period of seven years, used solely for the purpose of the arrest and prosecution, incarceration, treatment and prevention of drug related offenses and violent crimes; and the judicial processing of adult and juvenile violators of such offenses. Anti-Drug Sales Tax funds annually generate over $19 million and are used throughout the county to support these efforts.

COMBAT has played a vital role in law enforcement's ability to confront drug production and trafficking, as well as other drug-related crimes. COMBAT helps fund the Jackson County Drug Task Force, a multi-jurisdictional agency that helps smaller police agencies more successfully fight drug crime in their communities, and COMBAT funds both the Drug Trial Unit and the **Community**

Justice Trial Unit -- two special programs in the Jackson County Prosecutor's office dedicated to prosecuting offenses in which the use of illegal narcotics contributed to the commitment of a crime.

Furthermore, in its approach to dealing with non-violent drug offenders, Jackson County has become a leading innovator in the nation through the COMBAT-supported Drug Court. The best treatment outcomes are derived under court supervision. The Jackson County Drug Court diverts nonviolent offenders into court-supervised treatment in lieu of incarceration. More than 1,000 Drug Court "graduates" have turned their lives around through this program. A drug court commissioner selected by the judges in Jackson County presides over the Drug Court program in a quasi-judicial role.

Here are just a few of the law enforcement success stories made possible through COMBAT funding: The multi-jurisdictional Jackson County Drug Task Force and the Kansas City Police Department's Street Narcotics and Drug Enforcement Units have seized and recovered more than $300 million worth of controlled substances from Jackson County communities. COMBAT funds 50 correctional officers at the Jackson County Detention Center, which increases the facility's capacity by 200 inmates. More than 60 detectives and law enforcement positions throughout the County are funded by COMBAT. Since 1991, the Drug Abatement Response Team (DART) has stopped drug activity at more than 7,200 Jackson County properties.

So that is probably way more than you ever needed to know about the COMBAT program in Jackson County but you will surely use that info at your next dinner party to impress people with how much you know about law enforcement. Now back to the story. One of LeVota's job duties was to supervise the DART prosecutor. At this time, the assistant prosecutor assigned to run the DART unit was a young attorney named Bethany Campbell. Unfortunately for a budding trial attorney, managing the DART unit leaves little time for the attorney to actually get in the courtroom. But as her supervisor, LeVota knew that Campbell wanted to try cases and had the skills to be a great trial attorney. As the Dennis Moore and Natasha Morgan homicide cases progressed towards trial, LeVota called Campbell to his office to offer her the opportunity to go to trial on a double homicide case. The only catch was that it wasn't a great case.

It was no secret that the "great" cases in the prosecutor's office went to a few very veteran attorneys. When a case is described as great, it meant that it was most likely a "slam dunk" for the prosecution in front of a jury where there were a lot of witnesses and a substantial amount of evidence. As LeVota talked with Campbell about the case he said, *"Oh no. This wasn't a great case."* This was the dreaded "snitch" case where your only evidence was the testimony of one dirtbag against the other. These were the tough cases. These were the ones that most prosecutors shied away from because they were hard and challenging. They were the "dogs" of the homicide cases. These cases took precise organization and exceptional trial skills to win and these were the cases that always made it to LeVota's elite 10th Floor Community Justice Trial Unit. It seemed that all the "dogs" went there. LeVota was the opposite of other trial attorneys in the office. Even as a veteran trial attorney, he actually shied away from the easy 'slam dunks.' It seemed that LeVota loved dogs.

So even though Campbell was presented with a dog, she knew it was her opportunity to go to trial on a double homicide and she jumped at the chance. She was excited to participate in a double homicide as she had limited experience in trial. But LeVota wasn't done with his presentation about the case to her. Even though this case was a dog, LeVota felt that the young and ambitious Bethany was ready to "first chair" this case.

55

In trial work in the prosecutor's office, the "first chair" is the designated prosecutor who makes the main decisions of strategy and planning of the case. Formally it is called the attorney of record for the trial. In Jackson County, each first chair always had the luxury of a "second chair" and they would try the case as a team and split the case load of jury selection, opening statements, direct examinations, cross examinations, rebuttals, and closing arguments between each other. But it was the first chair who had the final word on the case. Actually most trial attorneys learn their craft after sitting as a "second chair" in many trials. It is at a second chair position that most attorneys learn real trial work and develop the successful traits like witness handing and the unseen aspects of organizing a case for trial.

Many prosecutors would select a young attorney to take with them as a second chair but only allow them to take notes and not actually participate. However as he progressed in his own trial career, LeVota was adamant about allowing young attorneys to sit as his second chair and not just take notes but actually allow them substantial parts of the case.

Getting in the game was the best way to learn successful trial skills. The good young trial lawyers were always seen running around the office eager for any second chair experiences they could get. The involvement in the trial setting participating at any level as a second chair was a learning experience and always improved the lawyer's craft. LeVota would speak that in his first year as a prosecutor he 'second chaired" eight jury trials with then prosecutor and now Judge Jeffrey Bushur. As a seasoned veteran prosecutor, Jeff Bushur was a great trial lawyer with a keen mind of his case and of what was important to the jury. When Bushur allowed LeVota as his second chair to actually call witnesses and present half of the closing argument to the jury on all of those trials, LeVota fine-tuned his trial skills rapidly. LeVota would say that he learned more about trying cases in that one year then some attorneys do in their whole career.

56

But in this case as he talked to the young attorney about it, LeVota had a surprise for Campbell. LeVota said that not only was she going to be involved with her first double homicide, but she was going to be first chair. The only condition was that LeVota would sit as her second chair. LeVota was confident Campbell was ready but he also knew he could be there to whisper in his first chair's ear as the trial progressed. Campbell was ecstatic and the trial preparation began. There was a lot of work to do in this "dog" of a case.

By the start of day one of trial, Assistant Prosecuting Attorney, Bethany Campbell had all the many players, witnesses, and evidence all organized and branded in her mind. In her opening statement, she would eloquently try to do the same for the jury. LeVota's advice was that in an opening statement stay away from "legalese" and lawyer mumbo jumbo. Just tell the jury what the story is about and what witnesses you are going to present to them. Finish by telling them that's what they will hear and when they are all done you will be asking them to render a guilty verdict. Speak to the jurors as you would speak to your neighbor or family member telling them about the case. Too many attorneys lose their connection to the jury in the opening statement because they are too sterile and emotionless.

As the fresh-faced brunette prepared for her opening statement, she planned to name all of Powell's accomplices. She would openly admit to the jury that they would hear multiple variations of the facts from these individuals. In jury selection, LeVota had already prepared the jury that they would probably be hearing from less than likeable people in the case. So in her opening statement, Campbell would just ask the jurors to keep an open mind and listen to all the evidence.

Marc Powell's public defender, Tom Symson would open for the defense and would admit that the only consistency they would hear to any testimony was that all the witnesses admitted to being at the scene. His plan was to then go on and stated that there was no evidence that indicated the defendant was actually involved. It was merely a group of boys attempting to fight their way out of serious trouble by pointing their fingers at each other.

Tom Symson had been a public defender for a long while and had tried many cases. He had long ago learned that he didn't have to fight every battle but just find the right holes and keep punching them in hopes a juror might grab hold of that point. Public defenders are a rare breed. Some are the "true believers" that are very frustrating to deal with because they lose their grasp of reality. These unproductive attorneys question and fight on every issue because even though the evidence might be 20 eyewitnesses, a video of the defendant committing the crime, DNA, and group of nuns that all saw the crime, they swear their client is not guilty. They are adversarial on every issue even though their noble actions are a detriment to the trial efficiency and a detriment to their client. They lack strategy and just yell "police cover up" or "the police are liars" to every issue. They are abrasive in the courtroom on every issue and continue to be abrasive outside the courtroom when they need not be.

But to their defense, there are bad prosecutors and bad actors in the police department so some defense claims are not always without merit. However, these over the top defense lawyers that use the same tactics that 'everybody but their client is always wrong' and 'their client is being treated unfairly' are not effective and those tired tactics are clearly seen by the jury. Most often they are young attorneys that just don't have trial or life experience to realize it. Everyone in the courtroom hopes they grow up eventually but know that they won't without causing some major issues. Their overzealous passion that they think is such an advantage is actually harmful to their representation of their current client and to future clients. They lose credibility without even knowing it.

Tom Symson was not that type of defense lawyer. He was smart and he was likeable and he used that in front of the jury. Tom was up front about the problems with his case when he talked to you privately but aggressive as a bulldog fighting for his client in front of the jury. Tom understood what trial work was about and he was good at it. Tom had a simple theory and one that the defense bar should follow. He didn't always try to prove his client innocent. He worked hard to make sure the government didn't prove his client guilty beyond a reasonable doubt. That made him a very successful defense attorney even when he was representing murderers that everyone knew were guilty.

Tom understood that every person deserved a fair trial and a quality defense. If you think that is wrong to give murderers a good defense, then you don't understand what our founding fathers were all about. The government has so much power to utilize over citizens and each and every person accused must be able to defend themselves against this power and force the prosecution to meet the burden of proving guilt. In the case of the State of Missouri v. Marc Powell, Tom Symson found himself with a lot of good issues to deal with for the defense.

The Jackson County, Missouri Circuit Court is the busiest circuit in the state of Missouri. Sometimes there are just more cases scheduled for trial than there are judges able to hear them. On this date, the circuit was utilizing a new division to send trial cases to and it was called "Division 70." No one actually received credit for the name but it was an extra division created that visiting and retired judges would utilize to come back and hear cases. It was called Division 70 as a reference to the age of 70 that is the mandatory age for state judges to retire from full time status. The judge could always be ready to be employed on a part-time basis and come back as a visiting judge or retired judge but just not full time. Division 70 marshalled those cases to be assigned a trial docket in Jackson County to help with the overload.

Marc Powell's case was assigned and set for trial in Division 70 and visiting Judge Carl D. Gum Jr. would be presiding. LeVota was excited to learn that Judge Gum would be hearing the case as this judge had over fifty years of experience and was always more than fair to both sides. Judge Gum also had a great sense of humor and was a pleasure to work with. He made each attorney try a clean case and didn't put up with any nonsense.

Jury selection was typical and 12 jurors and 2 alternates were seated and sworn as Judge Gum sat serious and solemn in his chair behind the large wooden desk and prepared himself for the start of the trial. Prosecutor Campbell delivered a short opening statement that outlined the state's evidence and defense attorney Symson told the jury that they must make the state prove Marc Powell guilty beyond a reasonable doubt.

TRIAL WITNESS: First officer on scene: KCPD Officer Brad Dumit:

The facts were graphic and horrifying but unfortunately that is what a trial is about. It is to tell the story. And unfortunately for a jury who has been chosen to decide the fate of the defendant, the graphic details had to be heard. It was upsetting and many of the jurors cried as they heard from the prosecution's first witness, Brad Dumit, a patrol officer on duty the night of the murders. Officer Dumit talked about the heartbreaking details of finding a toddler screaming and hugging the body of his dead mother.

Prosecutor Campbell, in a no less graphic display, presented into evidence a diagram of the house and pictures of both victims, just as the police found them, dead in their respective pools of blood. She presented a diagram in front of

60

the courtroom via a projector while the officer continued with his direct examination of the crime scene as he found it. Dumit ended his testimony by detailing how he secured the child and the house for safety and preservation of evidence. As the prosecution ended the direct examination, Symson told the court that he had no cross examination for Officer Dumit.

TRIAL WITNESS: Walter Moore

Unlike Dumit's testimony, which set up the scene after the murders, Phil LeVota requested that the next witness, Walter Moore, provide the details that led up to the crimes. Thirty-three-year-old Walter Moore sat confident in the witness chair and made direct eye contact with the prosecutor as he opened with a line of questions that allowed Moore to tell his story. Moore gave background information about his brother and then moved into testimony about the phone call he received from his brother that alerted him that something was wrong. Moore ended his testimony with vivid details of him exchanging gunfire while chasing his brother's car and another car down Indiana Avenue until he lost them.

Symson did not intend to let this witness go without a cross examination and to refresh the witnesses memory, he recapped some of the details of his prior statement. He then fired out a list of questions he thought would emphasize his facts and diminish the State's facts. Moore's demeanor changed from confident to restless and he awkwardly repositioned himself in the witness chair with each response. Symson asked if it was dark outside and Moore thought his three-letter response held the weight of a thousand words and knew it would lead the attorney down a path of additional damning questions but he was truthful anyway. Moore's notion was correct and Symson asked Moore if he was able to identify the two men that were running or if he could see who was driving the cars he was following. Moore nervously cleared his throat before he uttered the word "no" to each question.

LeVota popped back up for a re-direct with one question, "Mr. Moore, Mr. Symson tried to rattle you with all of those questions about it being dark and the time of day and all, but let's be clear, you were never asked to identify who killed your brother because you weren't in the house. You are just here testifying that he called you before he was killed and that you got into a rolling gunfight with someone, right?"

Symson immediately objected, "Leading question." LeVota responded, "Withdrawn," as he turned and looked at the jury as several jurors nodded back at LeVota. His point was made. Symson had tried to discredit Walter Moore about some specifics but LeVota wanted to remind the jury that the State nor Walter Moore were there to say Marc Powell was there. Walter Moore was just part of the story. Not every witness is put on the stand to say, "Yes, I saw the person do the crime." Some witnesses are just filling in the blanks or telling the story in all of its completeness.

TRIAL WITNESS: KCPD Crime Scene Technicians Curtis Boyd & Diane Lutman

Curtis Boyd was on duty as a Crime Scene Technician on the night of the murders. The prosecution called him to the stand and he sat down in his blue police CSI uniform. Boyd was experienced and knowledgeable in his profession and did exceptional work in the field. Boyd also had a welcoming personality that always a made a good impression on the witness stand. It was always interesting to see jurors perk up when a crime scene technician was called to the stand and you could almost read their minds as their eyes widened and they thought "Hey, here is the CSI TV show in real life."

As the prosecutor started her direct examination, Boyd recalled what he observed the night at the crime scene. Before

Boyd arrived, the officers had rolled out the yellow tape, secured the area, and preserved it for his investigation. Boyd explained that the area around the house was sparsely lit and made it very hard to see anything from the street. He stated they found no witnesses despite their neighborhood canvas. Boyd elaborated and stated that regardless of the poorly lit venue, they processed the exterior and the street and were able to recover ten bullet casings on Indiana Avenue. He identified them as 3 casings from an AK47 and 7 casings from a 9mm handgun.

Boyd moved his testimony from the exterior investigation of the house to the interior and discussed the messy condition of the home before he added the details of the gruesome circumstances of the bodies. Both the jury and the courtroom spectators were visibly shaken during his testimony as the prosecutor introduced 63 additional pictures of the crime scene and the bodies into evidence. One-by-one, Boyd expertly recalled and identified each of the eleven-year-old photos including several photos of unfired ammunition and one photo of a fired 20 gauge shotgun shell.

The defense's cross examination with Boyd was short and was directed primarily at what and where evidence was collected and who did the testing. Boyd gave a long list of the things collected including samples of blood, fingerprints, and hinge lifts. Symson asked him to explain hinge lifts for the jury and Boyd elaborated that they were a form of adhesive tape they patted down onto surfaces and bodies to collect fibers and hairs that could possibly contain evidence. Boyd indicated the crime scene technicians both collect the evidence and then send it off to the appropriate lab or fingerprint identification section.

In the same way Boyd testified about the evidence found and collected on Indiana Avenue, Crime Scene Technician Diane Lutman testified about the evidence she collected on the Impala. The information provided by the two gave the jury a clearer picture of some of the additional players involved in the lineup of crime solving; however, it was merely factual and did not identify Powell as being involved. However, it did explain to the jury the professionalism of what happens at a crime scene and how evidence is collected. Again, it was just part of the story of the trial. Without putting these witnesses on the stand, the jury may wonder why someone didn't investigate the crime scene and other questions. The prosecution didn't want the jury distracted by anything like that so the State gave them the whole story.

TRIAL WITNESS: Dr. Thomas Young – Jackson County Medical Examiner

Jury selection took up the whole first day so this was the second day of trial but only the first day of putting on evidence. It was almost midday and the prosecution was nearly half-way through all of their witnesses when Dr. Thomas Young was called to the stand to present his testimony of Moore and Morgan's autopsies. The silver-haired Jackson County Medical Examiner was a veteran when it came to sitting in the witness chair and upon questioning from LeVota, without emotion, he described the shrouds in which the bodies were transported to the morgue.

Young explained how the victim's blood adhered their skin to the white plastic like glue and instead of the shrouds just slipping off; he had to peel them off. He told the jury that detectives and crime scene technicians arrived at the morgue at the same time the bodies did and after he removed the shrouds from the bodies, the police personnel worked to collect and remove any trace evidence. Young then described the collection of evidence under the nails and photographs he witnessed the CSI complete.

Young then detailed a series of non-fatal injuries he observed on both victims, including the wounds he observed on Moore's head and hands. On Dennis Moore's body, Young testified that he believed both injuries were indicative of Moore's

64

hands resting in the same area of his head where his assailant shot him. He included in his testimony the obvious defensive wounds on Natasha in the form of two broken acrylic fingernails. After summarizing the list of injuries, LeVota asked Young to describe the injuries that proved to be fatal and, in the same dry manner, the doctor gave a very in-depth presentation of Moore's and Morgan's passage to death.

The jury listened as Young testified that gunshot pellets journeyed through layers of Moore's chest, first through his skin and then through his breast bone and right lung before it tore into his heart and caused copious amounts of blood to fill his chest cavity. Just as thorough, the doctor described Natasha's fatal head wound and stated that the gunshot blast travelled deep into her brain and caused extensive tears to the right hemisphere as well as multiple fractures to her skull and caused her head to cave in. Young went on to say he recovered all the shotgun pellets and wadding found in the victims and submitted them to Detective Robert Delameter from the homicide unit.

LeVota displayed for the courtroom additional detailed photos of all the injuries. While the jury reviewed them with apparent shock, the defendant remained sitting at the defense table with no show of emotion and stared at the ceiling tiles. LeVota watched each juror as they looked at a picture and passed it on to the next juror. LeVota noticed several of the jurors look at the defendant immediately after viewing the autopsy photos. These weren't looks of sympathy but looks of distaste.

With a host of unflattering photos and unfavorable testimony swimming through the jury's mind, Symson's objective, during his cross examination, was just to explore a list of all possibilities. He had Dr. Young focus primarily on the wounds to both victims' hands. He asked the doctor if all the injuries to Moore's hands could have happened inside a different scenario other than one gunshot blast and if there was a medical determination of how Morgan's fingernails were broken. Concerning Moore's hand injuries, Young indicated that another scenario was always possible but stated that his explanation appeared to be the best fit based on the evidence and his experience. Young continued testifying and indicated that there was, in fact, no specific exam to confirm how Morgan's nails were broken. When asked about fingernail scrapings, he stated he was unsure of any conclusions to any evidence collected from that area as that was a duty of the crime scene technicians. Symson ended his cross with a question concerning any toxicology results received from the victims. Young stated both victims' blood was tested for drugs and both of them showed negative results for drugs in their system.

Again, Symson's attempt to poke holes in the doctor's statement and derail the jurors led to a follow up question by LeVota. *"Dr. you weren't in the house that night when Dennis Moore and Natasha Morgan were brutally gunned down, were you?"* LeVota asked. Young replied, *"No, I wasn't."* It was a question presented solely for effect but it was necessary as it helped reframe Young's original testimony. LeVota then asked, *"Doctor, the medical examiner can't tell us exactly what happened and only the people in that room when those shotguns were fired know exactly what happened, right?"* Young replied, *"Yes, I wasn't there and can only speak to my review of the bodies."* LeVota reminded the jury again that the doctor was only testifying to the facts of how he found the body because Symson had tried to discredit the doctor with the questions of different scenarios.

"Doctor you are not here to say that Marc Powell pulled the trigger or even that he was there that night but you are just here to give us your expert opinion of what may have happened based on your education and professional expertise on what is consistent with the evidence, right?" Young replied, *"Yes, when you suggest a scenario, I can only testify if it is consistent with my*

66

examination of the bodies." LeVota responded, *"So one last question, are the injuries to Dennis Moore's hands consistent with his hands being tied and resting on the back of his head like this when the shotgun was shot into his head?"* Dr. Young said, *"Yes his injuries are consistent with that situation."* The doctor pushed his glasses back on to his face and leaned back in his chair. Dr. Young had been on the witness stand for LeVota many times and Young knew after that question, the prosecutor was finished with the questions. *"No further questions."* LeVota said as he sat down at the counsel table.

In an attempt to try to turn the tables on opposing counsel, Symson re-crossed Young with just one question. He asked him if he had every met Marc Powell before. Young indicated he did not know Powell and with that, Symson ended his re-cross.

TRIAL WITNESSES: Detective Robert Delameter and Detective Marcus Regan

Immediately following Dr. Young, the judicial administrative assistant swore in Robert Delameter to testify. Detective Delameter was as much of a tenacious investigator as he was a likeable guy. His affable personality had served him very well in suspects letting their guard down and him obtaining information. He was one of the most dedicated detectives on the police department and he took each case very personal and from his testimony, he took this one to heart after finding young J.D. sobbing over his mother's body. Even though it had been eleven years since the murder, Delameter did well in recalling the events and his involvement in the investigation of the eleven-year-old crime. Delameter was also humble and upfront during his testimony and stated that his best recollection was that regardless of the police department's thorough investigation and numerous interviews, there was nothing that could lead them to the killers.

67

Just as Delameter testified to the completeness of the investigation and the eventual fruitless investigation, so did Detective Marcus Regan. Regan gave the specifics of many of the leads they followed that were, unfortunately, empty of any useful evidence. He included in his testimony the details of a tip they followed from a woman who pointed a finger at one particular person. But he went on to explain that by the time the tip came in, they had already ruled that person out as a suspect. Regan continued and stated that because they had no additional leads and no DNA to tie any suspects to the crime, the investigation came to a halt by the end of 1995.

Regan testified that the case remained untouched until 2002 when the Kansas City Police Department formed a new cold case squad. Regan explained how this case and hundreds of other unsolved cases were then transferred to that unit for specialized attention. Regan explained that the case remained inactive until 2003 until a detective in the cold case squad received a phone call. The cold case detective then contacted him and Delameter about the new information.

Both Delameter and Regan's testimony painted pictures and opened the juror's minds to the unfamiliar occupation of detective work. They listened as both detectives detailed their procedures, methods, and complications of their job. Again, they were not witnesses that said Marc Powell was guilty but they were witnesses telling the complete story of the incident. These witnesses were also effective keeping the jury focused on the fact that it was about the brutal death of two people as both detectives were almost apologetic about the fact that despite their hard work, they couldn't find the suspects and bring justice to the victim

TRIAL WITNESS: Detective Anthony Cooper

Sometimes luck falls into the laps of the very unsuspecting and that's what happened to Detective Anthony Cooper on

October 23, 2003 when he received a collect call from Calvin Miller. Cooper, a twenty-year veteran of the KCPD took the stand as the State's next witness and gave accounts of the day the unsolicited call came into the department. For LeVota, Cooper testified that unlike Delameter and Regan, he was unfamiliar with the case and while still on the phone with Calvin, he asked another detective to search the database for any offense that matched what the caller was describing. Cooper provided the details of what Calvin had told him in their initial conversation and he stated that he and other detectives subsequently reviewed the file for consistencies. Those findings warranted a trip to the Missouri correctional facility in Jefferson City for a face to face interview with Calvin Miller.

Through his testimony, the jury learned that upon Cooper's first in-person meeting with him, Calvin claimed that his motivation for coming forward was a combination of guilt about the crimes and anger at the Chapple brothers as well as an expectation of sentence reduction. Cooper told the jury that in the meeting at the penitentiary, Calvin only identified Trevor Wilson and the Chapple brothers as being involved. Calvin first said that Ronald and Johnny Chapple were mainly responsible for the homicides. Calvin never mentioned himself, Matthew Gulley or Marc Powell as being part of the crime.

LeVota continued his direct examination and asked Cooper if he had the opportunity to question any of the men mentioned. Cooper replied that he was never able to talk with Trevor Wilson because he was already dead as a victim of an unrelated homicide. Cooper testified that after talking to Calvin, he issued a pickup order for the Chapple brothers. The Chapple brothers were brought in for questioning and he spoke with them. He went on and added that it was in the process of obtaining statements from the Chapple brothers that he found the names of the other three men that were involved including Marc Powell and Calvin Miller.

After the totality of the investigation, it was clear that Calvin had lied about his specific involvement and had hoped to just get the Chapple brothers in trouble alone. Cooper stated that after all of the interviews he was able to ascertain all of the players. He stated he finally had the names of all six men involved and from all the evidence he proceeded to contact the prosecutor to pursue the charges. Cooper concluded his testimony and emphasized that there was no question that this case would have remained unsolved forever but for Calvin Miller making that call. The state had no further questions. Tom Symson muddled, *"No questions"* and as it was 4:45 PM, the court adjourned for the day with only four more witnesses left to testify.

On the first day of hearing evidence in Marc Powell's trial, the jury heard from the responding officer, crime scene technicians, the medical examiner, and three detectives. The jury heard their stories that went from the initial call to 911 about the crime through the years of investigation to the final charging of a cold-blooded, double homicide case. On the following day, the jury was about to hear from four of the six men responsible for those crimes, Ronald and Johnny Chapple, Matthew Gulley, and Calvin Miller were on the state's witness list to tell the rest of the story about that night inside 5901 Indiana Avenue.

TRIAL WITNESS: Johnny Chapple:

Of the four men, Johnny Chapple testified first. The prosecutor asked the short and stocky witness to tell how he knew the five other participants and she reminded him to speak directly into the microphone. Johnny leaned forward and indicated that he had known them all since grade school and then pointed and identified Powell as the middle person at the defense table wearing a suit and tie. Johnny acknowledged that he knew Dennis Moore as well and stated he often rode around with him in his car. He added that Calvin was opposed to the two of them hanging together due to their conflicting gang colors. He continued his account of Calvin's objection and added that Calvin threatened him with a shotgun but promised he wouldn't hurt him if he helped him rob Moore.

Johnny admitted he was present at the Indiana address on the night of the murders and helped in the strategy of getting everybody inside by being a familiar face on the other side of Moore's door. He stated he wasn't aware that anything other than a robbery was going to take place and although he arrived with his brother, he left before everyone else. Johnny said he had been drinking and using drugs and it was late so his memory wasn't the best.

Johnny also admitted that the State charged him with the same offenses as Marc Powell and that he would receive a sentence of ten years in the Missouri Department of Corrections and a condition of that recommendation, he had to provide truthful testimony in this or any other trial related to the crime. Johnny Chapple was clear about Calvin and his brother, and Trevor Wilson as being there; however, Johnny Chapple's memory about whether Marc Powell was there was not as crystal clear.

In the public defender's cross examination, Johnny reiterated that it was the threat by Calvin that placed him at the crime scene but denied being there when the murders took place. After some pushing from Tom Symson, Johnny actually was more adamant about his foggy memory and denied seeing the defendant at the victims' residence. Symson had scored some points with the jury in pressing Johnny on whether Powell was there or not.

TRIAL WITNESS: Ronald Chapple

Just like his brother, Ronald Chapple admitted he arrived at Moore's residence in the same car with his brother and that his brother left prior to him. However unlike Johnny, Ronald was confident that Marc Powell was there. Ronald testified that

71

Powell and the other three defendants followed them to the residence in a Chevy Caprice driven by Trevor Wilson.

In a trial dealing with witness testimony, attorneys can ask the judge to not allow the testifying witnesses to be in the room when another one is testifying as to not allow one to hear what another is testifying to before they get on the stand. To allow one to hear the other may cause testimony to be swayed or poisoned. So while the others testified, the judge did not allow witnesses inside the courtroom. Ronald had not heard his brother's testimony and the details he gave were ones of only someone who had witnessed the event first-hand. As questions rolled off the prosecutor's tongue, so did answers from Ronald with ease. The information he provided flooded the jury with a gruesome sequential chain of the events and added strength to the medical examiner's theory of how specific injuries occurred.

As he continued his direct examination, Ronald indicated he spent the majority of his time downstairs with Matthew Gulley as they were trying to steal Moore's car. But Ronald did talk about his going back upstairs several times throughout the evening. He said the first time he came upstairs he saw Dennis Moore lying naked and face down on the living room floor with his hands tied behind his head. He said he also saw Natasha Morgan naked on the couch. Ronald said that before he went back downstairs, the victims were still alive and unharmed, but then he heard gunfire from the basement. Ronald said he ran upstairs to find Moore was shot and he saw that two of Moore's fingers were missing.

When asked about who was still in the house when he came back up after the first shot, Ronald indicated that everybody but his brother was still in the house. When asked directly if Marc Powell was in that house. Ronald said yes and said Powell was standing in the living room holding an AK47. Ronald was asked more questions about Powell's behavior like if he did anything to Natasha Morgan or if he had anything to do with her being forced to take her clothes off. Ronald indicated that he had not seen that Powell had anything to do with either of those things.

Ronald told the courtroom what he saw but he said his fear of retaliation from the other men was a major concern. On cross examination, Ronald confirmed that he did not want to be testifying and the only reason he was doing so was because of the deal he made. Like his brother, he pled guilty to murder and was to receive a ten year sentence with a condition being his truthful testimony. The Chapple brothers and their attorneys had met with the prosecution team in pre-trial and LeVota had made it clear that if they didn't tell the truth on the stand, this offer would be revoked and they could be looking at a sentence of life in prison. Both of the men and their attorneys agreed that pleading guilty with this deal, testifying in the case, and receiving a ten year sentence was much better than the chance of going to trial and receiving more time.

On cross examination, Symson also asked the witness if he was aware that Calvin Miller actually had told the police that it was he and his brother who were ultimately responsible for the murders and that actually Johnny pulled the trigger that killed the victims. Ronald wasn't shaken and confirmed that he and his brother were both present at the Indiana address that evening, but reemphasized that Johnny left very early and before anyone was killed. Ronald also went on to explain that he had no involvement in the shooting and the murders including the phone call made to Walter Moore or undressing and tying up the victims. Ronald never flinched in taking responsibility for his actions and never faltered on his testimony on who did what in that house but he came up short on saying exactly what Powell did.

Although Ronald made it clear that he was in the house on the evening of the murders, LeVota saw that some of his answers

73

on cross were not consistent and he was swaying from the truth as he looked in the eyes of Marc Powell in that courtroom. Ronald knew that he was going to prison and the last thing he wanted to do was to be called a "snitch" so Ronald was trying to say just enough to put Marc Powell in the Indiana Street house to get his deal but not to finger Powell for specifics.

On redirect, LeVota opened the door to impeachment on his witness. LeVota reminded his witness of what he had just said to Tom Symson about not seeing Powell tie up Natasha Morgan. Ronald quickly responded back saying he didn't see that. In laying the impeachment procedure, LeVota asked if Ronald remembered giving his statement to the detectives concerning Natasha Morgan being tied up. When faced with the statement he gave right after he was arrested, Ronald had no choice but to acknowledge his inconsistency. LeVota did not allow Ronald time to provide his answer before he quoted Ronald's statement to him verbatim where he said that he saw Marc Powell tie up Natasha Morgan. When Ronald heard his own words repeated aloud from his arrest interview indicating that he did see the defendant tie up Natasha; Ronald admitted he remembered saying that to the police.

This line of questioning is a great example of the pitfalls of asking "one too many questions" that many trial attorneys do. The prosecutor had a less than likeable witness on the stand that had testified differently than he had previously about whether he saw Marc Powell tie up Natasha Morgan. Then in re-direct, LeVota was able to get Ronald to admit that he did remember saying to the police that he told them two years earlier that he saw Marc Powell tie her up.

It is almost human nature to ask that next question….."So Ronald, were you lying then or are you lying now."…or something like that and hope for some sort of Perry Mason moment. However for trial lawyers, you don't ever want to give your witness that much room to answer because you never know what they might say because either way you've made your point and you shouldn't let anything derail it. So LeVota sat down without asking that question with the full confidence that he would be talking about that discrepancy. But just not with Ronald Chapple on the stand but in his closing arguments to the jury where they could infer from the evidence that the statement to the police earlier was probably more truthful than the statement Ronald just gave in court with Marc Powell staring at him. The prosecutor would be able to bring up that inconsistency in closing argument when it is just him and the jury.

In this back and forth of re-direct examination with Ronald, the prosecutor was more harsh and assertive. LeVota was eager to aggressively go after Ronald and demonstrate to the jury that the prosecutor had a disdain for Ronald but had to work with him to get this conviction. LeVota knew the jury hated Ronald Chapple and when Ronald was telling a different story about who tied up Natasha, LeVota pounced at the opportunity to rip into him and demonstrate to the jury that LeVota didn't like him either. But the goal of Ronald's testimony was to place Marc Powell in the room and he did that. Whether Ronald was lying about Powell and Natasha, there was never a discrepancy about the fact that Marc Powell was in the house when the murders happened. What the defense thought might have gained them points, actually backfired and allowed the prosecutor to beat up on his own dirtball witness. That beating and the damages that resulted in that turn of events, in turn, probably harmed the defense.

TRIAL WITNESS: Mathew Gulley

There were five people that gave different statements of the events of that night and not surprising, each person had their own account of the facts, including Matthew Gulley. Gulley's testimony was different in that he provided the least amount of

75

detail. He told LeVota that all six of them, including Powell went to the Indiana residence all in one car, but he thought they were only going to buy drugs. Gulley said that once inside, he saw someone hit Moore in the head. Gulley stated he didn't see who struck Moore but when he saw him fall to the floor, he immediately went downstairs so as to not be a part of what was going on. Gulley then indicated he only wanted to steal the car and stayed downstairs until he heard three gunshots at which point he backed the car out of the driveway and left everyone else behind. Gulley also admitted his recall of the night's events was clouded. Gulley didn't say that his memory was bad because of the many years that had passed, but because on that night he was high on both PCP and marijuana. Gulley testified that everyone had been doing PCP and marijuana before they went to Dennis Moore's house.

LeVota's intentions were obvious in his direct exam of Gulley and despite his declaration of memory loss, LeVota wanted to make sure the jury was aware of what Gulley did remember. He specifically emphasized that Gulley remembered Powell was in the house when he questioned him about the participants involved in the events. Gulley confirmed, no less than seven times, that Powell was inside the residence on the evening of the murders.

During cross examination, Symson preyed heavily on Gulley's memory loss and a discrepancy between his police interview and the testimony he gave to LeVota. With the implication that Gulley had said that Powell was not at the residence, Symson presented the witness with a transcript of his police statement in which he said there were only four other people with him that evening. Gulley immediately said he might have said there were only four other people with him but he was sure about the fact that one of those four people was Marc Powell. The defense's attempt to use Gulley's generic term of saying there were five people there to exclude Powell from being there as a defense, seemed to fall flat to the jury.

TRIAL WITNESS: Calvin Miller –"Cheesy Rat"

By midday on the third day of trial, the state had called all of their witnesses but one: Calvin Miller. LeVota announced, *"The State of Missouri calls Calvin Miller to the stand."* The sheriff's deputies escorted Miller into the courtroom and to the witness stand where he was sworn in. LeVota's first question was *"Please state your name for the record."* After that the six-foot tall Miller faced the jury wearing his orange prison jumpsuit and told his version of the murders on Indiana Avenue.

Calvin recalled the events that led up to the night Dennis Moore and Natasha Morgan lost their lives. He admitted that he saw Johnny selling drugs with Moore and that he didn't like it. However, Calvin Miller then testified that it was actually Johnny Chapple and Trevor Wilson who initiated the plan to rob Moore. There was no question from his demeanor that Calvin thought himself as very clever in using Trevor Wilson as a scapegoat since Wilson was dead and could never be called to testify. Clever Calvin continued to name Wilson several more times as one of the main instigators. He said Wilson approached him with the idea to rob Moore and he went along with it but didn't think Moore had any money.

In the same way LeVota kept specifically asking Matthew Gulley about Powell's behavior, he did the same in his direct examination of Calvin. LeVota asked Calvin if Powell was with him when as they drove to Dennis Moore's house and he asked him if Powell had a gun. Calvin indicated that six people, including Powell, rode to the residence in two cars and Powell definitely had a gun, an AK47. This was consistent with all the other witnesses about Powell's weapon of choice. Calvin then added everyone had a gun with the exception of Johnny who had two guns. Calvin said Johnny had a 20 gauge in his pants and a .45 caliber in his hand.

As the master of manipulation, Calvin continued to point the finger at everyone and 'sugar coat' his involvement in the murders and even went as far as to say he never went inside the residence until he heard the first gunshot. Calvin continued his account of the murders and indicated he saw Johnny shoot Dennis Moore in the chest and then he watched Johnny Chapple walk down the hall with Natasha Morgan and seconds later heard another gunshot. But little did he know that this was the first time anyone in the courtroom had heard that Johnny Chapple was the shooter when all the others had said he left early. LeVota watched the jury as they listened to "Cheesy Rat's" testimony. They weren't buying it.

In an almost smart aleck way of acknowledging to the jury that LeVota realized the jury didn't believe Calvin, LeVota asked, "Ok Calvin, we all understand that you had nothing to do with any of it but my question is, where was Marc Powell as all of this was going on?" Calvin answered, "He was right there pointing the AK47." And that's what LeVota needed. Calvin could try to skirt the other issues but the important point in the case of the State of Missouri v. Marc Powell was whether Marc Powell was in the house, not whether or not he pulled the trigger. Even though Calvin thought he was outsmarting everyone and trying to get Johnny Chapple in more trouble because the Chapples wouldn't give him money in prison, Calvin gave exactly the testimony the prosecution needed.

Usually when a witness is on the stand, the prosecutor will ask them about convictions and prior bad acts as to take the sting out of it because the defense attorney will ask them about it in an effort to question their credibility. But not this time and not this witness. LeVota realized the jury saw Calvin in a prison jumpsuit and didn't even touch on his priors. LeVota didn't care if the defense brought up his priors. Calvin was a violent criminal. LeVota didn't want the jury to like him or even think he was credible. The jury already saw that the important issue was that Calvin was consistent on who was there, especially Marc Powell and that's all the mattered. Let the defense attorney have at him.

Calvin had a terrible history of not learning from his mistakes and while being cross examined by Symson, he admitted to his many prior misdeeds, including robbing drug dealers and murder. To his own undoing, Calvin even admitted in his first police interview that he did not mention Matthew Gulley. Calvin said he failed to mention Gulley because he didn't want Gulley to get locked up because Calvin wanted to go kill Gulley himself. Calvin went on and testified that he was once Marc Powell's friend but no longer considered himself a friend to Powell. Symson continued to show the jury that Calvin Miller was a terrible person. He did a great job at it and even though Calvin said Powell was not the shooter, Symson could not shake Calvin on his testimony that Powell was in the house when the shots were fired.

Marc Powell chose not to testify in his defense and at the end of the trial in the many jury instructions given to jury, they would be instructed that they could not use that fact against him.

After Calvin's colorful testimony ended, both sides rested and closing arguments commenced. The prosecution focused heavily on the consistencies of the last three witnesses in that Ronald, Gulley, and Calvin all indicated that the defendant was at the residence while the crimes were taking place. In the first half of the state's closing argument, Campbell told the jury that all participants were responsible regardless of who pulled the trigger and that because Powell was there; he needed to take responsibility for his actions.

Defense closing arguments began and Symson attempted to deconstruct the prosecution case and argued that Calvin was already in prison and wanted to take others down with him. He pointed out the inconsistencies of the witness's testimony of where people were standing, what time it was, who had what gun, and who tied who up. Symson advised the jury to reject the witnesses because they only testified to get lighter sentences. He concluded and informed them that there was no physical evidence to support their stories and that Mark Powell wasn't there.

LeVota started his rebuttal and final part of the trial with a quote he had used so many times before in his closing arguments. As the defense attorney sat down after asking the jury to find Marc Powell not guilty, LeVota stood up and walked directly in front of the jury, cleared his throat and began with:

"I'm from Independence and one of my personal heroes is Harry Truman. President Truman had a saying that went, if you can't convince them, confuse them.......... and that's what Marc Powell is trying to do to you today," as he pointed at the defendant.

LeVota then meticulously went over the consistent testimony of people who were there, albeit bad actors themselves, and the glaring fact was that everyone said Marc Powell was there. LeVota told the jury that he didn't like the scumbag witnesses and he didn't expect the jury to like them either. But the jury had listened close to what all of them did say and it was the same. That simple fact was that Marc Powell was involved in the drive to Dennis Moore's and in all of the brutality inside that house. The evidence presented proved guilt beyond a reasonable doubt and there was evidence that Marc Powell was there. Witnesses may have gotten other things differently but the issue that was on trial was whether Marc Powell acted in concert in the murders. LeVota told the jury that after hearing the consistent evidence of Powell being there, the only verdict that was fair and just according to the evidence was to find Marc

80

Powell guilty of murder. LeVota ended by reminding the jury again that the case is not about whether Powell being the shooter but about Powell being at the scene and acting together with others to commit a crime.

It took eleven years to bring these men to justice and then another three days for Marc Powel's trial but it took less than eight hours of deliberation to convict Mark Powell of all charges. He was sentenced to thirty years in the Missouri Department of Corrections.

Even though Calvin Miller decided to "rat out" his fellow conspirators in helping the police solve one of their coldest homicide cases and despite the damning testimony in the trial of Marc Powell, his plan to get his sentence reduced backfired. He did get a deal for his testimony in the Marc Powell case, but unlike the Chapple brothers' ten years, Calvin Miller racked up an additional 17 years to his prison term for his role in the murders of Dennis Moore and Natasha Morgan.

Every prosecutor has that inner feeling of distaste when they have to deal with the likes of Calvin Miller and allow him to get only seventeen years when he might have been the actual shooter but it is a prosecution reality that deals must be made with the worst people in the world to get justice for victims. But in the end, finally, justice for the brutal murders of Natasha and Dennis finally had come to pass.

2

Racist, Criminal, Manipulator, & Murderer

Born August 20, 1961 at Research Hospital in Kansas City, Kathryn Brown entered life with the proverbial silver spoon. Nicknamed "Kat" at an early age, she was raised in an affluent Kansas City family and had many options available in her young life. However, just having positive images and options in a life does not necessarily result in positive choices. Even though Kathryn Brown had many choices, she made lots of bad decisions. She was pushed through her childhood by money and lack of responsibility and all the while she wanted for nothing. But her generous upbringing did not enhance her respect for money or authority and Kathryn eventually became very familiar with the inside of a jail cell at a young age.

A child of the early sixties, Kathryn innocently grabbed hold of the tail end of the hippie culture as she entered adolescence and connected to its carefree lifestyle. This was quite contrary to her regimented routine of Catholic school and afterschool religious studies. By the late seventies, even though the hippie movement was over, Kathryn held on to those same values and embraced that counterculture instead.

Kathryn was pushed quite aggressively by her parents to attend college but against those wishes, she pursued a less prestigious path of dance clubs and rock concerts. Her free spirited attitude made it easy for her to embrace the most current views on civil rights, women's advocacy, and the sexual revolution. She held no restraints in speaking her opinion or freely expressing her sexuality. Her mind was open to anything, found nothing wrong with exploring alternative states of consciousness, and happily accepted offers of marijuana and LSD from friends and even strangers. Kathryn's views were vastly different from her parents' views but she found living within their financial assistance was easier than not having any money. Her desire for fun and freedom grew and even though she was rebelling against her social status and said materialistic things were unimportant, she secretly needed her parents because she remained unemployed and well taken care of by their money.

Her access to money, lack of accountability, and "the girl-next-door" good looks continued to provide Kathryn lots of friends and attention in her late teen years. However, by the time she turned 21, she had gained a serious drug addiction. Her free spending of her parents' money and her bad choice of friends earned her this huge problem. The continued behavior took a toll on the family and was met with an example of tough-love from her parents. They made her to move out and cut off her money. Kat made the decision not to change her behavior and naively thought she could make it on her own without the help from mom and dad. Forced out of her parents' home and cut off from their money, her promising future was diminished by her bad decisions. Unfortunately, her adoration of drugs remained ever constant. Without her parent's money, Kathryn's choices became even more destructive and the consequences even more devastating.

Kathryn's most traumatic and life changing moment happened on the evening of February 26, 2000. Kathryn was pouring dog food into her dog's bowl in the kitchen while her boyfriend, Kevin Tucker watched TV on the sofa in the family room. Kathryn let out a big sigh as she looked around her new living arrangement. The once barely livable house was very low rent but in a quiet eastside area of Kansas City. Kevin had made arrangements with the landlord to remodel the home in exchange for rent and then towards the possible purchase of the house. Kevin spent the whole day on a drywall project and had just finished some mudding a final piece and had just called it quits for the day and sat down on the couch. Kevin didn't move when the doorbell rang but watched Kathryn as she dried her hands on a paper towel while walking from the kitchen to answer the door.

To rewind and give you the background, the story of Kat and Kevin was anything but typical in how they came to be there on that specific day. Years before, Kevin Tucker was just another tall, thin black male who started balding at an early age. He had full cheeks and light, smooth skin that made him appear cherub-like and happy. Kevin often shaved his head to avoid what he called the "bald men trying to compensate" look or covered his head with a hat. He never lacked in friends as his features and humorous demeanor often drew people to him and made them feel comfortable.

Kevin never had it easy. He was the youngest boy in a large family of eight and like many kids of large families, he lacked individualized attention but craved it nonetheless. Raised by an aunt after his mother died, he used humor as an attention-seeking ploy and as a way to fit in with his peers. Unfortunately for Kevin, his audiences were not always the best influences.

When he was growing up, he attended church regularly. He believed religion to be important on his list of priorities and it was a driving factor in his decision making process. But Kevin Tucker hated being alone and went along with most anything to gain companionship even if it conflicted with his religious teachings. Minor crimes and truancy often caused him trouble with authority figures and although his offenses were small, Kevin had multiple run-ins with the police and several school suspensions by the time he was fifteen. Society had already applied the 'delinquent' label to Kevin by the time he entered high school. Nevertheless, as Kevin matured, so did his desire to redeem himself from his past mistakes.

Kevin made good on his aspirations to stay out of trouble and was promoted to a full-time supervisor's job at a local motorcycle factory. However, an automobile accident kept him in constant pain and after an extremely long day in the factory months after the accident, he found himself in severe pain but with no paid meds. A helpful co-worker offered Kevin some Oxycodone which he had never tried before. The pill knocked out all the pain and on the next day he went back to his friend for more.

His simple desire to relieve the pain soon turned into a huge drug addiction. Like many other addicts, Kevin sought out even better highs and eventually turned to heroin. He realized that like Oxycodone, heroin was an opiate and actually even easier to attain than the legal drug. Kevin had no idea where the drug use would lead him but after only a week of continuous use, the desire grew. He was soon spending hundreds of dollars a week on the drug.

Kevin, like typical heroin users, felt heroic, more focused, and confident. However, the highly addictive drug depleted his concentration and confidence at work. His main effort was on securing his next high. As Kevin became habitually late and absent from work, he compromised his good reputation and found himself in danger of losing his job. He knew he had a problem and Kevin tried to kick the habit on his own, spending days in bed at home and going to the hospital. This met with no success. He kept using.

As he got into a routine, he found that Fridays were usually his day to stock up on his drugs and it was just a typical afternoon. Kevin was just looking for a helping hand when he found himself taken into police custody on drug trafficking and heroin possession charges in November of 1998. It was just another cloudy day in November when he had just picked up some drugs for the next week when his truck broke down. He had just purchased this GMC Truck from a co-worker who described it as "nice" and it was supposed to run great. He was surprised that it stopped running just minutes after he left the drug house and picked up his package.

After his initial anger, he looked more thoroughly at what might be the problem and he realized that he had ran out of gas. He hadn't had the truck long and he didn't realize the gas gauge didn't work. Penniless, Kevin processed his options. He could walk home or flag down a car and ask for help with gas. It was cold and a far walk, so Kevin waved down the first car he spotted. As the car stopped to help him, his happiness soon became anxiety when he realized he had waved down an unmarked Kansas City Police Department car.

Kevin immediately thought about the truck, the registration, and the license plate and then realized he had everything legal so he would have no problems with that. The only problem was the package sitting on the seat of the truck. The officer stopped and the men talked. It was only a matter of time before the officer, who had stopped to help, routinely asked if he could search the car. Within minutes, the Good Samaritan that was there to assist him was now handcuffing Kevin and arresting him for drug possession.

Kevin was taken downtown for processing and was sitting in a chair at the station waiting to be dealt with. Detective Gary Lynch was not the arresting officer who brought Kevin into the station on that Friday evening but was sitting close to the officer who was filling out paperwork about Kevin's arrest. Lynch recalled being a little surprised, at first, by Kevin's arrest as his demeanor and vernacular were different from most other drug addicts that came through the system.

Dressed in his generic grey factory uniform, he thought Kevin lacked the characteristics that usually accompanied drug addiction and Kevin seemed quite intelligent and polite. These different issues that seemed to set Kevin apart from many other drug addicts made Lynch pretty confident that Kevin was new to the drug scene. The young homicide detective was actually working on a case where the murder victim was a drug addict at the wrong place at the wrong time. He took a pause from his own case to wonder how long Kevin had been caught up in the poisonous culture or if his life was beyond the point of return. Unfortunately, Lynch didn't have time to linger on Kevin's situation too much and he went back to his business of solving his own case as Kevin was processed, fingerprinted, and placed in a jail cell for the weekend.

While Kevin awaited someone to bail him out jail, he remained in custody for forty-hours. Being without drugs for that long made his withdrawal symptoms set in. Nonetheless, determined to stop using this poison, he took advantage of the almost two full days without heroin. When he got out, he contacted his work and took a leave of absence from his job. He locked himself inside his house and vowed to conquer his drug addiction. Kevin was quitting cold turkey. After doing some research, he planned a self-detox program in which he relied on some leftover prescription painkillers to alleviate some of the withdrawal symptoms. Kevin didn't like the idea of swapping one drug for another, but was sure, at least by his standards, that being addicted to heroin was much worse than being addicted to pain meds.

Heroin withdrawal is tough.   Like others suffering from withdrawal, Kevin suffered severe body aches, diarrhea, vomiting, insomnia and leg cramps. He was violently ill. On the fourth day he was no longer able to stand the symptoms. After pain, tears, and agony, he gave in and started to find out where he could find a new dope man. Now dangerously desperate for a fix, Kevin jotted down an address he received from a friend and in less than an hour was knocking on a promising door in an unfamiliar neighborhood. The person that answered that door would be Kathryn Brown and it would be the first time they would meet each other. But for now, let's hit the "pause" button and catch up with Kevin Tucker a little later.

Years before she met Kevin Tucker and right after she left her parents' house, Kathryn Brown had nowhere to live until she found an abandoned house on Elmwood Avenue in Kansas City. Uncut grass and tall weeds enclosed the house and she had no idea why the house was abandoned but it was in terrible shape. A brown door with a gold knocker was useless lying on the ground in front of the house and the front windows were almost all broken out as shreds of glass stuck both to the window frames and gathered on the ground underneath. With no other option and little money, Kathryn unpacked her few belongings inside the deserted home.   In the mostly black neighborhood, the abandoned home on Elmwood was once an eyesore to its neighbors. The previous owners blamed the bank for its unsightly condition and the bank promised the neighbors they would send a lawn mowing service out to landscape the overgrown lawn. That never happened and soon the bank stopped even responding to the complaints from the neighborhood. However, Kathryn soon had some of her male friends mowing the lawn and making minor repairs to the residence.

Kathryn's life was far from the indulgent one she had once known but she was content with her small and simple home that she was squatting in. The problem was that her addiction and her

89

lack of a steady income left her with few choices for survival. One thing that she did find made her money was selling her body, so prostitution became one of her resources. But Kathryn didn't want to be a "street walker" as she described others, so she ran an ad in a local newspaper where she offered traditional massage therapy. One option of the therapy was sexual services. Within the month, she had a small but steady flow of clientele entering and leaving the once abandoned home on the city's east side.

Not long after her new career was established, it was obvious her customers had vastly different appetites and sex wasn't the only thing her clients had a taste for. With that information, she did what she did best and added drugs to her menu. Kathryn's Elmwood Avenue industry grew. She was making money. Her customers grew and even as her business flourished, one thing remained constant. She was constantly visited by her first and oldest client, Chester James.

In relation to crime in the Kansas City area, there are those who know crime exists but are so far removed from it they almost forget about it. There are those who are unfortunate enough to live in the middle of it and can't forget about it. And finally, there are those who embrace crime and make a living from it. Chester James was the definition of a career criminal.

When Chester James was born, it was a time of war and a time when women had gotten out of the house and into the workplace. WWII dominated the 1940s and it was not the happiest of decades for the James family. Chester's father died in an automobile accident when he was just nine-years-old, forcing his mother to leave the home to make a living and increasing their hard times twofold. Chester was the oldest of five children and took over the position of man-of-the-house at an early age. Until he was old enough to work outside the home, he supplemented his mother's income by hunting and fishing for food in the rural area outside of Kansas City where they lived.

After his father died, Chester never considered his role in the family as anything other than one of authority and, in turn, his siblings regarded him as more of father figure than a brother. He had an intimidating and persuasive personality and he used manipulation and threats as the compliance tactics he used to enforce household rules. His siblings loved him but feared him more and they heeded to his authority. He dominated his family by intimidation and he also carried his influence outside the household. In school, Chester was most definitely the class bully. However, despite his reputation, underneath, he was self-conscious, cowardly, and shy. These characteristics magnified his need to maintain authority.

Chester married as soon as he quit high school. He left school mainly because he was in trouble all of the time and missed more classes than he attended. Chester married Patricia who was a middle child two years his junior. If you would have asked Patricia about her new husband she would say she knew two things about her husband. He was a violent racist who hated blacks and that he had a roaming eye as far as other women. Patricia would say at the time she married, she was young and naïve and thought that marriage would settle him down. However, Chester did not take his vows seriously and often spent his nights somewhere else. He also forced his young wife to spend her time with his family who lived on the same desolate dirt road. Chester knew that Patricia, just like everyone else, would not question his decisions or talk back to him because they knew the consequences.

It didn't take long for Patricia to figure out that Chester was never going to settle down and that she would never be her husband's first priority. He had a long list of other hobbies for which he didn't need his wife for and that kept him copiously occupied.   Stealing from everyone, robbing banks, using prostitutes and taking drugs were among a few of his favorite pastimes and he was often gone for months at a time.

Chester was not good at his criminal enterprises and often got caught.   The Missouri Prison System was very familiar to Chester but unfortunately, it didn't serve as the crime deterrent for which it was designed.   Chester moved in and out of prison multiple times throughout his life. At one time Chester boasted he had been in prison more years of his life than he had been out of prison. When Chester wasn't in prison, he was always involved in some sort of illegal activities. In his "out of prison" time," he was never without a loaded gun, a roll of cash, and an alibi. That was the one thing he did rely on his wife for. Patricia always provided a shaky alibi. Patricia was a loyal wife and did what she was told, rarely knew of his whereabouts when he wasn't at home, but was quick to say he "had been with her" if needed.

By the end of the 1960's, the civil rights movement was in full swing and Chester had picked up another full-time interest. Chester and Patricia had moved from the country to the city where it was easier for him to maintain his hobbies. Chester found the racial issues far more exaggerated in the urban area. Chester knew that most places in the Kansas City area still had policies that segregated the blacks from the whites and for that, he was grateful. Chester didn't like sharing his personal space and he felt very strongly in excluding blacks from equal participation in public places. Chester's posture was more than just a minor discomfort around certain black people in his community. It was a profound intolerance aimed in the direction of the entire black population. Chester could often be found screaming racial epithets at blacks as he drove by or walked by them for no other reason than the racism in his heart.

Chester's strong prejudicial opinion kicked into full gear by the time Chester was in his thirties. Chester held membership in several anti-black organizations, including the Ku Klux Klan, an organization best known for its avocation of white supremacy. Chester used his involvement in those groups to oppose the Civil Rights Movement as well as desegregation. Well known for his membership participation, he led many of the biased group activities. Despite the declining membership of the KKK and other hate assemblies in the seventies, Chester's involvement was as intense as ever. Because of his membership involvement and his criminal history, he was consistently under the local authority's microscope when racial crimes were committed and was often arrested for those offenses. But unfortunately, he was never charged for some crimes and sometimes it was because of Patricia's alibis.

But sometimes, Chester's activities ended him up in prison. Although Chester appeared to have influence on the outside, the inside of prison was completely different. His power on the outside was not as valuable on the inside and a chain of command was already in place. He found that assuming authority and respect was something earned and not granted, nevertheless, Chester intended to climb the prison power ladder. He clung to those that shared his beliefs.

Chester joined the Aryan Brotherhood, a notorious white supremacist gang, where he fit in very well. But regardless of his involvement in one of the most powerful anti-black gangs, prison was not an easy time for him. Unfortunately, the gang had an initiation agenda that preyed upon the weaker inmates. More specifically, the initiation preyed on first-time inmates who were unfamiliar with prisoner protocol. In a huge contrast of how his life was on the outside, Chester was a personal servant in the penitentiary for the prison gang. He didn't like it as he was not used to doing other peoples' bidding. However, it appeared to be his best method of survival and with each new prison sentence, prison life became more manageable.

In his many prison stays, Chester was pleased with the unspoken rules that the inmates congregate to their own race. His involvement with the anti-black group along with the unspoken segregation practices only reinforced his racism. With every prison stint, he became more biased and blamed all results of his bad decisions on black people.

As a good business practice, Kathryn made personal notes of all her clients but as Chester poured his money into her business every week, she made sure she knew him well. She knew he was a creature of habit and she knew his likes and dislikes were inflexible. His visits to Kathryn's house were always on the same nights and times and his sexual demands never varied. Heroin was his drug of choice but he rarely purchased it from Kathryn as she always got him high for free when he was there. He was a punctual man and could not stand for anyone to be in Kathryn's home while he was there, regardless of his or her business. Upon his arrival, it wasn't uncommon for him to become violent with her clients if they did not appear to be leaving soon. Despite her regard for his needs, it eventually became obvious to Kathryn that Chester didn't care about her business as he kept messing it up and the two argued about the issue often.

Over the years, Kathryn saw Chester's violent side more than she cared to but he never directed his violence at her. He had a history of aggressive behavior towards many people and on that issue he was very non-racial about it. But ironically, Kathryn always felt safe and protected when he was around. In turn, regardless of their arguments, Kathryn tolerated most of his idiosyncrasies. However, she did have one rule for Chester to obey when he was around and that was for him to keep his mouth shut and never to practice his racial prejudice around her or her customers. Chester's fondness for Kathryn kept him in line most of the time.

To Chester, Kathryn was more than a friend and he had very strong feelings for her, but unfortunately for Chester, Kathryn's feelings toward him were not mutual. To Kathryn, who had a history of bad relationships, Chester was a just high-paying customer she had become friends with and one she would do anything to make sure she didn't lose that business. Those unbalanced feelings always bothered Chester and he was always jealous of other men around Kathryn.

Kathryn kept running her profitable drug house out of her new home she had spruced up even though she had no right to be there. The once neglected and paint stripped home was upgraded by Kathryn to a livable residence and no one suspected a thing. She repaired the door and painted the outside of it an inviting soft yellow. She painted the trim around the windows a rustic brown and lined the cracked sidewalk with flowers. Potted plants framed the steps to the door entrance. Even though, Kathryn maintained a tidy home and yard, many of her "guest's" cars often cluttered the street in front of her home.

Although Kathryn's maintenance of the abandoned home was respectable, the traffic coming and going was intolerable to her neighbors. In winter, the same bank that had once ignored complaints about the abandoned property, finally intervened. When they found the property was being lived in by someone who had no right to be there, the bank had no mercy on Kathryn or the repairs she did to the Elmwood home. When the bank learned that she had just decided to move into an abandoned house, they began the eviction process and served her with papers. Kathryn was devastated that she was being forced out of her home she had worked on but with the fear of the police uncovering her other wrongdoings, she told the bank she would be out immediately. But she had nowhere to go. Under strong persuasion by Chester, Kathryn moved herself and her business into Chester's home with his wife, Patricia.

Chester's home hid behind a yard full of trees and sat back off the street and even on the sunniest days, it appeared gloomy and dark. Privacy was something Chester preferred, as he did not like the neighbors seeing into his business. The house was small and Patricia did not welcome Kathryn as her live-in houseguest nor did she welcome the competition. However, Chester's decision concerning living arrangements for Kathryn was non-negotiable with Patricia. Kathryn remained there for several years until Chester's next stint in prison.

After one of his former prison sentences, Chester was released to a halfway house and is where he met Margaret Fowler years before Kathryn was being kicked out of her house. This former prison sentence was a five year sentence but after two years, Chester was released to serve the rest of his time in a half-way house. The two-story halfway house located in downtown Kansas City had room for only twenty people and was over populated like every other rehabilitation facility in the city. Chester was one of last ones accepted the month after his release from prison in 1996. The halfway house functioned inconspicuously as it housed, fed, monitored, and counseled inmates who had taken jobs with private employers while they awaited parole. Some inmates had jobs and left the halfway house to work and returned in the evening. The management of the home expected each resident to participate in the everyday activities. Inmates helped with housekeeping or meal preparation and if an inmate refused to cooperate, it was grounds for immediate discharge, which meant a trip back to the penitentiary.

Chester was compelled to accept his responsibilities because going back to prison was not an option for him. At least that's what he told Margaret Fowler who was an employee of the halfway house. Margaret had worked in the halfway house for many years and had a caring, nosy, needy, personality that got her way too involved with the inmates. Maybe because she was lonely or maybe because she was trying to help but she had always gotten involved with inmates. There wasn't a past or present resident she didn't know and she quickly made friends with Chester within days after his arrival. Chester immediately took advantage of Margaret Fowler's insecurities and started his manipulation of her.

Chester spent months in the halfway house and spent much of that time being close with Margaret. Within weeks after Chester was released from the halfway house, Margaret quit her job and she and Chester became even better friends and were even intimate for a brief time. However, Chester was already married and overly preoccupied with Kathryn. Margaret first became aware of Kathryn when Kat called Chester asking him for help with a hard-to-please client. At first, Margaret was not mindful of her profession; however, she knew Chester well enough and quickly figured out the various roles Kathryn played in Chester's life.

Margaret was thankful she didn't work at the halfway house anymore because as an employee, she was under a lawful obligation to report Chester's indiscretions to his parole officer. She was now learning all of his illegal activities with Kathryn as well as the gun he carried in the waist of his pants. These were major violations of his parole conditions. It became clear to Margaret that Chester wasn't as afraid of prison as he had once claimed. Like most people who knew Chester, she did not question him as she knew he was up to no good. Margaret had learned that it was in her best interest to keep her mouth shut.

Margaret never knew what Chester saw in Kathryn. Margaret described her as looking tired with her hollow cheeks and dark circles under her eyes. She felt that her straight blond hair was stringy and over processed and that Kathryn looked

97

older than her forty years. However, Margaret didn't know Chester and Kathryn's history and Margaret was no beauty herself. Margaret was less than plain looking with lines so deep in her face it was hard for anyone not to infer a tragic story from them. She was thin with dirty gray hair and blotchy skin. The dark stains on her teeth were evidence of many years of heavy smoking.

Other than what she did for an occupation to make money, Margaret knew very little about Kathryn. But what she did know was that Kathryn seemed to have a way with men. Margaret wasn't sure if it was what Kathryn was selling that drew the men in her direction or if it was her personality, but she always seemed to have them hanging around. Margaret had an unhealthy love for Chester and was jealous of any woman he ever even talked to. She had no evidence but suspected that Chester and Kathryn were intimately involved and she had a problem with that. She never expressed her jealousy and never let on to Chester that his fascination with Kathryn bothered her. She knew Chester would do what he wanted, regardless of her feelings. Like anyone desperate for attention, Margaret tolerated the other women in Chester's life.

To no one's surprise Chester was again arrested, charged, and convicted of yet another crime and sentenced to 4 years in the Missouri Department of Corrections. Chester had already done the math and figured he would be out in 18 months. In the meantime, Kathryn was clearly not welcome by Patricia in Chester's home so she decided to move. Kathryn found a house to rent and moved her "business" there. Free from Chester's influence, she even stopped using drugs but didn't stop selling them.

In November of 1998 and on an eastside urban street with no particular pleasing scenery or aesthetics, Kathryn sat with her feet propped up and petted her Pit Bull, Brandy. Despite the snow-covered ground, Kathryn's feet were nearly naked with the exception of a pair of flip-flops she purchased at the Dollar Tree the prior summer. She kept a pair of over-sized, pink galoshes near the front door for when she went out because no other shoes would fit her swollen feet. Kathryn was clean and sober and in the last weeks of her third trimester of an unwanted pregnancy. But even though she was pregnant, she attempted to preserve her previous drug business in order to maintain an income. However, as her pregnancy progressed, she noticed that the once busy house was quiet. It appeared that even her most immoral clientele had issues with buying drugs from a pregnant woman and had found alternative resources for their bad habits.

As she reflected over her life, Kathryn realized her life had changed very little since the months after she left her parent's house. She moved from home to home and in and out of unhealthy relationships. Her bad habits remained constant. The grey, cold skies seemed endless that winter for Kathryn and her small home appeared empty of any promises of good. Kathryn's long belief that she was forever trapped in a repetitive cycle of poisonous relationships had once again been validated. A close friend of Kathryn's had recently committed suicide and the overly obsessive attention from her oldest client Chester had kept her mind full of unwanted activity. Kathryn had little doubt that drugs and her dog were her only loyal companions. She had already decided on giving the baby up for adoption after birth and she felt she merely existed for the survival of the unborn and unwanted infant.

A red brick church was the only thing Kevin noticed on his way to 7333 Euclid Avenue but the religious reminder did not dissuade Kevin from his final destination. Kevin had tried to quit drugs but he had given up and was in dire need of a fix. He had heard he could buy drugs at the house on Euclid and he needed a new connection. He knocked on the door and was let in. Once inside the run down home, he shivered in the cold room as a very pregnant woman introduced herself as "Kat" and accepted his money without question. She had no words for Kevin as he used the drugs alone at her kitchen table.

Kevin was still chilled from the cold and to alleviate the silence he asked Kathryn about her pregnancy. He was happy to hear that she was not using and oddly relieved that a pregnant drug dealer had decided to give the baby up for adoption. Desperate for companionship, she welcomed the conversation and regardless of her condition, she offered physical affection to Kevin. Both Kevin and Kathryn took advantage of each other's needs that day. That particular drug deal cost him an extra hundred dollars but feeling better from the withdrawal pains and the good companionship, he thought he received quite the bargain. The euphoria of drugs and sex made the day pass quickly and the tiniest idea of quitting drugs was quickly gone from Kevin's mind. Soon thereafter, Kevin traded his dream of sobriety for Kathryn's companionship.

A year later, on a hot July Friday, Kevin stood outside a local convenience store and waited for his ride. It was an extremely humid ninety-eight degrees, but normal for Missouri during that time of the year. To block the hot sun off his mostly baldhead, he wore a Kansas City Royals baseball cap and held a forty-four ounce soda cup in his hand. In his pockets, he had nothing but fifty dollars and a half-pack of cigarettes. Kevin had plans for his fifty dollars but no plans on where, or if, he was going to sleep that night.

Kevin used to sleep soundly and comfortably in his own home but bad decisions and bad luck eventually cost him restful nights. He wiped the sweat from between his head and hat with the bottom of his thin, stretched-out grey t-shirt.   Recently showered and shaved, he thought of going back inside the cool store to wait, but he knew that his race and tattered appearance might earn him unprovoked suspicion and a quick phone call to the police for loitering. Kevin moved under an awning, slid down the brick wall of the store, and waited with his knees under his chin. He did not care about the three-inch long tear in his pants or his broken shoelace because he knew the drugs he just ordered would be making him feel better in a little while.

With his head bowed and relaxed, he dozed for a few minutes and didn't see her pull into the parking lot. Her shadow stirred him and he lifted his head. It was Kathryn and she stood over him wearing a pair of cutoffs and bikini top. She offered her hand to him. Kevin reached out, grabbed it, and sprang up from the hot concrete. Forgetfully leaving his soda behind, he climbed into the red pickup and lit up a cigarette. Kathryn put the truck in gear and patted her passenger's leg. He appreciated the human contact and placed his hand on top of hers.

Kevin and Kathryn had been friends since the fall of 1998 and were on the cusp of a boyfriend/girlfriend relationship or as close as two drug addicts could be. However, neither had openly admitted it. Kevin took off his hat and handed her his fifty dollars. He thanked her for picking him up and scooted as close to her as he could without compromising the latching of his seatbelt. Kathryn knew what Kevin needed and she pulled a tiny manila envelope from between her cleavage. Kevin wasted no time in emptying the envelope, tying the rubber tourniquet around his left arm, and injecting the contents from the syringe into his vein.

At one time, Kevin considered himself choosy when it came to picking his friends and had a tendency to remain loyal and protective over those he considered closest to him. However, his few years of doing drugs changed him considerably and his close friends were few. But one thing remained the same about his feelings towards those he cared about. Kevin was jealous and territorial if he felt others were threatening his relationships. Kathryn told him about one of her oldest clients and 'friend' that had just gotten out of prison and may be coming around. Chester was out of prison.

Chester and Kevin had many things in common but they were not friends. The two men met at Kathryn's home on Euclid Street and Chester believed his seniority of knowing Kathryn longer than Kevin had served him with some authority. On one occasion, while Chester was visiting, he refused to let Kevin inside Kathryn's house. However, to his disappointment, his view of superiority did not influence Kathryn and she chose Kevin's side and made Chester leave. Chester stormed out and told Kevin, *"This aint over!"*

Chester was furious that Kathryn preferred Kevin's company to his but he was even angrier that she was involved with a black man. Chester made it clear to Kathryn of his hatred of Kevin as well all other black people. Chester was very open about his feelings for Kathryn and he openly disrespected Kevin's relationship with her by deliberately making sexual advances towards her in front of him. However, Kevin was not afraid of Chester and the two almost came to blows many times. Kevin was not shy about telling Chester, *"I'll kick your ass, old man!"*

Kevin and Kathryn's fondness for drugs and each other kept them together most of the time. In the fall of 99, they moved in together, along with Brandy, the pit-bull. The house on Oakley was not the same home where they first met but the energy was the same. The house was cold, rundown, and not much more than a place to sleep but they had good intentions. Kathryn's tastes were simple and they started renovating soon after they moved in.

Kathryn's new address and new boyfriend were suggestions of hope and her business practices changed as soon as she met Kevin. She no longer offered "herself" as one of her menu items. Kevin helped turn one of the bedrooms into an office with a computer and Kathryn bought a 380 pistol for Kevin. For many, the story of a young relationship, a new home, and a loving pet sounds like the American dream, but that was far from what was going on. By Valentine's Day the following year, the house that was once empty with only a couch and a mattress was now fully furnished. In the living room, a large stuffed bear sat atop the television and subtly announced the commitment between Kathryn and Kevin.

However, there was always business to attend to and Kathryn's oldest customer had come to visit. Chester James walked into the kitchen and sat at the table. While at the table, Chester reached under the table and grabbed at Kathryn's leg. Kevin was in the other room but it didn't stop Chester from telling Kathryn how stupid she was for a white girl to be dating a black guy. Kathryn pulled her leg away but Chester persisted in touching her.

Kevin didn't like his girlfriend being alone with Chester even before he heard Chester throwing around the "N" word. But after he heard that, he got up from his favorite spot on the couch and went into the kitchen. Just as he had suspected, Kevin saw Chester groping Kathryn and he demanded he remove his hand off his girlfriend's leg. Chester mockingly placed both hands on top of the table but told Kevin he didn't approve of the way he spoke to him. *"Watch how you speak to me, boy!"* Chester muttered. Feeling back in control and that Chester would leave her alone, Kevin went back into the living room and ignored Chester's declaration of disapproval.

The two men had been in constant conflict from the moment they met but Kevin wasn't the only one that threatened bodily harm. Unbeknownst to Kevin, as soon as he left the kitchen, Chester asked for Kathryn's gun and said he had enough from this "N" and told her that he was going to kill her boyfriend. Kathryn knew Chester was full of bravado but she also knew his temper. She told him that she didn't have her gun and that Chester should just let it go. This was the second time Kathryn had taken Kevin's side in front of Chester and he didn't like it. Chester got up and walked toward the front door but he turned briefly to give Kevin Tucker an eerie stare and said, *"I aint done with you, boy!"* as he left the house.

A few days later was a cold February in Kansas City. Kevin Tucker sat on the couch with his shoes on but wrapped in a thick brown comforter to keep warm. He was watching TV when the doorbell rang and he watched as his girlfriend walked toward the door to answer it. *"It's Chester!"* boomed from outside. Kevin grimaced. It had been days since Kevin had seen Chester but in Kevin's mind, it was never long enough and Chester was never welcome. Kevin reached around to his backside to pull out his gun but when Kathryn saw that movement, she assured her boyfriend that she wouldn't let Chester stay too long.

The poorly insulated house seeped air through multiple crevices and the bitter cold blast of night air that pushed its way in was just as annoying as the houseguest that entered with it. Kevin tucked his feet tightly under the blanket and watched as Chester walked into their living room with barely an invitation. Kevin never said a word. Kathryn sat on the couch beside her boyfriend as Chester James walked in. Usually Chester would immediately go into the kitchen to conduct business with Kathryn but not this time. Chester only walked as far as the living room. He stopped and stood in the middle of the room and blocked Kevin's view of the TV.

Chester stared right at Kevin with a cold look that made Kathryn very uncomfortable. Kevin stared right back but there was no exchange of words between these two men that evening. Chester James was a violent man that was not used to not getting his way. He hated black people and those that stood in his way of what he wanted and those that didn't comply to his orders. Kevin was the epitome of all of that. Chester never said a word but pulled out a large handgun and pointed it at Kevin. Before Kevin could even react, Chester fired a bullet into Kevin's chest. Kevin slumped over immediately.

Kathryn jumped away at the sight and sound of the gun and screamed. She knew Chester was violent but she was shocked at what she had just witnessed. She was sure Kevin was dead after he fired the first shot and she was worried she would be Chester's next victim. She jumped off the couch away from the gunfire and as she covered her eyes, she heard Chester fire two more bullets at Kevin. Chester had now shot Kevin Tucker three times. Kathryn knew Chester had more bullets in that gun and Kathryn pleaded for her life as she crouched in the corner with her dog.

Chester still didn't speak or even acknowledge Kathryn as he stuck his gun in the back of his pants, removed the comforter off his victim, and threw the now bloodied blanket aside. He then proceeded to take inventory of his dead victim. He removed the watch from Kevin's wrist. He took the gun out of Kevin's pants. Chester put Kevin's gun in his own pocket; the same gun Kevin had decided not to pull out when Chester knocked on the door. Chester then ripped away a necklace that Kevin had around his neck as he rummaged through Kevin's pants. He pulled out a set of keys and put them in his own pocket.

Next, Chester grabbed Kevin's feet and pulled him off the couch. Kevin's untied shoe slipped off in Chester's hand as his lifeless body landed with a thud. Chester pulled off his other shoe and wrapped Kevin and his shoes inside the blanket. It was harder than he thought to wrap up the lifeless body in a blanket. Only then did Chester James speak. Despite Kevin Tucker being dead, Chester kicked the body several times while simultaneously calling him racially offensive names. He kicked and kicked as he taunted and hollered at the lifeless body of Kevin Tucker.

Kathryn screamed for him to stop, and for a moment, Chester let go of his anger and attempted to console the horror stricken Kathryn. He secured both guns inside his coat pockets and slid down the wall. He sat by Kathryn and gathered her in his arms. She clung tightly to her growling dog as Chester pulled her head towards his shoulder and stroked her blood spattered face with his blood soaked hand. She smelled liquor emanating from his breath as he tried to calm her as he swore her to secrecy. Afraid for her own life, she calmed Brandy and pretended to be less scared than she actually was. She offered him alcohol and sex as possible distractions and swore she would never tell. As she knew he would, he accepted both but unfortunately that was not all he wanted from her. Chester wanted Kathryn to help him hide her boyfriend's dead body.

As any prudent person who witnessed a cold-blooded murder would, Kathryn wanted only to escape. But just as any terrified witness would, she also wanted to guarantee her safety. In fear for her own life, she complied with Chester's demands and helped him move Kevin out of her house. She had been told that he wouldn't hurt her but she did not believe it for a second. Kathryn knew if Chester saw any refusal on her part, she might be next for a bullet.

Chester said it was too cold to dig a hole and dispose of the body, so Chester said he was just going to throw Kevin's body out his car door somewhere in a secluded area. Kathryn couldn't dream of Kevin's body being disgraced like that so she told Chester about the home's small basement where he could put Kevin's body until he figured something out. The entrance to the basement that was actually a crawl space was only accessible from the outside. The only way in was from a door only about four feet tall.

The two of them worked together in dragging the blanketed body outside to the only entrance to the basement located at the side of the house. Kathryn loosely carried the bottom end of the twisted comforter as Chester pulled most of the weight with his arms locked tightly underneath Kevin's armpits. As they carried him out into the night, the dark concealed their activity as well as the trail of blood they didn't know they left behind. Kathryn dropped her end of the load as soon as they reached the small door to the basement/crawl space and fell sobbing onto the cold ground. Chester insisted she assist in getting the body into the basement but she refused. She just saw Chester murder her boyfriend and there was no way she was going into a cold dark underground room alone with him.

She ran towards the house. Behind her, she heard the click of the padlock open and then the bang of the basement door as it opened and hit the side of the house. She flinched and paralyzing chills raced down her body at the unexpected noise. She didn't stop and she kept walking. She went in the house and got her keys and her dog and was ready to go get in her car to drive away leaving her dead boyfriend at the mercy of his murderer. In the cold, dark night, Chester had removed the unlocked padlock from the loop on which it dangled on the door. He flung open the door and rolled Kevin down the stairs as carelessly as one would throw a bag of laundry down the steps. Chester laughed to himself as he thought the body sure went down the stairs easier just dropping it than it would have to carry it.

Kathryn gathered her dog and left the residence of 3052 Oakley for the last time just after midnight on February 27. She walked quickly and tried to act nonchalant but nervously studied the dark area in front of her house. After hearing three gunshots, some neighbors might have been curious to see what happened but it seemed that no one was alarmed. It was quiet and deserted on the street with the exception of a vacant minivan

107

Kathryn noticed parked on the street. She had never seen that van before. As she got in her car and escaped, Kathryn couldn't help but wonder why she was so relieved to see that no one was around to witness the event that had just taken place. If someone would have seen something, maybe the police would come. She quickly shrugged off that idea because that wouldn't have saved Kevin. She just needed to worry about saving herself.

Meanwhile inside that minivan that Kathryn had seen across the street, Margaret Fowler sat in the driver's seat and for Margaret, time was moving slowly. Margaret watched Kathryn exit her house and leave in her vehicle. Margaret was waiting in her minivan because she had actually driven Chester over to the house and had been waiting outside for Chester for almost an hour now. Margaret doubted that Kathryn had seen her as she was crouched down in the seat of her minivan just as Chester had ordered.

Chester closed and locked the door to the basement that now held Kevin's body and hustled to the waiting minivan and his driver Margaret Fowler. Margaret took Chester home and she went home herself. The next day, Chester was determined to finish the job. Even though he had put Kevin Tucker's body into the basement, he wasn't satisfied he had done enough to remove himself from the eyes of investigation. So a few evenings later, he revisited Kathryn's residence and again enlisted Margaret as his chauffeur and her van as his ride. However, on this occasion, he wasn't alone with Margaret on the ride.

Vincent James, Chester's barely legal-aged son, had just turned eighteen the prior month but Chester expected much more from him than his age could comprehend. On this night, he would force even more from his son. When they arrived at the house, Margret waited in the van as Chester and Vincent went up to the front door. After knocking several times, they entered the unlocked door. He led his son on a so-called treasure hunt to find a set of keys that would unlock Kathryn's 1994 Chevrolet Club Cab pickup truck that sat in the driveway. Chester told Vincent he bought the truck for him but the owner misplaced the keys, so the two of them looked through the house for keys.

Late that Monday night, Vincent was only a few steps behind his father as Chester guided his trusting son into the house to look for the same set of keys he already had in his pocket. Vincent, influenced by the promise of a new ride, followed his father through the rooms of an unfamiliar residence, clueless to his dad's most un-fatherly intentions. When the two failed to find what they were looking for inside, Chester suggested they look inside the vehicle and the unsuspecting son followed his father outside. With that, Chester successfully set up his son for the discovery of his crime.

Chester had little regard for the feelings of others and had no concern about the possibility of implicating his son in the murder he committed. But Chester did know that if he told him what he really wanted his help with before they got there, he could not have persuaded his son to come. Of course, there was no one at home at 3052 South Oakley with the exception of Kevin Tucker's body in the small basement but Chester was back to finish his job. He was unsure if the body was where he left it or if Kathryn had done something with it but he came prepared with provisions nonetheless. His pockets bulged with ropes, a pocketknife, and a pair of work gloves. He maneuvered around those necessary essentials as he dug in his pants for the same set of keys he stole from Kevin the prior evening. In the dark, Chester, fumbled through the keys searching for the smallest one, the one that would unlock the padlock on the basement door.

Chester aimed a flashlight at the ground and Vincent followed the lit path. As he subtly forced his son into the direction of the door and role of a coconspirator, Chester began playing his part of innocent victim. Vincent at one time was behind his father but eventually ended up right next to him as Chester purposely slowed his movement. He opened the door and walked down the few short stairs. Before Chester took the seven steps that led to the damp room where he left his victim, he closed the door, reached up and felt for the thin hanging chain that would help light his feet. Chester found the corpse exactly where he left it. He was glad that he had left the brown comforter as it would help to camouflage his evening's activities.

He then spotlighted the area he wanted his son to see. Vincent's eyes instinctively followed the flashlight in pursuit. He finally saw what his father wanted him to see and his mind now shifted from the thought of a new truck to the thought of the unimaginable that was now before him. He walked closer to the body squinting his eyes as he tried to make out the image. What was there then became clear. The young man heard his heart pound in his ears. He heard his own heartbeat and he heard incoherent mumblings from his father as he stood in shock in that basement.

Chester felt no remorse as he looked down at the bloody, lifeless body, but instead, a slight feeling of euphoria over the challenging man-against-man competition he had finally won. Nevertheless, he was worried about getting caught and he had no idea what to do with his trophy. Chester got caught a lot but in the big scheme of things, he had a pretty good history of staying underneath the police radar but this time he knew it wouldn't be as easy to conceal his latest infraction. Dumping a body was not an easy task.

But first Chester had to tell his son about what had happened. Vincent said nothing as he vaguely listened to his father tell an ambiguous story about a recent argument between him and the vehicle owner's black boyfriend. For Vincent, there wasn't an immediate connection between the dispute and a dead man. The dead body held nothing significant to him except a confirmation of a bad deed. However, as he listened to his father's fragmented sentences about how he feared for his life and his concern about being blamed, Vincent looked down at the black man's dead body and put two-and-two together. Chester finally had his son's full attention and started telling Vincent a lie about what had happened. Chester was convincing as he doled out his version of an ill-fated event.

Just as Chester suspected, Vincent's strong family loyalty reared its ugly head. He was wise for his age and expressed his concerns about the complications that could arise from the death of a man with whom his father had argued. As Vincent was naively being played into his father's evil hands, Chester convinced his son that the only way to avoid any implications was to make the body unidentifiable. Chester went on and on about fingerprint identifications and if there were no hands, it would be hard to identify the body. Chester also suggested that they should remove Kevin's head also so they couldn't identify his face. Chester told his son, the harder it would be for the police to identify the dead body then the harder it would be for anything to be connected to Chester. Vincent objected but did not impede the actions of his father as he watched him follow through with his scheme.

Lit by only a single dusk-to-dawn light on the opposite side of the street and a fading flashlight, Chester searched the property for means to help exaggerate his already terrible crime. Chester found a rust covered hatchet leaning against the back of Kathryn's house and came back in the basement where Vincent stood motionless over the body. *"This would be simple,"* thought Chester as he chopped at Kevin's body. Vincent watched only a few seconds as Chester hacked at the lifeless body and realized the removal of a human's head and hands with a rusty axe was far from an easy task. Chester screamed obscenities at Kevin as he hacked and hacked without much progress. As one of the hands finally became severed from the body, Chester seemed to

111

almost enjoy his activities. After ordering his son to collect some trash bags from inside the house, Chester went back to his task of dismembering the body of Kevin Tucker.

Vincent rummaged through drawers and found several plastic bags. Some were black large trash bags and some were smaller plastic bags customers receive at the grocery store. Vincent came back in with bags and thought all was over when his father handed him the axe. Vincent wanted no part in it but knew that his dad would not take no for an answer. Whether he was being loyal to his father or if he was fearful for his own life from Chester, he took the axe and struck Kevin Tucker's neck five times until the head fell away from the body. Chester and Vincent then filled the bags with the fruits of their ugliness. In those bags that would carry bloody clothes and shoes were also the head and hands of Kevin Tucker.

With Kevin Tucker's head and hands now removed, the men wrapped the body back up in the blanket and tied it shut with ropes. Now they just had to take the body and dispose of it. They each grabbed an end and pulled the body back out into the night. Although the thick blanket surrounded the body, Chester could hear each thump as Kevin's body hit each concrete step as they pulled the body up the stairs. It was much harder moving dead weight up the stairs then the men thought.

Once outside, Chester dropped the body, locked the door behind him, and scoped out the neighboring area. Kathryn's house was the middle house of the only three homes on the street. Chester knew that one of the houses was vacant. Now all they had to do was get the body to the car and dump it anywhere but in Kathryn's yard. Chester thought the best idea was to ditch the body in the river, at a park, or in a vacant car wash. The ground was hard and the body-filled-blanket moved across it smoothly as they pulled it away from Kathryn's house and towards the empty house next door.

112

A four-foot gate was locked and that fence separated the two residences but his determination to rid 3052 Oakley of Kevin's body was unwavering. In his arms, Chester gathered both ends of the heavy blanket, hoisted it up, and dropped it over the fence. On its way down, a raw piece of wire snagged the blanket and the weight of the body snapped the thin ropes. Kevin's body rolled out of comforter just before it hit the ground of the next door neighbor's yard. Even though spring was just around the corner, it was still cold outside. Nevertheless, Chester was sweating by the time the men went around to the other side of the fence to finish the job and collect the body.

It was either the noise from the cutting or the thud of the body that had awakened a neighbor and Chester saw lights were being turned on. They heard the back door of another neighbor's house behind them open. They knew they could not be caught or seen with the body so Chester and Vincent left the body and ran to their get-away car. They did not finish the job of getting the body out of 3052 Oakley. However, in his hands, Chester James carried the bags containing the head and hands of Kevin Tucker as well as other incriminating evidence. They did, at least, get away from the house with those things.

Chester and Vincent James ran to and climbed into the middle seat of Margaret Fowler's minivan just shy of midnight. It was the same transportation then as it was a few nights ago when he shot Kevin Tucker. As the two men hurriedly jumped in the car, Margaret watched from her rearview mirror and felt the van bounce as Chester threw some heavy black plastic bags over his seat and into the back of the van. While she wondered what was in the bags, she did not ask. Margaret had established a good habit of not asking questions about his activities and she silently drove them to her apartment complex as he had dictated. When they got to her apartment, Margaret and Vincent stayed in their seats but she could still see the chrome-colored handgun in Chester's waistband as he got out of the van. Chester casually grabbed the bags and tossed them in the apartment complex's trash dumpster. The deed was done.

In the very early hours of February 29, Chester James threw two small plastic grocery bags and one large black trash bag into the back of a waiting 1994 mini-van. In one of the small bags was a set of human hands and a pair of black tennis shoes and the other contained a severed head. The larger bag held a bloody axe and a .45 caliber pistol. The contents of the two small bags once belonged to an unfortunate victim and the contents of the larger bag belonged to his assassin. The killer had removed what he thought was the only identifiers and Kevin Tucker's body would not be found for two more weeks.

Moc Tran had just recently purchased the property next door to Kathryn Brown. Mr. Tran was in the business of buying run down properties and fixing them up and selling them. He bought 3054 Oakley for cheap because there had been a fire in the kitchen. He was about halfway through with the remodeling project when he arrived that morning and walked around back. His first impression of the pile of 'something' he saw in the back was that someone had once again dumped trash on his property. At closer inspection and to his shock, he saw it was a human body that was missing its head. He immediately called 911.

Around 10:45 on March 15, Kansas City Police Detective Gary Lynch received a call advising him to respond to an address in regard to a dead body found in a yard. Lynch, a relatively young homicide detective for the Kansas City Homicide Unit, jotted down some key notes on a yellow notepad. These notes would be almost cryptic to anyone else, but would serve as reminders of important details for him later. The twenty-seven-year-old reported to the scene where he saw the body of a headless black male lying chest down near a chain-link fence.

114

Detective Lynch's initial summation of the crime scene revealed the body to be in the yard area between two single-family dwellings of 3052 and 3054 Oakley. He observed the victim on the ground and his legs partially leaning against a four-foot high chain link fence between a seven-foot wood privacy fence. With the help of the medical examiner's investigator, Lynch turned the body over and exposed the underside of the headless, stiff corpse. The turn of the body revealed two arms without hands and a gaping hole in the victim's abdomen as well as a large amount of maggots.

While he examined the body and the surrounding area, Moc Tran, the person who found the victim, spoke with Lynch. The detective spoke to the witness and determined he was the property owner of 3054 Oakley, a vacant home neighboring the location of the crime scene. Tran said he owned the house next door but did not live there as the home is uninhabitable due to a recent fire. He also told the detective he only visited the home in his spare time to work on the remodeling, but he was at the residence a few weeks prior and the victim's body was not there at that time. Lynch took notes as Tran went on to say he didn't know the owner of the residence at 3052 Oakley but he did see a dog chained to the porch during his last visit and heard some sort of a power tool noise coming from the inside the residence. He also stated he did see a black male walking around the home and he appeared to be working on the residence.

There was nothing extraordinary about the clothing on the unidentified victim that lie dead on Oakley Street. A small section of the chain link fence, northeast of the victim's body was bent downward toward the torso and a small piece of gray material not unlike the victim's sweater was found attached to the same area of the fence. This small piece of evidence spoke loudly to Lynch and he concluded that the person responsible for the crime threw the victim over the fence from the yard of 3052. Consent to search was signed by the owner of 3054 Oakley and a second search warrant would be requested and obtained for 3052 Oakley.

Until then, Lynch, looked for not only what was visible on the dismembered body, but also for what wasn't visible. He noticed the victim had no shoes and a slight discoloration around the victim's left wrist where a watch might have once been. The detective also found a partial shoe print next to the body; however, he was unsure if the print belonged to the victim, his assailant, or if it had any relevance to the crime at all. The dirt around the body contained no trace of the victim's blood and it was clear to those who had seen this type of crime before that the murder had taken place somewhere else.

Detective Lynch was careful not to compromise any evidence on the body as he examined it. He took notes of the victim's condition, clothing, and personal belongings. In addition to the missing head and hands, the detective observed a small hole in the victim's sweater. Then with closer observation, he recognized it to be a bullet hole in the victim's chest. Lynch carefully rolled the body on its side and noted a bullet hole in the middle of the victim's back. He also noticed that an area of the lower portion of the victim's left hand remained intact. Crime scene technician, Charles Clossen, took a print from what was remaining of the victim's palm. The killer may have tried to remove the hands to avoid identification but he left the victim with a partial palm print that may be able to be used to scan through the criminal database.

As the day went on, homicide detectives, police officers, and crime scene technicians flooded the two residences as well did the nosy spectators who gathered on the other side of the police tape. However, unlike the police, most of the curious neighbors added nothing of value to the investigation. When they were interviewed, no one had seen anything and even if they did, no one talked.

The two residences the police were focusing on were a mere ten feet apart and the local authorities trudged back and forth between the two homes searching for information. It was not a warm day and a thick overcast made the bad scene appear worse. The next step was to search Moc Tran's home. A fine mist fell from the sky as Closson photographed the interior and exterior of 3054 Oakley, but the search for clues at that residence proved fruitless. After the investigation of Moc Tran's house showed no involvement, the detectives and crime scene focused on the next door residence of 3052 Oakley.

Armed with a search warrant, there was no response when Lynch knocked on the door. CST Closson was by his side armed with a camera and covered in protective plastic as he knocked again and announced their presence at 3052 Oakley. However, no one was there to answer the door. To find another way in the home, the police turned their attention away from the front door and rounded the corner toward the southwest side of the house. Despite the mist and the unknown amount of time that had lapsed since the murder, a red-stained path still remained on the sidewalk. Dressed in raincoats, they followed the trail that ended at the padlocked door leading into the basement. Lynch and Closson cut the padlock and climbed down a concrete set of stairs that led them into a room covered in sticky blood.

The police professionals knew something terrible had happened in that basement and they each took a deep breath as they entered. What they found were large amounts of blood covering the floor, ceiling, and basement walls. The blood was dry so there was no telling exactly when the crime had occurred. One of the detectives muttered to another that he was just happy that they didn't find another body in there. The detectives took their look and then crime scene took over to investigate.

Crime scene technicians took pictures from every angle of every portion of the small basement area. They collected blood samples for later identification. They removed pieces of flesh from the ground and even on the wall. They collected two bloodstained blankets and anything else of evidentiary value. The basement was bare except for the blankets and the blood. After closer inspection of the floor, they found marks in the concrete that would be consistent with a cutting object striking the ground. Lynch knew that the victim was clearly dismembered here but he didn't know where he was initially killed.

The police then continued in their search back upstairs to the main living area of the home. Some of the rooms had recently received fresh coats of paint but it was unclear if the renovations were due to someone fixing up the home or if it was just a poor attempt to cover up a crime scene. Again, CSI took pictures and collected evidence. The amount of evidence they collected continued to pile up as several sets of fingerprints, pieces of bloodstained clothing, several shell casings, and discarded cigarette butts were obtained. The investigators also found bullet holes in the couch and they were able to move the couch and recover bullets from the wall. Within hours of receiving the search warrant, the investigators discovered the murder site, the type of weapon used, and obtained fingerprints. After 14 hours of investigation and collection, the crime scene had been gone through with a fine tooth comb.

On March 15, Karen Smith, a fingerprint classifier for the KCPD, was responsible for trying to identify the victim and possible suspects. She received a partial palm print of an unknown murder victim and went to work. She obtained prints lifted from the crime scene from a piece of mail and many other areas and items. She processed those prints through the local system and forwarded them to the Integrated Automated Fingerprint Identification System for comparison. Within two hours, they received electronic results of the comparison prints with their criminal master files back. The police now knew that their murder victim's name was Kevin Tucker. They also knew that some of the

118

collected fingerprints on various items from inside that house belonged to a person named Kathryn Brown with an alias of "Kat" Brown.

Just after 1 a.m. on March 16, Lynch laid his head down on the stained grey table in his break room at the Homicide Unit. The detective loved his job but was thankful the day was over. He didn't raise his head when his name was called out by someone. It wasn't until a female officer on duty called out his name a second time that he took a deep breath and answered with a fake smile. The officer advised the detective they had identified their victim. He put his hands on the table to push himself off the chair and headed towards the lab. His day was not over.

The detective flipped the chair around backward and straddled it as he examined the information. Lynch mouthed the victim's name several times as if hoping to dislodge forgotten information. He knew the name sounded familiar but wasn't sure why. No sooner than he had asked himself that question, he remembered the victim and the occasion he had taken time out of his day to reflect on a man arrested on a drug possession charge when the officer brought him into the station over a year ago. In police work, Kansas City can be a small world and here was just another example of someone being involved in drugs ending their lives way too short.

But more importantly, Lynch had a name of his victim and also a live lead to track down. He wanted to talk to Kathryn Brown. He ran Brown's name through his database and found a phone number for her. Easily enough, he called her and made contact with her and left a message to provide him with her current address and respond back. Kathryn got the message and called back. Lynch told her he wanted to talk to her and she was cooperative and agreed.

Lynch sent officers to pick Kathryn up to bring her to police headquarters for an interview. The officers picked her up from an address on Jefferson Avenue and transported her to the Homicide Unit the same day. Upon arrival, Lynch asked Kathryn to go over any information she had concerning the murder of Kevin Tucker. Kathryn stated she was a good friend of the victim and stayed with him on several occasions but Kathryn lied and told the detective that she had no information about the murder.

The months following the murder, Chester wanted to stay on the down low. Just like Kathryn, he was staying out of public. He bounced back and forth between his residence and Margaret Fowler's house, but despite his desire not to stay too long in one place, he had an agenda that was not as flexible as his mobility. Chester was looking for Kathryn. He knew that she was the only eyewitness to his crime and he needed to know what she was doing and/or saying. However, his attempts to make contact with her were unsuccessful and he hated the lack of control. Fearing she might not keep her vow of silence as promised, he was on constant patrol for Kathryn.

The next month's investigation by the KCPD Homicide Unit provided for additional evidence as well as additional witnesses. The interview with Kathryn and some of her associates as well as a few anonymous tips proved fruitful. The KCPD homicide detectives narrowed their investigation down to one suspect. That suspect was Chester James. Everyone in Kansas City Police Department knew of Chester due to his antagonistic personality and his history of racial unfriendliness. However, the investigation still lacked the one thing and that was an eyewitness who could place Chester at the scene of the crime or any evidence that linked Chester to the murder.

It is easy for a witness to say "I don't know nothing" but the detectives do not just stop the investigation because a witness would say that. Surprisingly enough, sometimes people who have witnessed a murder might not tell the truth. This homicide squad kept talking to more people that kept mentioning Kathryn's name, so it didn't add up that she didn't know anything. Unsatisfied that Kathryn had been completely truthful in her first interview, the cops wanted to talk to her again.

KCPD then found out that the Drug Enforcement Agency had been working on a drug case involving Kathryn, so they made contact with the agency on how to find her. To get Kathryn to come out of hiding, an undercover drug agent working on the federal drug case called her and took her to a parking lot where two homicide detectives were waiting. After arriving at the parking garage, Detectives Lynch and Sharp transported Kathryn back down to the station for a second interview and told her the information they received from witnesses was indicative of her having more information than what she originally claimed. Brown sobbed uncontrollably as she explained she lied in her first interview because she feared for her life and then confessed she was present when Kevin was murdered.

This time Kathryn didn't hold anything back. She described the events as they happened and admitted that a man named Chester James, who she knew, pulled out a .45 caliber gun, and without warning, shot her boyfriend three times while he was sitting on her couch. She went on to tell how Chester James shot Kevin in the head, stomach, and chest. Kathryn's graphic detailed account was proof that she was telling the truth as she gave the detective information that only the police and someone at the crime scene would know. Kathryn explained that she ran away that night and never went back. She left all of her belongings there and only went back weeks later to find that someone had cleaned the place out. Kathryn said she knew Chester was looking for her and she was scared of him. The detectives took a video statement and released Kathryn with the full disclosure that they were not done with her.

121

On May 3, Detective Lynch got a message from the homicide unit that between the hours of 11pm and 12 am, Kathryn Brown had called the station several times requesting to speak with him concerning an emergency. He called Kathryn back as soon as he got the message and when she answered, Kathryn was crying and hysterical. She told him that Chester had just left her apartment after forcing his way into her home. Kathryn said he kicked in the door and grabbed her. She was fighting him and then her pit-bull attacked him in an effort to protect her. Her dog, Brandy, bit Chester and cornered him in the apartment. As Brandy was attacking Chester, Kathryn was able to leave the other way and got out to her car. She told the detective that as she was driving away, she saw Chester leaving her apartment and he was bleeding from his arm.

What Kathryn didn't know was that while Chester was at her apartment, Margaret Fowler was watching her. For the second time in two months, Margaret Fowler watched Kathryn Brown hurriedly exit a residence that Chester James recently entered. As she was waiting for Chester to get back in her van, Margaret stared out at the bright TV tower in the distance and waited for him to come back out. As usual, he didn't explain why he wanted Margaret to take him anywhere and as usual, Margaret didn't ask. It was not uncommon for him to randomly contact her for rides and she didn't mind driving him around as she liked any attention from Chester. But because she never asked, she was never quite sure what role she would play when they were out and about.

During the four years Margaret had known Chester, she knew several things about him: he had a temper, he had a criminal history, and he was a very prejudiced man. She also knew he still had a long-term, albeit, one-sided love affair with a drug dealer and one-time prostitute Kathryn. But regardless of his background and reputation, Margaret understood that Chester was harmless as long as she cooperated with his demands. Even

122

though their relationship was now platonic, she thought he treated her well. However, she knew by all other accounts, he was a very bad man. Unfortunately for Margaret Fowler, her standards were low and she tolerated his flaws.

Margaret never asked Chester about his business, but she was surprised when she saw Chester walking toward her car holding his arm. He jumped in the van with his left hand wrapped around his right wrist. Chester's wounds were obvious regardless of his attempts to conceal them. Despite their unspoken rule of silence, Chester knew his injury required an explanation and without persuasion, he explained Kathryn's dog attacked him for no reason as he went in the apartment. Margaret had known him long enough to know he was up to no good and doubted the attack was unwarranted.

After Kathryn's phone call to Detective Lynch about Chester being at her new apartment, Lynch and an additional detective responded to the James' residence at 6628 E. 13th street. Chester's wife, Patricia answered the door but refused to allow the detectives inside. She admitted that Chester was there but told them she would get him herself. The detectives were ready for anything and were not sure what Chester might do when cornered.

Without incident, Chester exited the residence where the detectives took him into custody, transported him to the Violent Crimes Unit, and placed him in the interrogation room. He was Mirandized and asked a series of questions concerning his whereabouts on May 2, his fresh dog bite, and his relationship with Kathryn Brown and Kevin Tucker. After several hours of interrogation, Chester requested an attorney and the detectives booked and escorted him to the detention unit.

Next up was for the police to talk to Margaret Fowler. After multiple interviews, May 5 was the day Margaret Fowler finally came clean with the police about Chester James. Detectives

Lynch and Sharp videotaped Fowler's last statement just as they had on her previous interviews. Margaret's prior statements offered only a partial reality and she confessed that her fear of Chester had prompted her to withhold some information. Margaret was honest with the police when she told them she was very fond of Chester but was equally as honest when she confessed that she considered him the type of person capable of committing murder and that she was relieved to know he was in jail.

Although Margaret did not actually see Chester murder Kevin Tucker, she told the police that on a cold night in late February, she drove Chester to Kathryn's home and a couple of nights later she drove him and his son to the same address. After they came back from the house the second time, they loaded some bags into the back of her minivan. Margaret added that she then drove them to her apartment complex where Chester dumped the bags in her dumpster. Margaret provided the address of her apartment and other detectives responded to the dumpster.

Even though it had been months earlier, KCPD contacted the trash company and investigated their detailed pick up schedule and questioned the drivers. The police also were able to figure out exactly which landfill the trucks dumped at and were able to get a rough estimate of where trash from that truck would have been dumped months before. After several days of methodically sorting through trash at the landfill, the twenty or so officers and crime scene technicians never were able to locate and recover the head and hands of Kevin Tucker.

Margaret Fowler proved to be a valuable witness as she provided much needed details concerning Chester's activities during the night of the murder and the following days. In addition, she addressed concerns about Vincent's involuntary involvement in his father's misdeeds. She was able to provide the

124

information that Chester acted alone in the murder but then fooled his son into accompanying him when they went back for the body. However, as cooperative as she was in helping establish probable cause, it was questionable as to how she would do testifying in front of Chester in court.

On May 16, the detectives finally had the opportunity to talk with Vincent James. The first reaction from him was to take the entire blame for a crime even though he did not commit it. Vincent first told the police that he was the one responsible for dismembering Kevin Tucker's body. Vincent then went on to tell the detectives that his father had known the victim but Chester had no knowledge of the heinous act he committed.

The detectives already knew too much about the case to know what Vincent was saying was not true and they suspected that this was Chester still manipulating his son by making him tell this story. Vincent was placed in a holding cell and later visited that night by his mother. The following day, and with persuasion from his mother, Vincent asked to talk to the detectives again. This time he retracted his statement of guilt and then gave the specific details of how his father butchered Kevin Tucker's body. When asked about why he lied at first, Vincent said he knew his father was in trouble and he wanted to lessen the burden on Chester.

Although Vincent seemed to lack the maturity and wisdom to comprehend his bad decisions, the police took his actions no less seriously and submitted his case to the prosecutor. As he had just turned 18, under Missouri law he was an adult and could face adult criminal murder charges. Vincent James could be charged with accessory to murder, tampering with evidence, and abandoning a corpse; however, the prosecution knew the value of a good witness. The prosecution waited on the decision on that charge and with the intention of convincing Vincent that his full cooperation at trial would be in his best interest.

Jackson County Prosecutor Phil LeVota was assigned with task of prosecuting the case against Chester James for the murder of Kevin Tucker. The trial date loomed large for Chester and it had been almost a year and a half since the murder and Chester had spent the entire time in the Jackson County Jail. As well as the charges against Chester, LeVota also needed to make a decision on whether or not to charge Chester's son, Vincent. LeVota had not filed any charges against Vincent because he realized the intimidation and pressure that his father had placed on him. With no charges against him, LeVota hoped he could persuade Vincent to testify to the truth in exchange for not doing any prison time. As LeVota delved into the case of Kevin's Tucker's murder, he was quick to realize the bizarre cast of characters and a storyline so peculiar that it seemed scripted for a theater production. With no murder weapon and a list of witnesses that were less than upstanding, it was obvious that the trial would be no less bizarre.

The prosecution believed they had three key witnesses whose separate testimony would provide the jury necessary adhesion to put any unclear narrative pieces together. Kathryn Brown would provide the vivid details of the actual murder. Margaret Fowler would give information of the events before and following the murder. And finally, Vincent James would supply evidence of the dismemberment and disposal of the body.

Simple enough, but LeVota knew that getting the same police interrogation information from a person to then be given in open court at trial from that witness is often difficult. The act of testifying to a jury as the eyes of the defendant stares a witness down can lead to the witness being inconsistent with prior statements. Then when you add the other issue that the witness is a family member and/or friend, it is hard to get that witness to stay on course.

126

LeVota also appreciated the dilemma Vincent would face in being forced to testify against his own father and he knew it would be an extremely difficult feat for the now 19 year old. However, in the year and a half since the murder had occurred, Vincent had met a young woman who he was engaged to marry. Vincent also had grown very close to his soon to be mother and father-in-law who LeVota found to be great role models and advisors to Vincent.

LeVota arranged several pre-trial meetings before court to speak with Vincent and prepare for his trial testimony. Vincent's future wife and future in-laws were present for the meetings to support Vincent. Vincent was very troubled to have to testify against his own father but also seemed to understand very clearly that Vincent would not be in this situation if it were not for Chester. Vincent spoke of wanting to join the military and his plans to get married.

With his new family as a great support system, LeVota thought Vincent might just have a chance at a normal and productive life. LeVota found that Vincent finally had some quality direction from his fiancé's mother and father that he dearly needed after he had been tormented by his father and then pushed to cooperate in the unthinkable. LeVota assured Vincent and his new family that he understood it would be a difficult task but if he told the truth, he would not have a criminal record. LeVota told him that there was more than enough evidence to charge him with a crime now and that he could face prison time. That conviction would be more than enough to mess up any chance of being in the military. But LeVota told Vincent that it seemed that Vincent acted with his father under duress and in testifying, Vincent can demonstrate that. After that testimony, he would have no criminal record and he could be done with this whole ordeal and move on with his life. Vincent seemed to be onboard and ready to testify in the case.

127

It was cold and dark inside the courtroom on February 20, 2002. Judge Messina requested the windows remain shut to keep out the noise from construction. The old heavy drapes remained drawn to keep out the sunlight that often overheated the room. However, despite the uncomfortable conditions, the State was ready for a smooth trial. The prosecution team was organized and their witnesses prepared for their testimony. Jury selection took its usual one day of trial time and on that Tuesday morning, the state and defense gave their opening statements outlining what each believed the evidence would be. The presentation of evidence was to begin.

The police witnesses were the first to testify. Their testimonies were fluid and counsel moved through six of them before the end of the first day. Officer Brett McCubbin and Sergeant Sharp described the scene where they found the headless body as well as the surrounding area. Senior Crime Scene Analyst, Charles Closson detailed the evidence he secured, including blood samples and photographs from the blood-spattered basement, a palm print from the victim, a vial of blood removed by the medical examiner, a comforter found near the body, and a piece of cloth that matched the victim's clothing removed from the chain-link fence.

The Jackson County Medical Examiner, Dr. Thomas Young, testified about the victim's injuries and indicated a gunshot wound from the front to the back was the fatal wound. Fingerprint expert Karen Smith stated she identified the victim by means of a partial palm print. Linda Netzel, a criminalist at the Kansas City Crime Lab described the evidence she examined from two hinge lifts from a couch cushion and blood swabs from the basement. She specified that on one hinge lift, she found one Caucasian head hair that she compared to the defendant's hair but indicated it did not match. She testified that she found two

128

separate DNA samples from one specific area of a couch. The analysis of those two pieces of evidence showed that one was from the victim and one from an unidentifiable source. Netzel also testified that the DNA from blood swabs taken from the basement matched the victim.

The state then called Detective Gary Lynch to the stand as the next witness and he was a major contributor of information. As LeVota led the direct examination, Lynch told the jury that he found a list of over twenty witnesses, including Kathryn Brown, by running Kevin Tucker's name through their computer and gaining a list of "associates." Lynch also testified about leads he obtained by looking through the mail at Brown's residence. He explained that he and other detectives interviewed over 30 individuals. He then spoke about talking to Margaret Fowler who had initially called in anonymously. Lynch testified about his contact with Vincent James and told the jury that through all their statements and actions, they were able to place their focus on Chester James.

Lynch did not testify to what a witness said but only that he talked to these people and the fact that after talking to them the detectives focused on Chester James. Public Defender Tom Symson objected every time Detective Lynch mentioned a witness name as hearsay but he was overruled by the judge who allowed the evidence to be heard by the jury. The judge ruled it was not hearsay, but it was subsequent police conduct and a description of why KCPD focused on Chester James and the testimony was not used as evidence of the truthfulness of what the witness said.

Detective Lynch continued and stated Kathryn's interviews were never voluntary and their first meeting with her was not at all rewarding. Lynch said her subsequent interviews were rewarding and the knowledge she shared helped provide them with vital evidence. The detective went on to talk about the crime scene and itemized a list of items they collected including the couch where Tucker was sitting when he was killed and a .45 caliber bullet that was found in the baseboard of the wall behind where the couch originally sat. LeVota presented into evidence a couch cushion with a clear hole in it and pictures of the couch with bloodstains. He also introduced several pictures of the scene depicting a noticeable hole in the wall and additional pictures of the wall and the bullet hole. Lynch identified it all as being the same evidence they found during their investigation.

Tom Symson was the public defender representing Chester James. Defense lawyer Symson cross-examined Detective Lynch and asked if they recovered the couch from Brown's house on Oakley. Lynch indicated they learned from Brown that sometime after the murder, some of her friends removed the couch from her residence but with that information, they located it and removed it from the alternate address. With the detective's answer, Symson turned around and seemed puzzled. He started to ask another question but stopped. He then pulled out some papers and resumed the questioning.

With his focus back on the detective, the attorney asked him to step down and identify a drawing that rested on an easel in the north corner of the courtroom. The detective identified it as a diagram of the residence at 3052 Oakley. Symson asked the detective to point to the location where the couch had been prior to its removal. As he pointed to area, Lynch explained that boxes were positioned and covering the wall where the couch originally was and in their endeavor to move the boxes, they found the bullet hole in the wall. The public defender asked Lynch to return to his witness seat but continued his questioning. He asked the detective where in the couch the bullet traveled and if he saw any blood on the wall. The witness stated the bullet went through one of the pillows that sat against the back as well through the back of the couch and added he didn't see any blood on the wall.

The public defender finished his cross examination by re-probing the detective for the location where he found the bullet and if he saw any other bullet holes in the wall. Lynch reiterated that they found the bullet in the baseboard of the wall and there were no additional bullet holes discovered. Symson had tried to make some issue about the bullet holes but his point seemed lost on the jury.

On the third day of trial, the next witnesses up for the State would be witnesses that LeVota knew the jury would not like from the first minute. LeVota decided to put Kathryn Brown on the stand first. Between the first time of the police contact with Kathryn Brown to this trial date, Kathryn had been charged in federal court with drug possession. She was awaiting her own federal trial and was currently in federal prison in Texas. LeVota had made arrangements with the Federal Marshall's Service for Kathryn Brown to be transported back to Kansas City from Texas for the trial and she was being held in the Jackson County Jail.

LeVota called out to the courtroom, *"The State calls Kathryn Brown."* and she entered the courtroom in her orange prison jumpsuit flanked by Jackson County Sheriff Deputies. Kathryn walked to the front of the warm courtroom and sat in the witness chair. Before they moved forward in the testimony, LeVota immediately addressed her prison attire for jury. LeVota walked Kathryn through all of her past and present convictions to the jury. Kathryn Brown told the jury she was currently in federal custody on drug related charges and had some prior drug charges for which she served a year of prison.

After clearing the air on her own bad behavior, Kathryn testified to the defendant's bad behavior. She clarified her relationship with Chester James and her relationship with Kevin Tucker. She told the jury about how Chester was jealous of Kevin. She further went into detail about how Kevin had never done anything to Chester and how Chester just did not like him

131

because he was black. She went on to describe Chester as a racist and a member of the Arian Brotherhood.

Kathryn gave an example of Chester's animosity toward her boyfriend when she described an occasion in early February when Kevin got mad at Chester for touching her leg. She continued and explained Chester didn't like being told what to do and informed her he wanted to hurt Kevin and asked to use her gun. Kathryn looked toward the jury box and stated on that occasion, Chester left her house after she refused to let him use her gun. Kathryn said she didn't see Chester again until he came over, uninvited, and shot her boyfriend in her living room.

Kathryn remained calm during her testimony until she had to provide the specific details of the murder. She wanted to gloss over the details but LeVota pushed for specifics and backed her up on the particulars of the timeframe. As she broke down sobbing, she pulled several tissues out of a tissue box and tried to compose herself. Kathryn then described the gunshots fired by the defendant that went between her boyfriend's eyes, in his chest, and in his stomach. She depicted Chester's demeanor as unusual and added that he was drunk and forced her to help him carry Kevin's body out of the house and around to the basement.

Kathryn told the jury that she would not help him carry Kevin to the basement but Chester made her. She then said she left the house before Chester did. She told the jury that she truly believed that Chester was going to kill her. Kathryn explained that she hid out and tried to avoid contact with Chester but he eventually found her at her friend's apartment building. She told the jury that she felt that her life was over when Chester entered her new apartment. But when he lunged toward her, she was saved by her pit bull who bit Chester allowing her time to escape.

When LeVota asked why she didn't immediately report the murder to the police, Kathryn responded that she knew that Chester would kill her and as she was involved with drugs she never wanted to talk to the cops because she might get in trouble for that. She sarcastically said, *"See, look at me now. I talked to the cops and now I am in jail."* She said she wished she could have had other choices but she had so few options and hiding from Chester and not talking were the best ones.

Public Defender Symson cross-examined Kathryn with the intent to derail her previous testimony concerning the night Chester asked to use her gun and challenged her statements regarding the defendant's intent to harm the victim. Although to Kathryn, Chester implied the threat towards Kevin when he asked for her gun, the defense wanted the jury to know that Chester never threatened Kevin face-to-face.

Performing his own theatrics in the already extraordinary case, the defense attempted to confuse the witness with her own words. Symson asked if during the time Chester asked for her gun, he made threats to Kevin. The witness replied and stated that he did not make threats directly at Kevin. Symson grabbed Brown's answer and didn't let go. He found many different ways to reiterate and rephrase the same question. Repeatedly she answered the attorney's questions; however, the attorney was craftier than the witness was and with each of his redesigned questions, he ruthlessly found a way to turn her answers against her. On one occurrence, he asked Kathryn when Chester asked for her gun, if he made threats to her. She replied he did not threaten her but threatened Kevin through her. Symson quickly responded with the accusation that her reply indicated Chester did threaten Kevin. Kathryn restated her answer and said Chester made threats about Kevin only to her and he did not directly threaten Kevin.

Symson wanted to paint a vivid picture of Kathryn's credibility as a witness, and statements concerning Chester's threats were not the only thing on which Symson tried to impeach the witness. He also questioned her prior testimony regarding who

133

left the residence first. He reminded her that one of her statements, she indicated Chester left first, and on a different statement, she stated she left first. Kathryn replied that it was confusing on who actually left first but she remembered seeing a van on her way out. The public defender didn't like to hear that because it corroborated Margaret's testimony that she drove Chester there and was waiting for him.

Symson quickly revisited Kathryn's first statement to the police where she said she knew nothing but she had already explained why in her direct examination. She again explained she lied because she was scared but Symson disregarded her answer and asked her if she lied to the police about what she knew. Kathryn again admitted she lied and repeated that it was only because of fear. Before Symson could stop her, she also reminded the jury that she did eventually tell the police Chester James murdered Kevin. Symson did his best to impeach her but her testimony matched all the physical evidence and even the jury realized that it is not unreasonable for someone like her to lie to the police to try to not get involved at first

Margaret Fowler was the last to take the stand on the third day. LeVota had subpoenaed Margaret Fowler and knew that she didn't want to testify against Chester. Unbeknownst to Margaret, LeVota had also pulled the jail visitation records and knew that Margaret had met with Chester many times. It was also interesting that she had met with Chester always right before and right after she had met with prosecutors. However, in her pre-trial meetings, Margaret told the prosecutor she would answer the questions truthfully and that the statement she gave to the police in video tape was the truth. But LeVota was leery.

"The State calls Margaret Fowler," LeVota said and the fifty-four-year-old witness took the stand and swore to tell the truth. However within seconds, her short-lived oath of honesty was over as she conveniently couldn't remember things and had a hard

time with even identifying Chester James. She couldn't remember if she drove Chester anywhere and conveniently even forgot his son's name.

In prosecution, many times witnesses may get on the stand and give entirely different testimony than their police statements. Around the prosecutor's office that act of a witness doing that is called "pissing backwards." LeVota started his direct examination with Margaret unaware that she would "piss backwards" but quickly shifted gears to save his case.

The prosecution had excruciatingly reviewed Margaret's testimony with her but when she got up in front of the jury, and more importantly in front of Chester James, her demeanor did not match that of the woman in the pre-trial meeting. Even though Margaret had previously supplied the police with detailed descriptions in her videotaped interviews, now under oath in open court, she denied knowing many of those same important details. She also indicated she could not recall many facts of the events she had once acknowledged. In her court testimony, Margaret Fowler now stated she couldn't recall how many times she drove Chester to Kathryn's residence but after pressure from the prosecutor, she did slip up and say she did take him there.

Margaret even denied that Chester carried a gun and she also denied knowing Kathryn both of which she told the police the opposite. Margaret testified she didn't remember who took the bags out of her van and put them in the dumpster. When LeVota asked her if she was aware that her statements were inconsistent with her prior videotaped statements, Margaret agreed that some of them were but also stated she couldn't remember everything she told the police and then elaborated that the details she was now providing were the truth.

LeVota was given permission by the judge to treat this witness as a hostile witness which allowed the prosecutor to ask leading questions. LeVota spent the rest of the direct examination catching Margaret in inconsistencies while also getting her to admit the important parts of her testimony. Margaret admitted she had taken Chester to that house on one occasion by himself and another occasion with Vincent. LeVota got her to admit she had been intimate with Chester and that she had visited him in jail over thirty times in the last two months with the most recent being the day before this testimony.

When LeVota asked if Chester had threatened her about her testimony, she hesitated in answering. She took several seconds but then said no. LeVota really didn't care what her answer would be. He asked it only for the jury to watch her demeanor. LeVota actually was looking straight at the jury when she answered the question as if to non-verbally say to the jury: "Really?" It was exhausting for the prosecution as LeVota battled with the Margaret and her circle of lies but it was not lost on the jury that Margaret had told the police a very specific story about what had happened just after the murder but now she was far less than cooperative and antagonistic when she was in open court in front of Chester.

Chester's lawyer made a short cross examination reiterating that she couldn't remember things and that Margaret was not there when Kevin Tucker as shot. The defense quickly sat down. Margaret Fowler's testimony started off as helpful but then became devastating to the defendant.

The next witness was Detective Jones who had videotaped Margaret Fowler's police statement. Due to the fact that Margaret Fowler had been inconsistent with prior statements, the rules of evidence allowed for her entire videotaped statement to be played for the jury. LeVota rolled a large 40 inch television into the courtroom right in front of the jury box. After getting permission from the judge, he played the entire video to the jury that consisted of a thirty five minute statement of Margaret talking to the detectives to the jury. In the police interview room away from Chester's glare, months before, Margaret told the police about all the places she took Chester and about the bags and much more.   All Chester and his lawyer could do was hope that time would move faster to get this video over as the jury watched on the edge of their seats. The video was over the day was done. The third day of the trial of the State v. Chester James had concluded and the judge adjourned for the day.

So after some rough witnesses, the prosecution had saved one of the 'best' witnesses for last. The next morning the jury would hear from Vincent James who Chester admitted he had committed the murder to as well as witnessing his father decapitate the body. It would be a tough testimony for the young man but one that Vincent assured the prosecutors he could and would do.

At the end of a trial day, the judge releases the jury and they go home, but the lawyers aren't done yet. The prosecutors still had work to do to prepare for the next day of trial. As LeVota and his second chair reviewed the trial so far, they both felt that even though Margaret lied on the stand, her testimony didn't hurt their case. In fact, it showed her motive to lie and after a lot of pushing and pulling, she did finally admit to the crucial facts. Public Defender Symson would think to himself that Margaret did some good and some bad but both prosecutors believed the jury was following along well and getting the truth of the trial.

Finally the day was over for the prosecutors. It was about 8:00 PM when the prosecution team called it a day. They were confident that they were ready for the next day and the attorneys left the Jackson County Courthouse. Parking spots were scarce in downtown Kansas City and good ones were hard to find. The prosecutor's office did not pay for employee parking so each attorney was on their own to find one. LeVota had acquired a great parking spot just to the south of the Missouri Court of Appeals Building, right where Kansas City's new Sprint

Center now stands. His parking spot was very envious to others in his office as it was close to the courthouse and it was cheap on a monthly basis.

Walking to his car, many things were going through LeVota's mind but the most important thing to him is that he was tired and hungry. Trial work is not physically demanding but at the end of a day in trial, an attorney can feel as tired as if they had just ran a marathon because the mental demands the process can take and its toll can be much more than a strenuous workout. LeVota was eager to get in his car and get something to eat.

However when he turned the corner and was almost to his car, something surprised him. It was dark and as he walked closer to his car, he noticed someone was leaning against it. He wasn't very alarmed and didn't really give it much thought as there were many homeless people around downtown Kansas City all the time. But what surprised him as he got closer to the car was that he recognized the person sitting against his car. LeVota immediately knew that person should not be there. The poorly lit parking lot lights were enough for LeVota to see that the person waiting for him was Margaret Fowler.

Maybe he should have been more worried but LeVota's first thoughts were how did Margaret Fowler know what kind of car he drove and further, how did she know where he parked. Finding out that kind of information took some effort. LeVota had gotten to know Margaret as a liar and flake but he never thought of her as a threat.   But then it hit him. Chester James had manipulated this woman to do incredible things for him for years even so much that she just lied on the stand and faced perjury charges or worse. What was she up to? Was she up to no good? But just as soon as he thought it, right or wrong, the idea of Margaret as a threat left his mind just as soon as it entered.

One thing he was sure of was that Margaret had an agenda and this was no chance meeting. So even before she could say a word to him, LeVota said to her, *"Margaret, you know you shouldn't be here."* It was cold and LeVota didn't think twice that she had her hands in her pocket. Margaret then said, *"Chester has a message he wants me to give you."* LeVota quickly realized he probably ought to be taking this a little more seriously and he now had second thoughts about whether Margaret was a threat as he noticed she kept one hand in her pocket.

His mind raced with what might come next. Did Chester really want her to tell him something or was she about to pull out a gun and deliver him a "bullet message" from Chester? Margaret tried to continue, but LeVota assertively cut her off. He had just spent the afternoon verbally sparring with her and was not about to let her start with anything. With sternness and some compassion, LeVota said, *"Margaret, whatever you want to say or do, you need to think about it real hard. I know you are loyal to Chester but you need to realize that Chester James is going to jail for a long time and you are not. So go home and in a few days Chester is going to be out of your life forever. Don't do anything stupid right now."*

LeVota would never know what "message" Chester had sent Margaret to "deliver" to the aggressive prosecutor that night because after LeVota spoke, Margaret looked at her feet, mumbled something, and walked away. LeVota got in his car and headed to dinner never really understanding whether Margaret was there to harm him or not. If Margaret had intended to harm the prosecutor, that had been avoided. If she had some sort of communication from the defendant, LeVota wasn't exposed to it as it would have been inappropriate and he would have had to report it to the judge. Either way, LeVota had avoided any chance of being harmed and any chance of her actions causing a mistrial. The prosecution was still moving along and his fight for justice for the murder of Kevin Tucker continued even though Chester may have just tried to derail it.

The next morning was the prosecution's star witness Vincent James. In the last month, Vincent had waffled back and forth on his willingness to testify but LeVota was pretty confident Vincent would at least acknowledge some issues even if he was uncomfortable in front of his dad. Vincent was called to the stand and was sworn in. LeVota started slow with his name and his relation to Chester James which he acknowledged. But to LeVota's surprise when he was asked about the events at Kathryn Brown's house, Vincent James asserted his Fifth Amendment right not to testify because his testimony might incriminate him. LeVota did not see that one coming and now LeVota had a full on witness shitstorm on the stand.

Trial work is fluid and it was time to make a quick decision. Should LeVota pursue more questions and risk a mistrial or try some innocent questions that Vincent could answer to see what he could get. Sometimes changing strategies mid-trial is like a quarterback having to call a new play at the scrimmage line. Like calling an audible in football, if the quarterback sees a different defense, he has seconds to analyze it and make some changes without input from coaches or others. That split second decision could result in a touchdown or a sack and many other things in between.

LeVota's new plan was to tread ever so lightly because he knew this young man was in the worst position of his life and was being pulled in many different directions, so he was clearly unpredictable. LeVota also knew that he had spoken to Vincent many times and he never mentioned that his testimony might incriminate himself so he was clearly coached on this method and up to something. Was the plan to force a mistrial? LeVota wasn't going to let that happen and when he glanced at Chester James and saw him grinning like the *Cheshire Cat*, he knew the mastermind behind Vincent's plan.

A good trial attorney always remembers that the most important thing in that courtroom is the jury. It is all about them. LeVota remembered that he had promised the jury in opening statement that Vincent would testify about being with his father when his father cut off Kevin Tucker's head and hands and he wanted live up to that promise. But could the jury read between the lines and understand what was going on without any questions? LeVota knew that the jury already heard from Detective Lynch about speaking to Vincent. Even though Lynch didn't testify to the specifics of Vincent's statement, the jury already knew what Vincent was being called to testify to. They just needed to see why he wasn't.

Carefully, LeVota asked if Vincent was with his father when Kevin Tucker's body was dismembered. Vincent replied that he would not answer and asserted his Fifth Amendment right not to testify and incriminate himself. LeVota asked him if he told Detective Lynch that he was with his father when Chester James dismembered his body. Vincent answered that he asserted his right not to testify under the Fifth Amendment. LeVota finally asked if Vincent would be giving the same answer to every question and Vincent responded yes.

A good trial attorney also knows to never let the jury see you flustered so LeVota did the best he could at seeming casual and let the jury assume that this what he expected from the witness and he casually stated, *"No further questions."* Vincent's assertion made it impossible to play his video statement to the jury where he outlined Chester's actions and his part in them. Defense attorney Symson immediately asked permission to approach the bench and, in hushed voices the jury could not hear, Symson asked for a mistrial.

The defense lawyer believed Vincent's assertion was an indication he was hiding something he or his father did and that was so prejudicial to Chester that it rose to the level of declaring a mistrial. LeVota informed the court that even as recent as one hour ago, Vincent James was ready to testify and that Vincent had never told them about asserting "the Fifth" or they would have never called him to the stand. LeVota reminded the court that he had been very cautious as to the questions he asked as to not ascertain damaging testimony and even asked the final question if Vincent would answer the same way and sat down. There was no prejudice to the defendant in this witness surprising the prosecution with a Fifth Amendment assertion that was previously unknown to the state.

Of the hundreds of judges who have sat in the 16th Judicial Circuit in Jackson County, there are few that have had less decisions overturned by the Court of Appeals than Judge Messina. This judge was smart, fair, and knew the law. A great trait was her ability to not only make fair rulings but to always offer the opportunity for arguments and even discussion about issues before her rulings. There was no other judge in the circuit with a better judicial reputation than her. Whether you were a prosecutor or defense attorney and she ruled against you, her reasoning for her rulings was always valid and fair. There was much legal analysis in responding to Symson's objection from Judge Messina but basically it was a balance of whether the jury hearing Vincent assert his rights with no prior knowledge by the prosecution outweighed the defendant's right to a fair trial and did it prejudice him. Judge Messina denied the defense's request for a mistrial but Judge Messina instructed the jury, *"Ladies and gentlemen, a witness by the name of Vincent James began to testify. All of his testimony and all of the questions that were asked of him are stricken from the record, and you are instructed to disregard that testimony."*

The prosecution's final witness was Detective Mark Woods who went to Chester James home to arrest him on the burglary charge at Kathryn's apartment and the person that that took a statement from Chester that day at police headquarters. Out of the hearing of the jury, the defense had previously asked the court to suppress this detective's testimony and asked that this detective not be allowed to testify. The judge ruled that she would allow the testimony. LeVota just had to be careful not to let the jury know that sometime during giving his statement, Chester James asked for a lawyer and all questioning stopped.

Detective Woods testified that he spoke with Chester James and read him his Miranda Rights. Woods also testified that Chester signed a written statement acknowledging those rights and that he would speak with police. First, Woods asked Chester how he got the wounds on his arm and Chester said he had been playing with his own dog. Woods asked Chester if he had ever been to the Warwick apartment and he said no. Woods asked Chester if he knew Kathryn Brown and he said yes but he hadn't seen her for six months. Woods asked if he knew Kevin Tucker and he said no.

Woods testified that Chester was shaking and sweating profusely during the multi-hour interview but the temperature was 70 degrees in the interview room. Woods also testified that Chester was allowed to eat, go to the bathroom, or smoke whenever he wanted. But as Woods pressed Chester for more information and confronted him with things the detective knew, Chester changed his tune. When the detective said that they found his blood at the Warwick address and other questions, Chester acknowledged he was at the Warwick apartment but not to hurt anyone.

Chester acknowledged he did see Kathryn at the apartment the day before even though he had just said he hadn't seen her for six months. Woods said Chester went on to

143

say that Kathryn had given him a red truck to use for work but when Detective Woods asked where he picked it up from, he said the Oakley address. But only minutes before Chester said he had never been to that address where Kevin was killed.

The detective told the jury that he explained to Chester that he could have someone write down all the questions being asked or he could have the statement videotaped and Chester said he didn't want to do either of those. That was as far as LeVota could delve into the statement in front of the jury because actually in the statement it was right about there where Chester found himself caught in so many lies that he asked for a lawyer. LeVota made sure the jury didn't hear that bit of information because it would violate Chester's rights. With that, LeVota ended his final witness's direct examination. The defense attorney tried to make some points that even though Chester lied at first, he did later tell the truth about some things, but the damage was already done.

The prosecutor gave the first half of closing argument outlining the evidence. The defense attorney followed with his argument that Kathryn Brown and Margaret Fowler are liars. LeVota had the final word in his rebuttal. As taken from the trial transcript, LeVota finished his 15 minute closing argument to the jury:

LeVota said: *"What a long week. What a gory tale. But this is what we are here about. This is the end of the road for criminals. You hear these bad stories every day on the news, that a body was found, that someone was shot or someone was killed. It's the lead story every night on the TV news. But then you don't hear about it anymore, because it doesn't get a lot of reporting at this point. But this is the end of the criminal justice train."*

"This is the end, where justice is delivered. This is the end, where you get to evaluate the evidence and come to a verdict. On behalf of the State of Missouri, I want to thank you for the time

you've shown and the attention you've given in this case. We've heard a lot of evidence. We've heard from a lot of bizarre people testifying and it's been frustrating just trying to get them to tell us the truth. You all saw it."

"But now it's your time to do your job. And whether you know it or not, you've got the most important job here. More important than Judge Messina's and more important than any of the attorneys. It's your job to decide what the truth is, what the facts are, and who's really to blame in this case. You take that truth and you apply it to those instructions that Judge Messina just read you and you render a verdict. And when you render that verdict, I want you to remember your verdict speaks the conscience for this community. It sends a message that if you murder someone, you will be found guilty. If the State proves beyond a reasonable doubt that you murdered someone, you will be found guilty. As simple as that."

"In Jackson County, you don't get to get away with murder. It's that simple. The evidence has been supplied to you. You must find this defendant guilty of murder and armed criminal action. And when you do that, when you come back downstairs and you render a verdict of guilty of murder, you'll be telling this man something he already knows... that he's a butcher, he's a killer, and he's guilty of murder and armed criminal action. The State of Missouri awaits your verdict. Thank you."

Certainly not a slam dunk case but the jury did hear from an eyewitness who saw the murder. But did the defense attorney make any headway in raising reasonable doubt? Would the jury think maybe Kathryn Brown really pulled the trigger? But if so why would Vincent assert the fifth? His plan with his dad may have backfired. Would the jury get lost in the TV CSI analysis and remember that DNA evidence was inconclusive even though it was irrelevant? Also there was no murder weapon and the witnesses were all lying about something. LeVota knew that a jury can find doubt in any case and any jury may think that doubt is "reasonable" when it may not be to others but they are the final

145

word. Either way, Chester left the courtroom smiling and laughing as the jury was deliberating. Chester was fully expecting that he had won another round by manipulation of Margaret and Vincent.

The jury deliberated for several hours and then returned a question to the judge saying they were deadlocked at 10 for guilty and 2 for not guilty. The judge instructed them to continue on in their deliberations until they reached a unanimous verdict. After a few more hours, the jury returned with a unanimous verdict. Even after his life of manipulation and intimidation, Chester James was found guilty of both second-degree murder and armed criminal action. Sentencing was set for later and Chester was taken to jail.

The next day, begrudgingly, LeVota filed a felony charge against Vincent James for the crime of abandonment of a corpse. It was a charge that LeVota could not find had even been charged before in Missouri but Vincent James was guilty of it. After Vincent's attorney begged LeVota to dismiss the charge and even yelled at the prosecutor in open court, LeVota would not dismiss but agreed to offer him probation and no jail time.

Vincent's attorney complained that this would mess up his future in the military. LeVota wrestled with the issue but came to the conclusion that Vincent James knew about the consequences of not testifying and he made an adult decision after many meetings with the prosecution, his new wife and his new family. In those meetings, Vincent promised to everyone that he would do what was right and move on with his future and not let his father bring him down again. He broke that oath to his supporters and he had to face adult consequences.

Vincent promised to testify in exchange for his life free from his father's influence and free from his own criminal record and now he had to face the repercussions. He had an opportunity for a clean path to a new life free of his father's horrible influence.

But unfortunately for Vincent's future, something changed his mind and he followed his father's advice. This father hurt his son once again. Vincent was an adult and he could never say that he wasn't explained all the pros and cons. The only good thing for Vincent is that he had a prosecutor that did empathize with his position and instead of trying to throw him in prison, he offered a sentence of probation.

Sentencing day came for Chester James and he walked in the courtroom with his usual carefree demeanor. LeVota made his argument for sentencing saying a jury found this man guilty of murder and the range of punishment is 10 years to 30 years or life. LeVota said that Chester James is the poster boy for maximum sentencing and the State recommended the judge sentence him to 30 years in the Missouri Division of Adult Institutions on the first count of murder and an additional 10 years on Count II, armed criminal action.

The defense argued for only ten years, but Judge Messina had the final word and concluded her ruling by saying:

"The circumstances here really do bespeak of a callousness that makes this a very heinous crime. And so the Court, considering all of that -- the jury's verdict, needless to say, first of all, is the threshold question, but also considering Mr. James's record and considering the nature of the offense itself, it seems clear to me that Mr. James should not be out of jail again for a very long time, if ever at all."

"That being the case, on Count I the Court hereby imposes a sentence of 30 years in the Missouri Department of Adult Institutions. The Court on Count 2 imposes a sentence of ten years on the ACA, said sentence to run consecutively with the sentence previously imposed in Count I."

When Judge Messina sentenced Chester to a term of forty years in prison, the confident, 61 year old Chester James' knees buckled. When his attorney told him that he would be serving his sentence in the Western Missouri Correction Center and would be eligible for parole when he turned 100 years old, Chester got oddly quiet and stared at his hands.

Finally as Chester James was led off in handcuffs and leg shackles, he stopped in front of LeVota. He looked straight at the prosecutor, cleared his throat, and said the same words he said to Kevin Tucker before he shot him. Chester told his prosecutor, "*I aint done with you yet, boy!*" LeVota shook his head, smiled, and said back to his defendant, "*I'll be right here, Chester.*"

3

The Girl That Wouldn't Die

In 2001, Delisha Williams was not your typical twenty-nine year-old. The pretty girl with brown hair stood out in most crowds because her light blue eyes stood out against her dark skin and striking features. Born to a mother who was just a child herself and abandoned by her father when she was small, Delisha's Aunt Therma helped raise her from infancy. Therma was ten years older than her sister who had given birth to Delisha at a young age and Therma took the role of parent and caregiver to both Delisha and her mother. The three lived under one roof at Therma's modest home in Kansas City, Missouri. A typical house that was once in a safe neighborhood but had become an area of high crime over time and an area where drug trafficking was part of everyday living.

Delisha's mother was rarely home when she was younger and had little interest in raising her daughter. In 1987, when Delisha was fifteen, her mother moved in with a new boyfriend and out of Delisha's life forever. Even though Delisha had her Aunt Therma, she still felt alone and abandoned. She attempted to combat the stress and the pain of her most recent desertion turning to marijuana that was as readily available as milk was at the grocery store. However as many young people find out, shortly thereafter, her palate for marijuana craved something more exciting and it wasn't long before she was vigorously participating in a smorgasbord of drugs in the local drug community.

Almost to the day, nine months after her mother moved out, Delisha's abandonment issues peaked with some terrible news. Late one night, Therma received a call advising her that Delisha's mother had died in a car accident while traveling in Alabama. Delisha was devastated and went into a depression. As they tried to deal with funeral issues, her family could not come up with the money for a funeral. With no funds to bring her body home or even have a ceremony, Delisha's mother was buried in a pauper's cemetery in Alabama.

Even though Delisha's drug habit started out like most users that were experimenting with just a little at first and advancing into a more progressive kind, the loss of her mother increased the speed of her use and the excessiveness of it also. As her drug use evolved, crack cocaine ultimately became her drug of choice. She managed to hide her addiction from her aunt for several years but Delisha's once compliant personality changed to rebellion and defiance replaced her once easy-going behavior. Aunt Therma became aware of Delisha's untraditional conduct and counseled her constantly about the dangers of drug use. She worried her story would end like most drug users with an arrest and a criminal record or death from a drug related incident.

Therma's fears were not unfounded and Delisha had several minor but unofficial brushes with the police. There was also an incident that brought her home late one evening scared and covered in blood. Delisha never talked about what had happened to her to Therma. Since the police were never involved, Therma never asked. But it was that issue that made her reach her limit with her niece. In 1992, just one day before her twenty-first birthday, Therma forced Delisha into a thirty-day drug treatment program. She completed the program and retuned home but Delisha was silent and bitter. Therma was happy Delisha was clean but skeptical about whether she would stay clean. To her aunt's delight, Delisha managed to maintain a drug-free lifestyle for the next two years.

In 1992, the people of the state of Missouri voted to allow riverboat gambling. The legislature passed an amended version of the gambling issue the next year and in 1993, Governor Mel Carnahan signed it in to law. Harrah's Casino was one of the first casinos to open in the Kansas City area in September of 1993. One of Harrah's first employees was Therma as a blackjack dealer. The management of the North Kansas City casino ranked her as one of their best dealers and, as time went on, she developed seniority which allowed her to choose which shifts she wanted. Therma opted for the 9:00 pm to 6:00 am shift as she made more money in tips then. As "graveyard" shift workers do, Therma grew accustomed to the lifestyle of being up all night and sleeping during the day.

While her aunt dealt cards on the riverboat all night, Delisha had a wide open schedule and no supervision at home. Surprisingly to her aunt, Delisha stayed clean. The next year Delisha landed her first real job as a factory worker at a local engraving company. Therma's night work schedule worked well for both of them even though they never saw each other. Therma slept during the day while her niece worked. In the evenings, Delisha attended her drug treatment classes which was something she thought was necessary in order to maintain her sobriety. Living with her aunt was still quite a good deal for Delisha because Aunt Therma did not charge her rent. However, Delisha had a dream to live on her own and was working towards that goal by saving as much money as she could.

Despite the circumstances of her childhood and early adult life, Delisha grew wise and recognized she was the owner of her choices and unlike many addicts, she stayed sober. Delisha never wanted to return to her past destructive conduct and learned quickly she would have to always remove herself from everything and everyone associated with the behavior. However, it was that resolution that left her without friends and few resources to make new ones. She found most people at her work were older, married, or had children and found she had little in common with them. She continued her evening drug treatment classes and when they were not in session, she spent most of her nights at home alone. It was a stark change from her previous lifestyle where she spent her nights and days worrying about her next fix.

Delisha was lonely but knew it felt good to be clean and she needed to continue to refrain from revisiting anything related to her old way of life even though her loneliness tempted her. To pass time, she sometimes visited her aunt at the casino and found that her frequent visits not only kept her off the streets and away from temptation but it helped her aunt feel more at ease knowing her whereabouts.

Delisha worked hard for five years at the engraving factory and even applied her trade outside her work by engraving her own jewelry and even on some of her aunt's leather handbags. She continued to save her money and although she did not work at the casino, she was unknowingly learning a new trade while hanging out there when her aunt was at work. She watched her aunt and other casino dealers and became very familiar with many of the casino games. Delisha always felt that she might be able to have a career at the casino if she wanted to.

On that year's New Year's Eve, Delisha reflected that maybe it might have taken more time than some, but her life now was more "normal" than it had ever been. However, she realized that she was almost thirty years old and she had depended on her aunt in the same way she had depended on drugs. She realized that as she was just as unyieldingly about her convictions to remain clean as was her decision to become self-sufficient. Delisha had managed her money wisely over the years.

In January 2001, she withdrew her money from her savings account and rented a small house in an attempt to establish a life of her own. Unfortunately, her meager savings and salary did not allow her a luxury address but she rented a home in a neighborhood that had its fair share of crime. However, it was located just one block from a bus stop which allowed her easy access to the transportation she needed to get back and forth to work.

Delisha became comfortable with living on her own and slid into her new life without much effort. She kept to her normal regiment but left her job and started a new career at the casino. Even though she worked at the same casino as her aunt, she still was independent. She found her own way to work and back on the bus and not with Aunt Therma. Living on her own helped Delisha feel as if she had accomplished something. But regardless of the "successful" years that had passed, Delisha still felt pangs of loneliness and desertion. She contemplated them as she looked out the bus window as she went to and from work. She wouldn't let on but those issues still haunted her.

Despite the dashed opportunity of ever being able to confront her mother, she could never convince herself that her father had truly abandoned the notion of parenthood. Delisha took a clean-slated perception and persuaded her aunt to give her all the information she had about her father. In her spare time, she searched for her father. Her efforts did not go unrewarded. She was lucky and located her father. She found him playing music at a local club in the jazz district in downtown Kansas City.

The reconnection with her estranged father was awkward but not ill received, as she had feared. The two made slow but ritualistic efforts to get to know each other but mostly by Delisha's visits to the club. In the same way she had visited her aunt at work, she visited her father at his. Due to her disciplined work

155

schedule, she only visited the club twice a week and only stayed for an hour or two each time. It was her way of keeping busy and it diluted her loneliness.

The club was a well-liked and popular establishment. It didn't open until 5pm but was a trendy place for tourists and locals alike. Unappealing small wooden tables filled the inside and an empty stage was bland to its patrons when it was daylight. However, its charm came alive at sunset when they dimmed the lights and the musicians took the stage. Jazz music, rich with charisma, seized the attention of all who entered and the hazy cigarette smoke only enriched the atmosphere.

The bar was equipped with several moneymaking gimmicks and scantily clad cocktail servers went from table to table selling cigars and selling photographs to the patrons. Delisha liked to watch couples huddle close together when the photographer offered to take their picture. She knew it was an overpriced gimmick intended mostly for tourists, but all who came, including the locals, liked to take a memory home with them. After all, New Orleans may have given birth to the Blues and Jazz but there is no question that Jazz "grew up" and became its own in Kansas City. Without the 18th and Vine District in Kansas City where Delisha's father worked, there would simply not be this thing called "Jazz Music."

Delisha's sobriety was never just a fleeting thought and she had to work on it because the world has many temptations. Delisha felt her disciplined life helped keep her on track and away from the boredom that she knew could cause her to stray off path even with her many years sober. She got up at the same time every morning, worked the same schedule every week and, on most days, she caught the same bus. Although she never spoke to anyone, she became familiar with many of the passengers who took the same morning route.

However, on one particular Thursday in March of 2001, Delisha stayed much later at the club visiting her father. It was later than her disciplined internal clock normally allowed. She was having fun and when a man wearing a Yankee's jacket came up and put his arm around her, squeezed her shoulder lightly, and asked to get his picture taken with her. She politely told him yes. The man leaned his face into her cheek and motioned for the photographer to take their picture. They both smiled and the camera flashed.

After the camera flash, Delisha looked at the man who had persuaded her into the picture and expected not to recognize him. However, he looked familiar but she couldn't place it. Offended at first by his intrusiveness, her demeanor softened when she realized she recognized him from the bus and she saw no threat in the man's nice features and small stature. She talked through the loud music with the man that introduced himself as "New York" and her normal two-hour visit lasted until the club closed that night. Even though she found conversation with New York easy and amusing, she quickly learned his choice for topics of discussion about drugs were, unfortunately, ones she wanted to avoid. She decided further communication with him would not be in her best interest. For Delisha, the relationship with the interesting man ended that evening and she declined his suggestion of meeting up in the future.

More than a week passed before Delisha visited her dad at his club again. On this day, the club was just beginning to fill up when she arrived. Although she didn't want to see him, she wasn't surprised to see New York standing against the bar. She could barely see him through the thick smoke, but she knew it was him. The barely five and half feet tall man wore the same New York Yankee's jacket as he had on when they met. Delisha tried to ignore him and sat down at her regular table but he sat down next to her and started talking.

At first, she made small talk with him even though she didn't really want to. They talked about the neighborhood and who they knew and before she could stop herself, she was enjoying the company and the conversation. They found some things in common and even that Delisha worked at the same casino as did one of his friends. Before she knew it, she was opening up to a man she barely knew and talking about her life story. Before she left the bar that evening, New York knew all about her history of drug abuse and she knew New York's cell phone number.

New York and Delisha talked many times over the next several weeks and he made his interest in her incredibly obvious. She never anticipated that and thought they were just friends. However, she was uncomfortable when New York made light of her past struggles with drug addiction as he boasted of his extraordinary drug connections and repeatedly reminded her that he could score whatever drugs she wanted. It was clear that New York was romantically interested in her but Delisha's interest in him never grew into anything more than casual companionship. His extracurricular activities appeared to be the kind she outgrew many years prior. Even though the temptation to use drugs again was great, she stood her ground.

Delisha knew very little about her new friend's life or history but she knew he wasn't her type. However, what she did know was that his careless attitude toward her rehabilitated life was only a warning sign of a toxic lifestyle. It was a life she once knew and never wanted to revisit. Nevertheless, desperate for peer companionship, she put up with his attention but declined his romantic proposals.

To Delisha, it appeared his affection for her continued to grow despite her rejections. It seemed that with each occurrence, he became more persistent in his propositions for a more serious relationship. Finally, his dealings started to become more annoying than friendly. Even though New York would state his faithfulness to remain platonic, he still was pursuing romance. The oddness of the relationship grew more unnerving when New York started questioning her whereabouts and timing more like a jealous boyfriend than a good friend. He wanted constant access to her and she became uncomfortable with his clingy behavior and attempted to gradually wean herself from him.

Unfortunately, the time she spent alone increased as she tried to eliminate New York from her life. Delisha's dad was concerned about her safety and suggested she stay with him. She accepted his offer. She had learned a lot in the few months she had lived alone, but despite her desire for independence, she knew that having a roommate would be safer for her and alleviated some of her loneliness.

Regardless of its awkwardness, Delisha took to the idea of moving in with her dad even though he really was a man she barely knew. She moved her belongings out of her house and into his home within a few weeks. She also considered the arrangement as an opportunity to free herself from the undesirable relationship she had with New York. Although she had kind feelings towards him, she also felt suspicious of him and knew she needed to stay away. She did not tell him she had moved and did not return his calls or go to the club for the sole purpose of avoiding him for two weeks. When he did see her on the bus and questioned her behavior, she explained to him her concerns and told him that it was in her best interest to sever all ties.

Delisha thought she knew what he wanted from her and it was something more than she wanted to give. Delisha knew in her gut that she shouldn't be around him. Most of the time, you should listen to your gut. Her gut was right. What she didn't know was New York's objective with her was far beyond the physical relationship she thought he wanted. Even though New York expressed his desire to be her boyfriend, it was actually just a scam to get close to Delisha for other reasons. New York was in the middle of working on a plan when she abruptly cut all ties with him. However, this did not deter him. It only put a crimp in New York's scheme and he started recruiting a partner to aid his redesign of the plot.

The house Delisha shared with her father was a small, two-bedroom home located in a modest neighborhood of both poor and middle class residents but outside the crime arena where she had always lived. The houses were close together but its owners strategically placed trees on their property to add privacy as well as to add charm to the humble neighborhood. The new area offered Delisha an unfamiliar sense of safety she had never known before. The main living area was the heart of the residence and both the kitchen and Delisha's room were accessible from that central room. Only a three-foot divider wall separated the kitchen and living room and both rooms were fully visible from the front door. Delisha's room shared a common wall, unfortunately, it was same wall that framed the large flat screen television. However, Delisha's dad was gone most nights and TV noise was rarely a problem.

Most people will generally describe parts of town as a good side or a bad side and people could debate about what area is really "bad" or not or even what defines a "bad" part of town. One thing that no one would argue about is that Bovi Combs was from the bad part of town. Combs was shorter than the average male. The so called "Napoleon Complex" is a term describing the theory that short men sometimes overcompensate in an overly aggressive or domineering behavior because of their small stature.

If ever anyone had this complex, it was Bovi Combs. He was brash and aggressive. He had more aliases than the average criminal had. He had dark skin and a friendly face but he was a hustler with a long criminal record who made his money selling drugs and breaking into houses. He was also a motivated drug dealer who worked hard to elevate his street status; however, he was once convinced that his small stature only earned him disrespect and reduced his opportunities of rising through the ranks of gang membership. His reaction was to act tough and create a reputation for himself. He spoke a lot of street slang and became well known on streets of Kansas City, but he was always looking for more creative ways to climb the corporate street ladder of gang hierarchy.

Like Delisha, Bovi had a schedule, but unlike hers, his list didn't include anything productive. He spent his days hustling and selling drugs on the streets. When he wasn't burglarizing homes, his nights were spent partying and club hopping to build his clientele. He had a set of distinctive characteristics about him. First was his northern accent, which was entirely different from the Kansas City vernacular and second, was his kind features which helped offset his hidden agendas. The combination of the two offered a unique formula of charisma and trust that helped him draw in his clients.

Like many relationships on the threshold of failure, a certain amount of break-ups and reconciliations are necessary before the final consideration of permanency is reached. New York preyed upon Delisha and her affections and she couldn't help but be entertained by the attention. Occasionally she agreed to see him and the two would meet up at the club. Nevertheless, her tolerance was only temporary as New York pressured her for a physical relationship and was always asking for her new address.

Once again, New York's extreme pushiness lost him access to her. Regardless of her continued unenthusiastic responses towards him, New York had not completed his final plans for her. Despite her resistance; he was never going to let her go. From a distance, he watched her almost every move. He knew her work schedule and learned of her new address as he followed the bus she rode home on one night. Like clockwork, he monitored her regular visits to and from the club. Delisha did very little that New York didn't know about.

Near Midnight on a cool spring evening in 2001, Bovi Combs was taking the bus back to his mother's house, where he stayed and he noticed 21 year-old Shecora Clanton sitting in the middle of the bus on her way home from work. Shecora was a shy but attractive girl. She also worked at Harrah's as a cocktail server from Monday through Friday on the 3pm-11pm shift. On the bus, Shecora stared out the window and clung tightly to her light overcoat that covered her revealing black Harrah's cocktail uniform. She was single at the time but was unknowingly riding the same bus as her soon-to-be first boyfriend, 29 year-old Bovi Combs. As she sat directly behind a man she had never met, little did she know Bovi's manipulations were already at work in a plan setting Shecora up to do his bidding.

Being the hustler that he was, Bovi was always looking for a new minion and unfortunately for Shecora, he turned on his charm and initiated a conversation with her. They made small talk and she let go of her inhibitions that night and gave him her cell phone number. Within the next few days, they started seeing each other. She was pretty but her introverted personality often cost her attention from the opposite sex. Her past included only a few sexual encounters which never evolved into any type of serious relationships, so she was eager to be in her first committed one. Despite her intelligence, she bought into Bovi's gangster image and was immediately under his charismatic spell. After only a few weeks of dating, she believed him when he said he wanted to be exclusive with her. From that point, Shecora considered herself Bovi's girlfriend.

Not long after they met, Bovi was spending most of his nights at her house. Shecora lived in a split-level house that was located on the corner of 26th Street and Walrond Avenue. Shecora shared the a-framed house with her father who lived upstairs in an attic-like apartment while she acquired and maintained the entire lower level. Shecora's mother had died when she was just 10 years old and she felt the need to stay close to her father and watch out for him. This arrangement worked well for the both of them as both floors had their own separate entrances and allowed for privacy but also allowed for more financial freedom as they shared in the cost of living expenses. Shecora's living arrangement also worked well for Bovi as it gave him another location to run his profitable drug dealing business. It helped with business because he just didn't have the same freedom while he was living at his mother's house.

Thieves and hustlers can be dumb but at least the successful ones have a special way of handling people and Bovi turned on all the charm for Shecora. He had special skills when it came to drawing people towards him and was charismatic but that was about it. He was not a smart man. Shecora often found herself aiding him on simple tasks like counting money and reading. She was so infatuated with her new boyfriend that she was blind to his faults. She was more than happy to overlook his educational shortcomings and lack of common sense. Shecora also loved that her boyfriend was a storyteller and that he enlightened her with unending accounts of his adventures on the street where he always made himself out to be the hero in a villainous story. In one of his stories, Bovi talked about his sister, Carla who had been murdered many years ago. In most of his stories, he provided only vague details, but in this one, he provided vivid and elaborate details.

Bovi's itinerary rarely was one that embraced honesty and sincerity so the sharing of his sister's murder wasn't without a hidden agenda. He used Shecora's sympathy to reel her in to his side as he pitifully elaborated on his sister's death. Basically the story went like this: He told Shecora that some people had gotten a key to his sister's apartment to steal from her. The people went to her house to steal some money and found her there and killed her. Shecora felt bad for her boyfriend; however, she had heard many of his tales and she was never sure if they were true or embellishments. Bovi then shared with Shecora that he had made a vow to find his sister's killers and murder them as they had done to her and hold them responsible. The fascination with Bovi's exciting anecdotes had long ago worn off and eventually Shecora stopped paying attention. However, when she heard him talk about his sister's murder and of revenge, she paid full attention.

The Harrah's riverboat casino cocktail servers who were dressed in shiny bustiers set the tone for the casino located on the Missouri River. But the casino had more of a royalty theme. The palace-like interior greeted each of its patrons with a sense of grandeur with brass railings adorning the marble floors and staircases. Regardless of their social standing, all who visited the favorite Kansas City hotspot were acknowledged with high esteem and respect by polished and attractive employees.

Delisha had never missed a day of work and had never been late, but on an early May Friday, she had to take a different bus because she had traded her normal 9am-5pm shift for a 10-pm-6am shift. She wasn't as knowledgeable about the later buses. Even though she had a new shift, New York still had a relentless eye on Delisha and he knew her new schedule. As a matter of fact, New York knew a lot about several employee's schedule at the casino. However, Delisha's schedule change that day worked out well for him as it helped him put his plan into action.

The same evening, shortly before the end of her shift, Bovi Combs surprised Shecora at work and told her that he had missed her and couldn't wait to see her. Shecora was excited that her boyfriend was there and that they would see each other after her shift but then he dropped a bombshell on her. Bovi pulled her aside and told her that he just saw one of the people that was involved in his sister's murder at the casino and that person was a casino employee. Shecora's euphoria that her boyfriend had surprised her at work was quickly deflated when he pointed out a pretty blackjack dealer as one of the persons involved in killing his sister. Shecora was uncomfortable and tried to ignore him when he followed her around as she delivered drinks to the last of her customers.

Shecora was stunned when her boyfriend pointed out Delisha Williams as the person he said had something to do with his sister's death. He did not elaborate on how he knew her coworker was involved but Bovi was very firm in his assertion. Shecora only knew of Delisha from work but knew she had a good reputation and was one of the most trusted employees at the casino. Like many of his stories, she wasn't sure she believed it in its entirety but when Bovi talked about murder, he always got her attention.

Shecora didn't know what Bovi was up to. She knew that Bovi didn't know Delisha and she was concerned as Bovi walked towards her table. Before Bovi settled down at one of the half-moon shaped blackjack tables, he had stopped by the cashier's cage to exchange some cash for poker chips. Inside the elaborate facility, uniforms were specific for each gaming section and blackjack dealers wore black slacks, white long-sleeved shirts with black tuxedo vests and bowties.

Despite the monotony of colors, Bovi had no trouble finding his target and placed a small pile of chips down on the green felt fabric in front of Delisha. Bovi Combs was the sole player at the table. Shecora watched as Bovi sat at Delisha's table but she found it odd that the two of them seemed to know each other. Shecora also found it even more strange when Delisha said, *"New York, you aren't supposed to be here."*

For the sake of her job and other patrons, Delisha remained composed when Bovi Combs sat down because regardless of what Shecora thought, Delisha did know him. However Delisha did not know this man as "Bovi Combs." No, Delisha knew the man who sat down at her table as "New York," the man she had been trying to get away from for the past few weeks. "New York" and Bovi Combs were one and the same.

When Delisha saw him, she briefly considered notifying security; however, he had never done anything to make her feel unsafe so she refrained. Bovi (New York) knew Delisha did not approve of his being at her work so Bovi played down his visit by telling her that he was there visiting his friend. Delisha did remember that he had mentioned he had a friend that worked in her casino in a prior conversation so she felt more at ease and softened her attitude towards him for the rest of the evening.

While she finished settling with her tables for shift change, Shecora watched Bovi as he played blackjack at Delisha's table. It was obvious by their interactions, they knew each other, but she didn't know why he was being so friendly if he thought she was involved in his sister's death. After her second pass around Delisha's table, she thought that Bovi was clearly flirting with Delisha and Shecora was annoyed by that. She consoled herself for a brief moment and wondered if it was all just a story he was making up to reinforce his gang image. Shecora's naivety was never in short supply. Her opinions about Bovi's gang posture were only a minor setback to her real concern as she pondered how he and Delisha knew each other. Although she didn't know Delisha very well, she had nothing against her. However, from that moment on, Shecora felt overwhelming jealousy.

It had been more than two weeks since Delisha had seen or heard from the man she knew as "New York," so when Bovi sat down at her table, she assumed he had finally taken her seriously when she told him she didn't want to see him anymore. Nevertheless, she admittedly still liked the attention and allowed him to stay at her table until her shift was over. Later after her work day was over, Shecora joined Bovi at Delisha's blackjack table and impatiently waited for him. While she knew what his implied intentions were for her co-worker, she took the threat of Delisha stealing her boyfriend more seriously than his grandiose boasts of revenge.

Unbeknownst to her, Shecora had already helped kick start her boyfriend's plan when she sat down that night. Bovi paid Shecora extra attention as they sat in front of Delisha. As Shecora relaxed in the arena of Bovi's fraudulent affection, his actions allowed for a temporary camaraderie between the two girls that had no idea how he had been interacting with each other. For the rest of the night, Shecora felt confident in her relationship with Bovi and Delisha felt less pressure knowing he had a new love interest. Regardless of Bovi's intellectual limitations, he was clever and conniving. Bovi had played a different character for each girl and continued on that evening. Even more devious was that each girl knew him by an entirely different name.

Blinded by Bovi's exaggerated charm after leaving the casino, Shecora listened obediently as he persuaded her to engage in a friendship with Delisha. He thought a friendship between the two girls would provide him with better chances of seeing Delisha outside her work and in a more private setting. This

167

would create an area where he could complete his revenge. Bovi then detailed his plans for Delisha to Shecora. He told Shecora that he wanted Delisha to die in her own home just like his sister. However breaking into the house would cause unwanted attention and Delisha needed to invite them over in order to assist them in her own murder.

In theory, Bovi's idea was complete and he knew when and where he wanted to end Delisha's life. He knew where she lived. He knew her living arrangement and he knew her dad was gone most evenings. Bovi convinced Shecora that she and Delisha had a lot in common as they both lived with their dad and they both lost their mother at an early age. Shecora's feelings softened for her co-worker as she recognized they shared similar life circumstances, but Shecora never would ask how Bovi knew so much about her.

For the most part, people who utilize the public transportation system in Kansas City are hardworking, law-abiding citizens, just trying to get from one place to another. However, in mid-May, the Kansas City Area Transportation Authority bus was a place for the planning for a murder plot. Bovi and Shecora were on the same bus where they had met, when Bovi called for recruitment in his murder plot. Bovi had made arrangements to meet a man on a certain bus at a certain time. The person he was to meet was Andrew Jackson but of no relation to the president and namesake of Jackson County, Missouri where Kansas City sits. Bovi only knew Jackson from word-of-mouth. Unlike the seventh President of the United States, Jackson was no hero. He was an unemployed and uneducated 43 year-old career criminal that was for hire.

Quite often, Bovi used the bus system as his office but Shecora didn't know of this pre-arranged meeting. Bovi pursued Jackson and Jackson knowingly and willingly kept the appointment. Several minutes into their conversation, he knew Jackson was the just the type of person that would be able to help him carry out his plot.

Jackson did not dress in the emblematic attire that was synonymous with the distinctive gang member uniform. He was a dark-skinned man with a clean haircut, pressed khaki pants, and blue polo. His face was clean-shaven and he carried an old brown blazer. Bovi, who was more loyal to the classic gang clothing rituals, would have never identified him that evening, had he not approached him first. Jackson knew of Bovi's reputation but also knew that reciprocity was an unwritten law among dealers. The more connections you had within the business, the better protection you had when you needed it. Jackson needed the money and wanted to stay on Bovi's good side, so the two men exchanged information. Jackson told Bovi he could fix him up with anything and could help him accomplish whatever he wanted.

That same evening, for affirmation, Bovi called several other people and asked them all similar questions. He asked them what they would do if someone killed their sister and if they knew how to "off" someone. Shecora knew what he meant and although she couldn't hear the responses, she knew from his reaction that his contacts were helpful in providing the information he needed. Bovi was good at dealing and stealing but despite his desire to kill Delisha, he had no experience as a murderer.

Shecora and Delisha did not work the same shift but they did share two of the same hours in their shift when the two girls were at the casino together. Their shifts overlapped between 3pm to 5pm. Shecora made a promise to Bovi to get close to Delisha and used the time to get to know her coworker. She knew Delisha couldn't leave her table unless she was on break so

Shecora made an effort to go to her blackjack table often to get her drinks. In the beginning, she forced polite conversation on Delisha but it wasn't long before Delisha opened up and reciprocated in the exchange.

Delisha was excited to be making a new friend at work. Small talk eventually evolved into the two sharing personal information. Delisha told her that she was once drug addict and had just recently moved in with her father and Shecora told Delisha about her boyfriend. Shecora felt guilty as she framed Delisha into a fake friendship, but she withheld his hidden agenda as a loyalty to Bovi. Similarly, Delisha didn't want to hurt her new friend's feelings, so she remained silent about the past she once had with her boyfriend she had known as New York.

Two young women who were both lonely and desperate for a healthy relationship found comfort in each other and looked forward to the two hours they shared during their shifts. However, Shecora's drive to gain Bovi's approval was much stronger than her ambition for long-term friendship. She obediently, but guiltily, asked the next question to Delisha that would be the next step of Bovi's plan. In one innocuous conversation, Shecora innocently suggested that her and her boyfriend ought to come hang out and watch movies together sometime at Delisha's home. Delisha no longer felt threatened by Bovi and she agreed to have them over the following Saturday. However, she laid down strict rules and told Shecora that under no circumstance would she allow drugs in her house. She explained that she did not want to compromise her father's trust and she didn't want to be in any position to be tempted to use.

On a Thursday evening, nearly two weeks after their meeting on the bus, Bovi made contact with Jackson again and the two collaborated and worked up a murder scheme. The plan they agreed upon involved Jackson using a homemade chemical with a syringe that ended with a dead Delisha. Bovi told Jackson he wanted to carry out the plan as soon as possible, but Shecora, realizing how serious her boyfriend was, begged him to let it go. But Bovi insisted he wanted Delisha dead by Saturday.

Saturday morning, on June 2, Bovi took the bus to Shecora's house. He insisted the murder happen that day and pressured her to call around to find a big moving truck they could rent. Shecora was puzzled by the need for a U-Haul type of truck. Bovi informed her that after he killed Delisha, he was going to take anything of value from her house. Shecora knew it was short notice and moving trucks would be hard to find but she obediently called. She called every rental facility in the area but just as she expected, there were none available.

By this time Bovi was hyper active and full of adrenaline. When Shecora told him there were no trucks available, Bovi lost his temper and slapped her hard in the face. Shecora reeled from the strike and realized the seriousness of the situation. She thought about getting out of the whole plan but realized she was in too deep to back out. Shecora was terrified of what Bovi might do if she tried and she did not want to be his next victim.

Regardless of the truck dilemma, she knew by her boyfriend's demeanor that no amount of issues could change Bovi's mind about his plan. Bovi ordered Shecora to call Delisha and cancel their plans for the evening. She lied and told Delisha she had to work and suggested they move their plans to the following evening. Delisha explained Sunday might not work because she had to go to bed early Sunday evening because she had to work Monday morning. With Bovi listening, Shecora told Delisha she really wanted to hang out and was she sure she couldn't do Sunday night? Delisha heard the frustration in her new friend's voice so to soften her disappointment, she reluctantly agreed to their Sunday night plans. But she again told Shecora they could stay as long as they wanted as long as they were gone before her father came home from work.

The next morning was Sunday and on that morning, Shecora continued to work on her assigned responsibility. She found an available U-Haul truck not too far from the Wal-Mart Supercenter near her home. So as to not connect himself to any crime, Bovi was very firm with Shecora when he told her the reservation and rental contract would be under her name. Bovi reminded her that he was going to kill Delisha, take all of her possessions, and load it into the U-Haul. Shecora had to do nothing.

Shecora and Bovi took the next bus in the morning to the Supercenter where they ate lunch and waited for his uncle to pick them up to take them to the rental facility. Bovi explained to his uncle he was helping his girlfriend move some stuff but his uncle didn't care and was just happy to get out of the house and give his nephew a ride. They exchanged pleasantries and jumped out of the car at the U-Haul store.

When they arrived at the rental facility, they said goodbye to Bovi's uncle and he and Shecora disappeared inside. She signed all of the rental documents and paid the deposit. Bovi then put his hands on her back and guided her towards the driver's seat of the rental truck. She drove them back to her house as Bovi called Jackson and advised him that they were waiting on just one thing. They had to wait for the contact with Delisha to say it was ok to come over.

At the demand from Bovi, Shecora attempted contact with her several times throughout the day and left several messages but it seemed that Delisha was in no hurry to return her calls. In the meantime, Bovi received several messages from Jackson advising him that he was ready to put the plan into action

Bovi and Shecora left the house only one time that afternoon when they drove to a local chicken restaurant to eat and arrived back around 6:30 pm. Bovi became annoyed when they still had not heard back from Delisha but knew they could do nothing but wait for her to call. Jackson called several more times throughout the evening and left repeated messages. Bovi returned his calls and, even though he and Jackson had already worked out the plot together, he nervously reiterated his questions about their plan. He asked Jackson to recap the details of how they were going to kill her and how long it would take. Jackson reassured him that he knew what he was doing and it wouldn't take very long. Bovi told Jackson that he would come pick him up as soon as he heard from Delisha. About 9:30 pm and with no contact from Delisha, Bovi and Shecora changed clothes, left the house, and headed to Jackson's apartment on 40th and Harrison.

Bovi expected the hired killer to be bearing a load of equipment but Jackson walked towards the truck almost empty handed. From there, with Shecora still driving, the three of them headed toward Delisha's house on Benton Avenue located just ten minutes away from Shecora's home. As the three drove down the highway, the conversation in the cab turned from nervous small talk to compensation.

Jackson advised Bovi that before he would do anything, he wanted three-thousand dollars plus some of Delisha's property. Bovi agreed to split the property and paid Jackson fifteen-hundred dollars in cash but told him he would have to wait until Delisha was dead for the rest. The U-Haul death truck was on its way to its first pick up.

Prior to getting into the truck, Shecora did not know how Delisha was going to die, but she knew it was the plan. She tried not to listen as Jackson, similar to a well-spoken professor, broke it down in microscopic detail. Jackson fed Bovi the specifics of how they would kill her and like a student hungry for facts, Bovi ate up his lecture. Fascinated by Jackson's cleverness, Bovi continued with his questions. By then Bovi was well versed in the murder plan but he liked to hear the narrative repeated as it fueled his energy. The killer-for-hire consultant, Jackson knew what was expected of him and started preparing his tools. Unlike Bovi, Jackson appeared fluent in the language of murder.

As the three rode over to Delisha's house, Bovi thought about how flawless the plan was. He had an invitation to Delisha's house, a hired killer to do his dirty work, and a naive girl who rented a truck in her name, which would allow him to clean out Delisha's belongings after she was dead. Bovi was pretty satisfied and lit up a joint and passed it around the cab. Shecora took a hit with one hand and drove with the other while passing it to Jackson. He took a hit off the joint, handed it back to Bovi, and then unzipped a small black zippered bag.

The inside of the truck cab was dark so Bovi turned on the dome light as he was engaged by the contents of the bag. The bag opened up like a notebook and in the small loops, where pencils might slide into were two fluid-filled syringes and a small vial of liquid. Jackson pulled out one of the syringes, flicked it with his middle finger, and explained its content and purpose.

Jackson explained that one syringe contained a simple window cleaning fluid which when injected into the body would cause the person to become paralyzed and fall into a coma but the second one contained a different cleaning fluid which would put the person into cardiac arrest. He further explained the vial was extra solution in the case the victim would need a second injection. Bovi had no medical training and had no idea that Jackson's description of the lethal effects of the chemicals was as much embellishment as it was rumor. However, after hearing the recitation of the deadly influences along with Jackson's confident demeanor, Bovi was convinced that he hired the right man for the job.

Bovi excitedly continued his obsessive inquiries but Jackson responded to his line of questions with a firm command to stop as he was already annoyed with the incessant talking. Bovi quickly regained control back from Jackson and changed subjects. He assured them that the outcome of the events that lie ahead of them would be good and they would be better off with Delisha dead and extra money in their pockets

When the trio pulled up to house, Delisha's dad had still not left for work and they were surprised when a man answered the door. Delisha rushed through the introductions to her dad and hurried her dad out the door unknowingly leaving herself alone with three killers. Bovi introduced Jackson as his cousin, "Junebug", and explained away the truck by indicating he was moving into the neighborhood.

Bovi made himself at home and looked inside the kitchen cabinets and asked Shecora and Jackson to go to the store for snacks and cigarettes. Exactly as he wanted, Shecora and Jackson drove the huge vehicle to a nearby convenience store leaving Delisha and Bovi alone. In the uncomfortable silence and to pass time, Delisha asked him if he wanted something to drink and before he answered, she was up and putting ice and soda in a glass. At the convenience store, Jackson paid for cigarettes, a fifth of Wild Turkey, and a two-liter bottle of Sprite. Even though she knew of Delisha's ill-fated future, Shecora sat in the truck seething over her boyfriend being alone with Delisha.

Bovi met the U-Haul as it was about to pull into the driveway and told Shecora to back it in towards the garage instead. Jackson jumped out of the passenger's seat and Shecora drove past the driveway and put the truck in reverse. The back-up warning alarm loudly sounded off until she had the back end square against the garage and the truck in park. Annoyed by the loud beeping, Bovi angrily slapped Shecora on the side of her head when she got out of the truck.

When the three went back in, Delisha was in the kitchen making something to eat and asked if anyone else wanted anything. They all shook their heads but sat at the kitchen table nonetheless. Delisha was a good host to her ungrateful guests and took their drink orders while she finished her dinner. She poured a Sprite for Shecora and thanked her for going to the store. She then made Bovi a mixed drink of Sprite and Wild Turkey.

After accepting their drinks, Shecora and Jackson went into the living room and watched TV. Bovi stayed in the kitchen while she cleaned up and he made himself and Delisha a drink. She protested at first but reluctantly agreed that one drink wouldn't hurt her and they both joined Shecora and Jackson in the living room. Just as he had the night at the casino, Bovi kept up his ruse that he was interested in Shecora and sat close to her on the couch. He kissed her every time he got up to go to the bathroom or fix another drink. It was something he needed to do to keep her loyal to him and to the events that would transpire later in the evening.

Bovi was also very attentive in making sure Delisha's drinks were strong and never empty. He continued to make drinks for her and she, uncharacteristically, continued to accept them. After about four drinks, Bovi knew Delisha was drunk. Shecora and Jackson needed to stay clearheaded and did not partake in any alcohol consumption but Delisha was getting drunk and she was clueless to what was about to take place.

To Delisha it was an awkward situation as the four sat in front of the TV and pretended to watch two movies. She never really wanted them there but agreed only for the sake of her new friend. The three guests fabricated interest in the movies as they watched Delisha slowly drink herself into complete intoxication. As the alcohol consumed her, she was unable to stay awake. In one of her last mistakes, Delisha announced to everyone she was going to bed but advised her guests they could stay as long as they wanted as long as they were gone before her father came home. She fake smiled at everyone and stumbled into her bedroom. Bovi smiled back and waved but his smile turned into a sneer as she shut the door.

He looked at Jackson and Jackson pulled out his black leather case. It was time. Jackson fished out a syringe and whispered that they needed to make sure she was asleep before they could act. Bovi went into the kitchen and made another drink for himself. He sat back down as they waited for Delisha to fall asleep.

Shecora panicked in the realization of what was looming. She told Bovi she was scared and wanted to leave. Bovi quickly pounced on the couch where she was sitting, laid himself softly on top of her, and stroked her face. He assured her that everything was going to be okay. Her posture softened with Bovi's reassuring words but she quickly reclaimed her frightened disposition as Bovi's charm disappeared and his threatening demeanor returned. He reminded her that she was part of the plan and made it clear that if she didn't cooperate, there would be two dead women instead of one. He leaned over and got off of her but Shecora couldn't stop shaking.

Ten minutes had passed since Delisha went to bed and the men were certain that she was asleep. Jackson held up the syringe and got up from his seat. He didn't say a word but disappeared into Delisha's bedroom. He quietly closed the door behind him. Shecora was terrified but Bovi giggled uncontrollably and turned off the TV as to maybe hear the sounds of Jackson in action. Complete silence filled the living room while they waited for Jackson to come back out of the bedroom.

In the bedroom, Delisha was comfortably numb in her state of unconsciousness and didn't hear a thing when Jackson crept into her room. With her blankets pulled tightly around her neck, she was attempting to sleep off the alcohol she consumed throughout the uncomfortable evening. Jackson stood over her for about 20 seconds to make sure she was asleep. Jackson tugged lightly at her legs several times and after Delisha didn't move at all, he removed the blankets from around her. Dressed only in a thin pair of shorts and a tank top, Delisha rustled and Jackson could see her body shivering from being uncovered. However, too drunk to care how she got uncovered, she only opened her eyes long enough to pull the covers back up around her.

Jackson moved in closer and decided he would stick Delisha in the neck with the needle but every time he got close and pulled the blanket down to expose her neck, she would pull the covers tightly back around her. He saw her eyes open each time he moved her covers but she never looked at him. He knew the needle was too thin and short to go through the heavy quilt, so after several attempts Jackson left the room.

Jackson may have seemed confident to Bovi but he was an evil person that was incompetent in his life and incompetent in this action also. Bovi might have believed Jackson's tale about Windex in a syringe rendering a person immovable or into a coma but there was not a part of that story that was true. Jackson's brilliant plan was foiled by Delisha just covering herself up. Jackson left the bedroom unsuccessful.

Bovi and Shecora waited for Jackson to come out and announce he accomplished his mission but instead he reappeared with the syringe in his hand. He told them he couldn't find a good spot to inject her but the injection was only the first part. The plan was for the syringe to incapacitate her then they would still have to kill her. Jackson said we are just going to have to do it without the anesthesia. Jackson threw the needle down, went into the kitchen and rustled through the drawers. He found a wooden hammer that is used to tenderize meat and he returned into the living room.

178

Evil was in great measure in that house that night as all three of them stalked towards the bedroom door where Delisha was asleep. Delisha had gone to bed thinking she had been a good friend and invited some people over. She went to bed as a naïve woman who didn't dream her "friends" meant her harm. She went to bed after telling her friends to take their time and leave when they wanted to. Well they were going to leave when they wanted to but only after their dastardly deed was finished.

All three stood outside the bedroom door. Jackson went in first followed by Bovi. Each men went to opposite sides of the bed, Shecora stood in the doorway. Without hesitation, Jackson grabbed the blankets with one hand and raised the hammer above Delisha's head with the other. He winked at Bovi before he ripped them completely off and delivered a smashing blow on her right temple. Delisha immediately screamed out but was unable to move before Jackson reared back and smashed the hammer into her head again. She received multiple blows to her head before Jackson realized the mallet wasn't the best weapon for murder. He was beating on Delisha but it was not striking any fatal blows.

Jackson weighed his options. It wasn't working so he could walk away, leave his victim still alive, and risk going to jail for assault or he could finish what he started. He chose evil. Jackson threw the hammer across the room and wrapped his hands around her neck. Delisha fought him and with his hands still around her neck, the two wrestled each other out of the bed and onto the floor. Delisha screamed and fought for her life. She clawed and hit him with her fists but he only tightened his grip. Bovi cheered as the two struggled with each other on the floor but his girlfriend couldn't watch and stood statue-like with her back against the wall just outside the bedroom. She was watching a murder and she couldn't believe it.

179

As Jackson wrestled with Delisha, he ordered Bovi to find the syringe so he could inject her with the chemicals. After what must have seemed like an eternity, Delisha lost all of her fight and her body went limp. Jackson had strangled her until she finally stopped breathing. Shecora could hear gurgling noises coming from Delisha's throat, peaked into the bedroom, and saw her new "friend" unconscious on the floor.

As instructed, Bovi ran into the living room and returned with the syringe and tried to hand it to Jackson. But with his tired hands still wrapped around her neck, Jackson ordered Bovi to remove the cap off the syringe and jam the needle into her neck. As Bovi uncapped the syringe and moved toward Delisha's neck, he found that his victim was breathing again and back to fighting for her life. Delisha was strong and found the strength to breathe again. She kicked and tried to wiggle herself free.

Bovi tried to stick Delisha with the needle but her limbs flailed in her desperate attempts to survive and he was unable to control her enough to succeed. Bovi yelled for Shecora and ordered her to sit on her legs and keep her from moving but she disobeyed him and remained by the door. Jackson grabbed the syringe out of Bovi's hand and jammed the needle into her neck. He emptied the contents out of the syringe, pulled it out, and gave it back to Bovi. Jackson barked at Bovi and ordered him to get the extra vial so he could reload the syringe. Bovi ran to the living room and came back with the bottle of chemicals. As Bovi held Delisha down, Jackson refilled the syringe and forced the needle into Delisha's neck for a second time.

Adrenaline was streaming through Delisha's veins and she knew these men were trying to kill her but the combination of whiskey and overexertion in her fight had compromised her reflexes. Regardless, she continued to fight the two men trying to kill her. She struggled hard to get the men off and tried to stand up but they overpowered her and Jackson emptied another chemical filled syringe into her system.

As Jackson injected the last of the chemicals, the thin needle broke off into her neck and the weakened Delisha vomited and fell unconscious onto the floor. Shecora left the doorway and ran into the living room but Jackson and Bovi stayed on top of Delisha and checked for a pulse. To their contempt, Delisha's heart was strong and continued to pump blood through her body. The two men were shocked when they realized that she was still alive. Bovi, exhausted and crazed from the fight, screamed obscenities in her unconscious face.

He picked himself up off Delisha and scoured through the dresser drawers and closet looking for a different weapon. He was on a deadly mission and wanted something that would put an end to Delisha once-and-for-all. He looked for something he could wrap around her neck and something that would steal her air like Jackson's hands had been unable to do.

Delisha's face was wet with sweat, blood, and vomit. She lay unconscious on the bedroom floor with Jackson still on top of her. With the bedside lamp still attached, Bovi used the electrical cord and wrapped it around her unconscious neck. After wrapping it several times, he pulled hard. Jackson jumped and ripped the cord out of the base of the lamp and both men pulled at the cord around Delisha's neck. They struggled and pulled and attempted, once again, to finish her off.

Delisha was not moving or breathing and she was finally surely dead. Blood covered her face, neck, and hands. Blood trickled from multiple wounds on her head. From her struggles, large abrasions covered all exposed parts of her body and lots of bruising was noticeable around the injection points. From the strangulation attempts, friction burns tattooed her entire neck. A deep scratch paved its way down her chest and blood spilled and fell between her cleavage and stained the front of her shirt.

The men sat back exhausted from their actions and took deep breaths. However, even though she looked dead, both men noticed that Delisha's chest continued to rise and fall. She was still alive. Clearly unconscious and severely injured but still breathing.

Jackson, out of breath and soaked with sweat, anxiously indicated to Bovi that he was done with his part. Jackson told his co-conspirator that he would not do any more and that if he still wanted the girl dead, he would have to finish her off himself. He pointed to the kitchen and suggested that a sharp kitchen knife may help him complete the job. The architect of the plan was Bovi and his flawless plan had been a disaster. He wondered what to do now but jumped at Jackson's suggestion to get a knife. It would be easy. Delisha was unconscious so he would just stab her. But to his surprise, as he left the bedroom he realized Delisha was no longer unconscious and he heard her moans as he headed into the kitchen to get a knife.

In the dark living room, Shecora sat near the bedroom doorway rocking back and forth with her hands over her ears and her knees up to her chin. Bovi raced past her and went into the kitchen and came out with a black handled kitchen knife. She saw the knife and scanned the room quickly for the TV's remote control. She hoped to silence the horrifying noises of Delisha's impending suffering by turning on the TV, but could not find the remote fast enough. She heard the stabbing noises and the weak screams coming from her friend so she closed her eyes and with her hands still over her ears, she hummed loudly to herself.

Shecora opened her eyes when the screams stopped but morbid curiosity got the best of her and she peeked inside the bedroom and saw Delisha on the floor in a pool of blood. She watched Bovi as he hurriedly gathered all the weapons and the small black case that once housed the syringes. Jackson ripped the extension cord from Delisha's neck. Shecora watched

Delisha's head lift up and fall back down onto the hardwood floor from the force as Jackson ripped the cord from her body. Jackson grabbed the murderous tools from Bovi and jammed it and the cord into a red leather shoulder bag hanging from Delisha's bedpost. The room was covered in blood. The blood was everywhere. It was on the bed, the floor, and the walls.

Bovi and Jackson quickly moved into the next phase of the plan in taking all of Delisha's property. They ran back & forth and in & out of the house as they loaded the contents into the U-Haul. Bovi yelled at Shecora to scan Delisha's home for valuables and load whatever she could lift onto the truck. Shecora did not comply but sat frozen in the same spot. Bovi and Jackson grabbed lamps, chairs, and electronics and threw them in the back of the truck that was conveniently backed up to the now open garage door. Jackson found some workout equipment in the garage and started loading it up as Bovi went back into the house for more.

Shecora still sat paralyzed by the events that had just taken place and was as motionless as the victim was. Her eyes scanned the living room in a useless effort to pass time, but she winced when she heard weak whimpers coming from the bedroom and her heart started beating very quickly again but she said nothing. Bovi had ripped a microwave from the wall and was carrying it through the living room but he stopped in his tracks when he thought he heard something from the bedroom. Bovi yelled out loud for everyone to shut up so he could hear but no one else was actually talking. Then he heard it again. Low moaning sounds were coming from the bedroom where there was supposed to be a dead girl. Clearly agitated, he threw the microwave carelessly into the back of the truck and ran back into the kitchen and grabbed yet another knife.

As he started back to the bedroom, he noticed Shecora just standing there and grabbed her and pulled her with him

183

towards the room. Bovi attempted to force the knife into Shecora's hands and once she had it in her hand, he ordered her to go in and finish off Delisha. She saw her boyfriend's mouth move as he delivered instructions but Shecora didn't hear a word he said. The blood that stained Bovi's jeans and white t-shirt screamed louder than Bovi's commands and she pulled away from his grip.

Shecora held out her arms, examined herself for blood, and then defiantly refused to take any additional part in the inevitable demise of her coworker. Shecora attempted to run but Bovi grabbed her and tackled her before she made it to the door. Bovi put the knife to Shecora's neck and forced her into the cab of the truck. He ordered her to remain there until they were finished loading it and for the first time in many hours, she complied with his order.

Shecora heard the back door of the truck slide shut and Bovi slid in beside her with the leather bag he had taken from Delisha's bedroom. Jackson was right behind him. He climbed into the passenger's seat, slammed the door, and ordered her to drive. She saw Delisha's splattered blood on Jackson's light khaki pants and he had blood dripping from a cut on his right arm. Shecora was unsure if he had cut himself during the struggle or while loading the truck but unlike the shy submissive girl he knew, she firmly ordered him to clean it off before he got out of the truck. She wanted as little evidence left behind as possible.

Shecora pulled out slowly and headed east. The three rode in silence until they arrived at Jackson's residence. Jackson and Bovi got out of the truck and Shecora stayed at the wheel. The truck back door was opened and the men unloaded some things into Jackson's apartment. The two came back out and Bovi got in the truck. Before they pulled away, Jackson pointed at both Bovi and Shecora told them to forget who he was or he would kill them. This time Shecora did not pull away slowly but hit the gas as hard as she could.

They entered the Superstore for the second time in less than twenty-four hours, purchased a padlock, and placed it on the back door of the U-Haul. With Shecora still driving, they headed back in the direction of her home. However, Bovi redirected their path and told her to turn around and take Interstate 70 toward his brother's house by the Kansas State line. She complained and told him she was too tired to drive but he promised her that they would unload only a few things at his brother's house and then they could go home and rest. Shecora drove towards Interstate 70 as directed but she wasn't driving long before she heard something other than overturning furniture coming from the back of the truck.

Business was good that Sunday evening, which forced Delisha's dad to stay at the club later than usual. He was the last one to leave as he was the only one who had keys to the establishment. He took his normal route home and stopped by the same 24 hour Wal-Mart Supercenter for some coffee and bread where his daughter's killers had just been. He knew he was out of that and he would need it for breakfast the next morning. Nothing seemed out of place as he pulled into the store's parking lot as a U-Haul truck pulled in. It was a U-Haul truck not unlike the one parked at his house earlier that evening but he didn't give it a second thought.

He purchased his items and drove the straight path towards his home just a few miles away. It was too early for Delisha to be up for work but the lights were on inside the house. Delisha's dad pulled into the garage and entered his home through side door that opened into his kitchen and immediately found his home had been turned into a horrific crime scene.

185

As Shecora drove the truck after dropping off Jackson, she had no idea the men had thrown Delisha's lifeless body in the back of the truck. When Bovi told her they needed to find a spot to dump the body, Shecora screamed. Bovi backhanded Shecora hard across her face. Still shocked from both the unexpected slap and the revelation that Delisha's body was in the back of the truck, Shecora initially refused when he demanded she help him think of a way to get rid of Delisha. However, she was now driving on the interstate and she had no other options than to do what she was told.

Bovi nervously ordered her to drive into the next open wooded area she saw. The truck had just crossed the state line between Missouri and Kansas when they heard the unthinkable from the back. Even though it was loud on the freeway, they could clearly hear Delisha screaming in agonizing pain from the rear of the truck. Bovi immediately stopped barking orders and seemed to be having a nervous breakdown. He then yelled *"How could this bitch still be alive after all of this?!"* Delisha's screams never stopped as Shecora drove over the Kansas State line and into a narrow dirt road that was hidden only by the trees on either side adjacent to a park. The truck, not meant to travel in rough terrain jumped and shook the stolen contents inside and Shecora shamefully hoped one of the large TVs would fall on top of Delisha and end her suffering.

Bovi told her to pull over and she aimed the truck into a small clearing barely concealed by the surrounding trees and the approaching daylight. Bovi jumped out of the truck before it came to a full stop and headed for the back. She put the truck in park and followed him to the back just in time to see him drag Delisha, bound by her own bed covers, out of the truck and onto the ground. Her body landed with a thump as it hit the ground and Bovi struggled to figure out what to do. He must have come to the realization quickly because he then grabbed Delisha and rolled the still alive woman and placed her head behind the left rear tire. Shecora was again paralyzed in terror. Bovi pushed her to the ground as he ran past her and jumped in the driver's seat.

He fired up the truck and put the truck into reverse. He floored the gas as it hopped and smashed over Delisha's body. He then pulled back forward and did it all again. After his third time of running the truck wheels over Delisha, he parked the truck and went back to her body. Three times he had driven the several ton truck over her body and now he rolled her body out of her bedcovers. Bovi Combs dragged Delisha's lifeless body deep into the woods and he turned to walk away. No one will ever know exactly what it was Bovi heard next but he heard a gurgling sound from Delisha. It was either gas escaping from her dead body or it was her final gasps of life as she was still alive. Bovi found a thick heavy log and smashed Delisha's head several times until there was no further question whether she was alive or not. Delisha Williams was dead.

Finally confident that he had killed Delisha and he had a great location to leave the body, he ran back towards the truck, picked up the blood-soiled covers, and threw them onto the floorboard of the truck. Exhausted, he almost couldn't lift himself back into the vehicle. The two murderers drove in silence back from Kansas to Missouri and to Bovi's brother's house.

They never made it to Bovi's brother's house and instead turned back and headed to Shecora's house. Bovi knew that Shecora was devastated so he confidently promised her the police would never be able to trace the murder back to them. However, words from him were the last things she ever wanted to hear. As they drove, Bovi threw the bedcovers that Delisha was wrapped in out the window. Bovi then made two phone calls on the ride back from Kansas. Bovi had called someone to arrange a meeting at her house to dispose of the remaining property.

Shecora was relieved to know he was getting rid of evidence but was not pleased that he was taking care of his business at her house.

By 7:30am, the U-Haul backed into her driveway and Shecora made her way into her home exhausted. She watched briefly from her window as Bovi and two other men transferred the contents from the truck into three separate vehicles. She was asleep when he came into her room carrying the leather bag taken from the victim's bedroom. Common sense told him he should keep the bag close until he had time to dispose of it; however, common sense was never Bovi's strongest character trait. Unbeknownst to him, the contents of the bag not only held the tainted paraphernalia that started Delisha on her long journey of death, but also a personal identification mark that could be traced back only to Delisha.

Back at Delisha's house, it was almost 5am when Delisha's dad screamed in terror for her as he walked into the living room. As he shouted for his daughter, the missing TV, rummaged house, and blood stained floor silenced him. He went for the phone but he found it missing as well. He searched his pockets for his cell phone and dialed 911. As he talked to the police, he walked through each room, and noted what was out of the ordinary and the missing items......the most important thing being his missing daughter,

Delisha's dad did not know Shecora's last name and only knew the men by their nicknames; nevertheless, the police took notes as he gave them a list of his stolen property, the description of the people, and the moving truck. An instant image of the truck at the Wal-Mart Superstore flashed through his mind the very second he mentioned the U-Haul to the officers. Delisha's father paused for a brief second to recall the memory before he advised them on any more details.

188

The detectives immediately conducted an area canvas for the truck but their efforts were fruitless until 8am when they drove to the nearest U-Haul facility. The detectives provided the rental manager with their modest information and they weren't too positive about getting any results. However, using the rental date and the only name of the three that they knew, the manager was able to provide the police with Shecora Clanton's full name and address.

Shecora and Bovi were both sleeping at 10am when the police arrived and asked Shecora's father a series of questions and also asked for his permission to search the premises. He was honest and told the detectives his daughter and Bovi had been gone all night and had just returned home a few hours earlier and were inside. Mr. Clanton signed a Consent to Search Form and advised the detectives that along with the rented U-Haul truck parked at his residence, there was an Audi that belonged to Bovi he would like removed.

The detectives completed a search of the outside of the U-Haul and found apparent blood on the passenger's side door and the cargo trucks bumper. Detectives immediately knew that this truck was involved in something and protected the area to preserve evidence. Crime scene technicians arrived and confirmed both areas tested positive for blood.

Bovi didn't wake up when Mr. Clanton knocked on his daughter's bedroom door and informed her the police were there and wanted to talk to her. Shecora met them in the hallway and wanted to tell them the truth; however, her fear of Bovi and prison forced her to lie. When asked why she had a U-Haul in the yard, she told them that she helped move her boyfriend's cousin into a new apartment.

Although Shecora lied about the truck, she did give up the identity of her boyfriend. At least part of his name. She told them that Bovi CAMDEN was asleep in her bedroom. Willingly and

189

almost with a sense of relief, she signed a consent to search form for the U-Haul and gave the detectives the combination to the lock on the back of the truck.

After his exhausting night of killing Delisha Williams several times, Bovi was out cold. Bovi was even still asleep when the detectives entered Shecora's bedroom. They ordered him awake and asked for his identification. Bovi pointed the detectives in the direction of the door where they found a blue New York Yankee jacket hanging on the doorknob. Upon searching the jacket for his identification, they found the U-Haul truck keys. The detectives also found the red leather bag with the initials D.R.W engraved on the inside flap. They transported both Bovi Combs and Shecora Clanton to the Kansas City Police Headquarters and housed them in the Detention Unit for questioning. The Crime Scene Unit collected the leather bag, New York Yankee jacket, and U-Haul truck along with additional clothing items for evidence.

Shecora Clanton was escorted to KCPD HQ to the Homicide Unit for questioning. Bovi Combs was arrested and placed in holding. In the small interrogation room, Shecora Clanton did not hold anything back when she was questioned by the police. She told the entire story and gave them Andrew Jackson's name also. There was an aggressive 2 day successful police hunt for Jackson and all three were now in police custody.

Many times you hear on the news that "the police charged someone with a crime" and that is not exactly procedurally correct. In Missouri, at least, the police do the investigation and submit their reports to the prosecutor's office who decides to file charges or not. The prosecutor can file a document called an "Information" which is the charging document that lists the crime the person is charged with and the process begins. Or the other way a criminal charge begins in Missouri is that the case can be forwarded to a grand jury that is a group of citizens that review the case presented to them to decide if charges are filed. If the grand jury agrees to file criminal charges, they create a document called an "Indictment" that is filed and the process begins.

Regardless of which manner a charge may begin, the first initial review is by a prosecutor to evaluate the facts of the case in relation to the law to see if a crime has been committed and if there is enough evidence to prove the offender guilty beyond a reasonable doubt. In this case, homicide detectives called the on-call prosecutor who was wearing the "homicide pager" that day and that lucky prosecutor was Assistant Prosecutor Brian Wimes.

Wimes had been a prosecutor in the Jackson County Prosecutor's office for 7 years and was assigned to the Drug Trial Unit that handled all variety of crimes that had any drug related aspect to the case. Wimes was a seasoned trial attorney who had a good rapport with the police department. In the office, the drug trial team was a close group of four male attorneys and one female attorney. These young prosecutors took the work seriously but also had a great working environment with other prosecutors and police. It was not uncommon to see the trial team and homicide detectives talking business over beers and wisecracking with each other at the 13th Street Grill & Bar at 5:00 after work.

Homicide detectives caught up with Wimes late in the day and told him they had a case to review and would be right over. At this same time in his professional life, Brian Wimes had another situation going on in his career. Wimes had recently applied for the position as Drug Court Commissioner which was the judicial position that supervised the Jackson County's Drug Court Program. The new commissioner would be selected by a vote of all the current judges and Wimes had just finished the interviewing process and the decision was to be announced soon. In the

Jackson County Courthouse, the odds on favorite to get the new job was Brian Wimes but Wimes was not counting his chickens before they hatched.

However, that didn't stop Wimes from hollering down the hall at his colleague and friend, fellow prosecutor Phil LeVota to come to his office after he hung up with the detectives. LeVota's office was next door to Wimes and after LeVota finished with what he was working on in his office, he went into Wimes office. Wimes explained the call and that he had the on-call pager, but asked his friend if he would sit in on the meeting with detectives. Because if there was a chance that he may be moving on from the prosecutor's office to take a new position, Wimes wanted to make sure someone else had eyes on the case from the start.

LeVota couldn't resist giving his friend a hard time about thinking about his new job when it hadn't been announced yet and also joking with him about why he hollered at him when there were six other prosecutors there. There was the typical banter back and forth from friends giving each other trouble but both men were professionals and when the detectives arrived, they focused and listened to the facts of the case.

First and foremost when a person is arrested, there is a time frame of charging them before the clock runs out and they have to be released. In a horrific case like this, a prosecutor wants to get a violent offender charged so they enter the system with a bond and cannot be released. In the review of the case, the evidence was great in proving a crime. Shecora Clanton had even since told detectives where they could find Delisha's body. However the question was what specific crimes should be charged.

Of course, a murder charge was initially to be filed but the issue of jurisdiction was questionable for a murder charge. Clearly, Bovi Combs and Andrew Jackson thought they had killed Delisha Williams at her house in Jackson County, MISSOURI but the facts would be that she took her last breath before she died after being driven over and her head smashed on the other side of the state line in Wyandotte County, KANSAS. So as it stood, the state of Missouri only had jurisdiction to charge the crimes of property theft, kidnapping, and assault.

Wimes and LeVota and the detectives discussed the case and agreed to immediately charge those crimes and ask the judge for a "no-bond" to hold the three immediately as this case was about to get more complex. The next morning members from the Wyandotte County Sheriff's Department, the Wyandotte County District Attorney's office, the KCPD Homicide Unit, the FBI, and the United States Attorney's office all met in the conference room at the Jackson County Prosecutor's office to discuss the case. Kansas City detectives had already been meeting with their Kansas and federal law enforcement colleagues in finishing the investigation across state lines and making sure each state authority had all the same information.

In the meeting, the Wyandotte County District Attorney presented her positon that they would file the murder charges in Kansas and she was reviewing whether this case would rise to the level of pursuing the death penalty. In the state of Kansas, the death penalty is a legal form of punishment in a capital murder case but it had not been carried out since the 1976 reinstatement of capital punishment in the United States in the Supreme Court case of Gregg v. Georgia that permitted states to reinstate the death penalty.

Sometimes government works against itself but in that room on that day, the professionals worked through the process without any turf issues or jealously on who got the media attention or glory in the case. The driving interest was justice for Delisha Williams. After the discussion, the group agreed that Kansas would file the murder charges and possibly seek the death penalty but if not, in the least, pursue sentencing under the "Hard 50" sentence against the individuals. Kansas did not waste any time in filing first degree murder, conspiracy to commit murder, and kidnapping charges.

Wimes and LeVota left the meeting satisfied with the path to justice the case would take; however, now the state of Missouri would have to dismiss all the cases against them so they could be taken to Kansas. Filing a dismissal is not ever a prosecutor's favorite thing to do but the criminals could not be transported to Kansas without doing such. Wimes and LeVota joked with each other about whose name was going to be on the dismissal because neither wanted to do it.

Before they finished the conversation, Wimes was requested out of LeVota's office for a phone call. When he returned, he informed his friend Phil that the Delisha Williams case was all his and that LeVota would have to sign the dismissal. LeVota looked at Wimes with a puzzled look. Wimes told his friend that he was just told that he was just appointed as the new Drug Court Commissioner for the 16th Judicial Circuit in Jackson County Missouri. LeVota joked with his friend that it was a better reason than usual for him to dump a case on him and he congratulated his friend. Even though Brian left his buddy holding the bag, Wimes would go on to bigger ways to help to serve the public as Wimes would later be appointed as a circuit judge by Missouri Governor Matt Blunt and then appointed as a United States Federal District Judge by President Barrack Obama.

With LeVota now flying solo on this case, he wasn't about to let anything fall through the cracks. Kansas had filed their charges but the three could not be released until the Missouri charges were dismissed. LeVota completed the dismissal and KCPD homicide detectives along with Kansas law enforcement walked the dismissal through Jackson County along with the Kansas charges through the records together. Then Bovi Combs,

Shecora Clanton, and Andrew Jackson left the state of Missouri to face their crimes in Kansas.

Even as they were leaving the Jackson County Jail, LeVota was filing new charges in Missouri. He charged Bovi Combs with Robbery in the First Degree and Armed Criminal Action and he charged Andrew Jackson with Assault in the first degree and Armed Criminal Action. Shecora would be the star witness in the Kansas prosecution of the two men, so no Missouri charges were filed against her for the time being. Kansas would be prosecuting the individuals with homicide so these Missouri charges were basically just to make sure if anything did happen to the Kansas case, the state of Missouri would still have a hold on the violent men. LeVota assured Delisha's family that even though Kansas would be pursuing charges, the state of Missouri would be waiting for those cases to finish and they would still face charges there.

LeVota watched the Kansas process over the following years and both men took their cases to trial and were convicted and sentenced under Kansas's Hard 50 sentence meaning they would serve 50 years before being eligible for parole. However after the convictions, both men appealed their conviction and actually raised some interesting legal issues: Bovi Combs appealed his sentence indicating three things: (1) He was not properly Mirandized; (2) His confession was not voluntary; and (3) He contended that Williams died in Missouri and not in Kansas. The Kansas Court of Appeals, on all accounts, found otherwise and affirmed the convictions and sentences.

Andrew Jackson appealed his sentence indicating a number of issues as well: (1) Kansas did not have jurisdiction over all of the crimes charged; (2) He was denied a speedy trial; (3) The jury was not properly instructed; (4) The trial court erroneously admitted evidence; (5) Cumulative errors denied him a fair trial; (6) Insufficient evidence to support his conviction; (7) His hard 50 year sentencing scheme was unconstitutional; and (8) There was insufficient evidence to support the hard 50 year sentence.

The Kansas Court of Appeals, on all accounts, found otherwise and affirmed the convictions and sentences.

For any of you legal scholars that want to read the actual ruling by the Kansas Supreme Court for Andrew Jackson, it is included below just in case you are interested. Others of you may get real bored by the court order and if you are ready to move on to the rest of the story, skip past the shaded pages and **jump to page 218.**

Supreme Court of Kansas. No.□89,620.
STATE of Kansas, Appellee, v. Andrew JACKSON, Appellant.

Sandra M. Carr, assistant appellate defender, argued the cause and was on the briefs for appellant. Sheryl L. Lidtke, assistant district attorney, argued the cause, and Nick A. Tomasic, district attorney, and Phill Kline, attorney general, were with her on the brief for appellee.

This is Andrew Jackson's direct appeal of his jury convictions of first-degree premeditated murder, kidnapping, and conspiracy to commit murder. Numerous trial errors which we will separately consider are alleged. □ We first set forth the sad facts and proceedings giving rise to this appeal.

Jackson met Bovi Combs and Shecora Clanton while riding buses in Kansas City, Missouri. □ Their chance meeting resulted in the murder of Delesha Williams, a woman Combs met at a bus stop in Kansas City, Missouri. Combs wanted to kill Williams because he believed she was involved in his sister's death. □ Clanton, who was Combs' girlfriend, agreed to help. □ They planned to steal items from Williams' house after the murder. □ Combs and Clanton initially planned to poison Williams with strychnine but were unable to make such a purchase over the counter.

Clanton rented a U-Haul truck to carry the stolen property from Williams' house. □ After picking up the truck, Combs and Clanton returned to Clanton's house, where Combs called Jackson and inquired as to how Jackson would kill someone. □ Combs then paged Williams several times and waited at Clanton's house until 9:30 p.m., when Williams returned Combs' page. Combs and Clanton then drove to Jackson's apartment to pick him up. □ When Combs and Clanton arrived, Jackson produced a syringe and a white chemical substance he had prepared for them. □ Jackson told them to stick Williams

196

with the syringe and she would die. ⏃ Although Jackson initially refused to go with Combs and Clanton because he thought they had waited until too late at night, he changed his mind and accompanied Combs and Clanton to Williams' house in Kansas City, Missouri.

As the trio was pulling up to Williams' house, they noticed a car in the driveway with its lights on. ⏃ They drove past the house a couple of blocks before turning around and coming back. ⏃ When they returned, the car was gone. ⏃ Clanton parked the U-Haul truck, and Combs knocked on Williams' door. ⏃ While Combs was at the front door, Williams' cousin walked up to the door. ⏃ He had been in a minor car accident and needed a ride home. ⏃ Williams opened the door for Combs and her cousin. ⏃ Combs returned to the U-Haul truck a few minutes later with Williams' cousin and told Clanton and Jackson to drive Williams' cousin home.

After taking Williams' cousin home, Clanton and Jackson joined Combs and Williams at Williams' house. ⏃ Williams did not have anything for them to drink, so Jackson walked to a nearby convenience store and purchased soda and cigarettes. ⏃ After visiting with Combs, Clanton, and Jackson for a while, Williams decided to go to bed. ⏃ She invited the trio to spend the night at her house.

Combs, Clanton, and Jackson waited for Williams to fall asleep so they could inject her with the chemical in Jackson's syringe. ⏃ When Williams was asleep, Jackson hit Williams with a mallet and then jumped on top of her and started strangling her. ⏃ Williams struggled with Jackson. ⏃ The two fell off the bed and continued fighting on the floor. ⏃ Jackson eventually subdued Williams and told Combs to get the syringe from his coat pocket. ⏃ However, Jackson broke the syringe before he could inject Williams.

Without a syringe to poison Williams, Combs suggested that Jackson strangle her. ⏃ Combs found an extension cord and gave it to Jackson. ⏃ Jackson broke the extension cord before he could strangle Williams, so he asked Combs for another one. ⏃ Before Combs could find another extension cord, Jackson told Combs that he was tired of struggling with Williams. ⏃ Combs suggested that Jackson stab Williams, but Jackson told Combs that if he wanted Williams dead, he would have to do it himself. Combs took a knife and began slashing and stabbing Williams until he bent the knife. ⏃ While Combs went to the kitchen to get another knife, Williams managed to crawl out of her bedroom into the hallway. Combs slashed at Williams again and kicked her in the face and the stomach. ⏃ Williams appeared to be unconscious, lying in a puddle of blood in the hallway. ⏃ She had multiple injuries to her head, neck, and shoulders caused by blunt force impacts, the attempted strangulation, and the stabbings and slashes with the knife.

197

Because Combs wanted to have all Williams' things loaded into the U-Haul before Williams' mother returned home from work, they left Williams lying in the hallway and began loading things into the U-Haul truck. ⏺ They took a big screen television (TV), two smaller TV's, a videocassette recorder, and several telephones. ⏺ Before leaving, they loaded Williams into the back of the U-Haul truck. ⏺ Jackson told police that Williams walked to the back of the U-Haul truck and Combs threw her in.

Clanton drove Jackson back to his apartment in Kansas City, Missouri, where he got into the back of the U-Haul and retrieved a small television to take with him. ⏺ Jackson told Combs to never call again and "you never heard of me." ⏺ Combs and Clanton then drove to a store and purchased a padlock for the back of the U-Haul truck before driving back to Clanton's house in Kansas City, Missouri. ⏺ After staying at Clanton's house for about 30 minutes, Combs and Clanton left in the U-Haul truck to deliver the big screen TV to Combs' uncle. ⏺ While they were driving, Clanton heard Williams' screams from the back of the U-Haul. ⏺ Combs suggested that Clanton find a wooded area to dump Williams' body, so Clanton drove to a wooded area near Washington High School in Kansas City, Kansas. ⏺ At this point, Combs threw Williams from the truck, hit her with a large log, drove back and forth over her upper torso several times, and threw her body into the woods.

Combs and Clanton were arrested a few hours later, and both gave statements to the police implicating Jackson. ⏺ Jackson turned himself in to Kansas City, Missouri, police a few days later. ⏺ Clanton testified extensively at Jackson's trial. ⏺ A jury convicted Jackson of first-degree premeditated murder, kidnapping, and conspiracy to commit murder. ⏺ The district court sentenced Jackson to a hard 50 life sentence.

Jackson appeals his convictions and his sentence directly to this court pursuant to K.S.A. 22-3601, raising a number of issues. ⏺ He first claims that Kansas does not have jurisdiction to prosecute him. If we conclude that Kansas has jurisdiction, Jackson contends his statutory right to a speedy trial was violated; the trial court failed to properly instruct the jury; the trial court erroneously admitted evidence, including gruesome photographs, hearsay statements, and his involuntary confession; he did not receive a fair trial because of cumulative errors; and, finally, his convictions are not supported by sufficient evidence. ⏺ If we affirm Jackson's convictions, he argues the hard 50 sentencing scheme is unconstitutional or, in the alternative, that his hard 50 sentence is not supported by sufficient evidence.

JURISDICTION

Jackson claims that Kansas does not have subject matter jurisdiction over the charged offenses because he never entered the state of Kansas or committed any act within Kansas. ⏃ An appellate court reviews a question of subject matter jurisdiction using a de novo standard. ⏃State v. James, 276 Kan. 737, 744, 79 P.3d 169 (2003).

Subject matter jurisdiction for crimes in Kansas is controlled by K.S.A. 21-3104, which provides in pertinent part:"(1)⏃A person is subject to prosecution and punishment under the law of this state if: (a)⏃He commits a crime wholly or partly within this state; or (b)⏃Being outside the state, he counsels, aids, abets, or conspires with another to commit a crime within this state; or (c)⏃ Being outside the state, he commits an act which constitutes an attempt to commit a crime within this state.

"(2)⏃An offense is committed partly within this state if either an act which is a constituent and material element of the offense, or the proximate result of such act, occurs within the state. ⏃ If the body of a homicide victim is found within this state, the death is presumed to have occurred within the state."

Although K.S.A. 21-3104 has been interpreted broadly, State v. Grissom, 251 Kan. 851, 889, 840 P.2d 1142 (1992), this court has recognized limits to its application. ⏃ See State v. Palermo, 224 Kan. 275, 277, 579 P.2d 718 (1978). ⏃ In Palermo, the State sought review of the district court's decision to set aside the verdict and acquit the defendant on a charge of selling heroin. ⏃ Palermo sold the drugs to a person in Missouri, who then sold the drugs to an informant in Kansas. ⏃ Because Palermo did not come into Kansas and did not personally participate in the drug sale in Kansas, he was tried under an aiding and abetting theory. ⏃ The Palermo court affirmed the district court's dismissal, holding that Kansas cannot assert jurisdiction over a crime under an aiding and abetting theory if the defendant never entered Kansas and could not reasonably foresee that his or her act would cause, aid, or abet the commission of a crime in Kansas. ⏃ 224 Kan. at 277, 579 P.2d 718.

Relying on Palermo, Jackson argues it was not reasonably foreseeable that Combs and Clanton would take Williams to Kansas and kill her. ⏃ He argues that his participation in the events leading up to Williams' death ended hours before Combs and Clanton drove to Kansas, killed Williams, and dumped her body. ⏃ Because he was not involved in any of the last-minute decisions, he contends he could not have known that Combs and Clanton would murder Williams and could not have aided and abetted in Williams' murder and kidnapping in Kansas. ⏃ To analyze this argument, we must look at each charge individually to determine whether Combs' and Clanton's actions were reasonably foreseeable to Jackson.

Regardless of whether Jackson was involved in the last-minute decision making, it was certainly reasonably foreseeable that Combs and

Clanton would finish the murder that Jackson helped start. ⏹ Before they left the house, Jackson became weary of struggling with Williams and told Combs that if he wanted Williams dead, he could do it himself. ⏹ Jackson told police that Williams walked to the back of the truck and Combs threw her in, indicating that Jackson knew Williams was alive in the back of the U-Haul when he got out at his apartment in Kansas City, Missouri. ⏹ Jackson would have seen Williams in the back of the U-Haul truck when he retrieved a TV from it before he went into his apartment.

Moreover, it was reasonably foreseeable that the beating, stabbing, and strangulation inflicted on Williams would disable her, making it easier for Combs and Clanton to finish the murder in some manner. ⏹ Jackson's refusal to participate in the final decision making or the final acts that ended Williams' life does not relieve him of responsibility because he knew or should have known that Williams would not survive.

Under the same reasoning, Williams' kidnapping was foreseeable and, in fact, was already occurring. ⏹ Jackson knew that Combs and Clanton had Williams in the back of the U-Haul. ⏹ It was foreseeable that Combs and Clanton would continue to confine Williams in the U-Haul until they could complete her murder. ⏹ Jackson knew that Combs planned to get a padlock for the back of the U-Haul and told police about it during his interrogation. ⏹ Jackson made no attempt to rescue Williams from the U-Haul truck or to prevent her impending death. ⏹ He did not offer to take Williams with him when he got out of the U-Haul. ⏹ He did not encourage Combs and Clanton to let Williams go, and he did not call the police to alert them to Williams' presence in the back of the U-Haul truck. ⏹ Instead, Jackson told Combs to get rid of his telephone number, not to call him anymore, and to forget he ever knew Jackson.

Even though it was reasonably foreseeable that Combs and Clanton would continue the kidnapping of Williams and complete the murder that Jackson had started, Jackson argues that it was not reasonably foreseeable that they would perform these acts in Kansas. ⏹ This argument, however, overlooks Jackson's close proximity to Kansas and the mobility of the U-Haul truck. ⏹ Jackson's apartment, Clanton's house, and Williams' house are all within 5 miles of the Kansas border. ⏹ Clanton could easily drive the U-Haul truck 5 miles into Kansas to finish what the trio had started. ⏹ The fact Jackson was not involved in the decision to go to Kansas does not make the trip unforeseeable.

The State prosecuted Jackson under an aiding and abetting theory for the crimes of first-degree premeditated murder and kidnapping. ⏹"Any person who counsels, aids, or abets in the commission of any offense may be charged, tried, convicted, and sentenced in the same manner as if he or she were a principal. ⯑[Citation omitted.]" ⯑State v. Wakefield, 267 Kan. 116, 142, 977 P.2d 941 (1999). ⯑ Because it was reasonably foreseeable that Combs and Clanton would continue to confine Williams and drive to Kansas to complete the murder, the State has jurisdiction to prosecute Jackson for the crimes of first-degree premeditated murder and kidnapping under an aiding and abetting theory even though Jackson never personally entered Kansas.

Although the foreseeability analysis applies to the first-degree murder and kidnapping charges, it does not apply to the conspiracy charge. ⯑ A conspiracy may be prosecuted in any jurisdiction where an overt act in furtherance of the conspiracy occurred, regardless of whether the defendant actually entered the state or district of trial. ⯑State v. Campbell, 217 Kan. 756, 779, 539 P.2d 329, cert. denied 423 U.S. 1017, 96 S.Ct. 453, 46 L.Ed.2d 389 (1975). ⯑ The defendants in Campbell contended they could not be charged with conspiracy in Shawnee County because neither the agreement nor any overt act in which they participated was alleged to have been committed there. ⯑ The court noted the indictment alleged the conspiratorial agreement occurred in Shawnee County and 10 of the separately numbered overt acts occurred there. ⯑ The Campbell court said: "It is immaterial that the particular complainants may never have entered Shawnee county during the existence of the conspiracy." ⯑217 Kan. at 779, 539 P.2d 329. ⯑ The Campbell court relied on Downing v. United States, 348 F.2d 594, 598 (5th Cir.), cert. denied 382 U.S. 901, 86 S.Ct. 235, 15 L.Ed.2d 155 (1965), and its holding that " '[a] conspiracy may be prosecuted in the district where it was formed or in any district in which an overt act was committed in furtherance of its objects.' " ⯑ 217 Kan. at 779, 539 P.2d 329. ⯑ The Campbell decision further relied on K.S.A. 21-3104.

In our case, the actual killing was an overt act in furtherance of the conspiracy to commit murder. ⯑ Kansas clearly has jurisdiction to prosecute Jackson for conspiracy to commit murder because an overt act in furtherance of the conspiracy occurred in Kansas.

We hold that the State properly exercised its jurisdiction in prosecuting Jackson for the crimes of first-degree premeditated murder, kidnapping, and conspiracy to commit murder. ⯑ We proceed to the other trial issues Jackson raises.

SPEEDY TRIAL

Jackson was arraigned on October 10, 2001, and his trial was originally set for January 7, 2002, 89 days after his arraignment. ⯑ Jackson was held in custody solely for trial on these charges, so the State had 90 days after arraignment to bring him to trial. ⯑ See K.S.A. 22-3402(1). ⯑ However, after continuances for the court's calendar and the availability of evidence, Jackson's trial date was continued until May 1, 2002. ⏹ Jackson claims that his trial did not comply with the speedy trial requirements of K.S.A. 22-3402(1).

Jackson raises two arguments in support of this claim. ⏹ First, he argues the trial court improperly granted two 30-day continuances due to congestion in the court's calendar. ⏹ Second, he argues the State failed to make a sufficient showing of materiality or reasonable efforts to support a 90-day continuance to secure evidence. ⏹ An appellate court reviews the application of the speedy trial statute as a question of law using a de novo standard of review. ⏹State v. White, 275 Kan. 580, 598, 67 P.3d 138 (2003).

K.S.A. 22-3402(1), in applicable part, provides: "If any person charged with a crime and held in jail solely by reason thereof shall not be brought to trial within ninety (90) days after such person's arraignment on the charge, such person shall be entitled to be discharged from further liability to be tried for the crime charged, unless the delay shall happen as a result of the application or fault of the defendant, or a continuance shall be ordered by the court under subsection (3)."

K.S.A. 22-3402(3)(d) allows the trial court to continue a trial without violating the defendant's statutory speedy trial right if "[b]ecause of other cases pending for trial, the court does not have sufficient time to commence the trial of the case within the time fixed for trial by this section." ⏹ The trial court may only continue the defendant's trial one time for no more than 30 days based on this exception to the speedy trial rule. ⏹K.S.A. 22-3402(3)(d).

The trial court in this case issued a 30-day continuance pursuant to K.S.A. 22-3402(3)(d) on April 1, 2002, because the trial of Combs, Jackson's codefendant, extended beyond the time previously allotted by the court. ⏹ Although Jackson did not object to this continuance, he claims that the continuance on April 1 was the second 30-day continuance pursuant to K.S.A. 22-3402(3)(d), in violation of the statute. ⏹ To support this claim, he points to a note on the trial judge's criminal docket notice of scheduled trials, dated November 28, 2001, stating: "It is expected that Jackson will be severed from the co-defendants set on 1-7, but will not waive speedy trial. ⏹ Thus I am giving this setting for the expected 30-day continuance." ⏹(Emphasis added.)

On December 4, 2001, the State moved to sever Jackson's trial from Combs' trial. ⏹ On December 28, 2001, the trial court granted the State's motion to sever; however, it did not set a new trial date for Jackson. ⏹ The State moved for a 90-day evidentiary continuance on December 31, 2001. ⏹ The trial court granted the State's motion for a continuance on January 2, 2002, and set Jackson's trial for April 1, 2002. ⏹ The record does not contain an order continuing Jackson's trial from January 7, 2002, until January 28, 2002,

202

as the court anticipated on November 28. ⯑ Jackson cites no authority to support his contention that the note on the court's November 28 docket notice was the equivalent of a court order for a continuance. ⯑ Because the court's anticipatory note does not amount to a court order, the trial court did not erroneously grant two 30-day continuances in violation of K.S.A. 22-3402(3)(d).

For his second argument, Jackson asserts that the State failed to meet the statutory standard for a 90-day evidentiary continuance to complete the DNA testing. ⯑ The State requested a continuance to complete the processing of DNA evidence from the multiple crime scenes. ⯑ Pursuant to K.S.A. 22-3402(3)(c), the trial court may grant a continuance without violating the speedy trial rule when "[t]here is material evidence which is unavailable; that reasonable efforts have been made to procure such evidence; and that there are reasonable grounds to believe that such evidence can be obtained and trial commenced within the next succeeding ninety (90) days. ⯑ Not more than one continuance may be granted the state on this ground, unless for good cause shown, where the original continuance was for less than ninety (90) days, and the trial is commenced within one hundred twenty (120) days from the original trial date."

We have previously upheld continuances of up to 120 days for DNA testing in murder cases without specifically analyzing whether the DNA evidence was material. ⯑ See State v. Green, 254 Kan. 669, 672-73, 867 P.2d 366 (1994); State v. Green, 252 Kan. 548, 551, 847 P.2d 1208 (1993) (codefendant brother to prior Green case, 112-day continuance). ⯑ Nevertheless, Jackson argues that the DNA evidence was not material because he did not contest the identity of the victim, the location of the murder, the cause of death, or the identity of the murderer. ⯑ However, contrary to Jackson's argument, these issues were material because the State prosecuted Jackson as an aider and abettor. ⯑ In order to establish Jackson's guilt, the State had to prove that a crime was committed by Jackson's codefendants. ⯑ The DNA evidence established that Williams' blood was on Combs' clothing and the knife found in Combs' possession. ⯑ Even though the DNA evidence did not directly implicate Jackson, it implicated his codefendants and corroborated Clanton's testimony.

Jackson further argues that the State failed to use reasonable efforts to procure the DNA evidence. ⯑ The DNA evidence was initially collected in June 2001 by Kansas City, Missouri, crime scene investigators and submitted to the Kansas City, Missouri, crime lab. ⯑

Due to a backlog of 2,000 homicide cases, including 119 cases that required DNA testing, the DNA evidence for Jackson's case was not available in

January 2002 for his original trial date. ⏎ The prosecutor began contacting Kansas City, Missouri, prosecutors and crime lab personnel about processing the evidence on June 6, 2001, 2 days after Williams was murdered. ⏎ The prosecutor continued her efforts to procure the evidence by sending letters and making multiple phone calls to crime lab personnel. ⏎ On December 28, 2001, the prosecutor was informed that regardless of the letters and telephone calls, the evidence could not be processed any faster because of the large backlog and insufficient resources.

Jackson argues that the State should have transferred the evidence to the Kansas Bureau of Investigation or another lab to expedite the testing. ⏎ However, the State advised the trial court that the KBI had a backlog as well and had been forced to close its lab for 2 weeks because of facility problems, further aggravating the KBI's existing backlog. ⏎ The State argues that it could not have had the evidence processed any faster at another lab and that transferring a large amount of evidence would have raised numerous issues regarding the chain of custody.

We hold that the State's efforts to procure the DNA evidence for trial were reasonable. ⏎ Although the State can inform crime labs of trial deadlines and encourage them to process evidence as quickly as possible, it cannot control the crime labs' schedules or caseloads. ⏎ In this case, the State informed and encouraged the crime lab at reasonable opportunities, beginning immediately after Williams' body was found, to expedite the evidence testing. ⏎ The State is not responsible for the other 119 backlogged cases that required DNA testing. ⏎ Likewise, the State is not responsible for the resource scheduling at the crime lab.

Jackson has failed to demonstrate any error in commencing his trial. ⏎ The trial court only issued one order for a 30-day continuance due to the congestion in the court's calendar and that continuance complied with K.S.A. 22-3402(3)(d). ⏎Additionally, the State's request for an evidentiary continuance complied with K.S.A. 22-3402(3)(c). ⏎The trial court did not violate Jackson's statutory right to a speedy trial.

JURY INSTRUCTIONS

Jackson raises several arguments regarding the trial court's jury instructions. ⏎ First, he argues that the trial court failed to instruct the jury regarding his defenses of withdrawal and compulsion. ⏎ Second, Jackson asserts that the trial court improperly expanded the instruction for aiding and abetting. ⏎ Next, Jackson contests the jury instruction about jurisdiction in Kansas. ⏎ Finally, Jackson argues the trial court should have instructed the jury on felony murder as a lesser included crime of first-degree premeditated murder.

Defenses of Withdrawal and Compulsion

Jackson contends he acted under duress and withdrew from the criminal enterprise before Combs and Clanton drove to Kansas and murdered Williams. ⏺ Because he relied on the defenses of compulsion and withdrawal, Jackson asserts the trial court should have instructed the jury as to these defenses as he requested.

A trial court is required to instruct the jury regarding the law applicable to the defendant's theory when there is evidence to support the theory, even if the evidence is slight and supported only by the defendant's own testimony. ⏺ An appellate court must review the evidence in a light most favorable to the defendant if he or she requests the instruction. ⏺State v. Scott, 250 Kan. 350, 357, 827 P.2d 733 (1992).

Jackson first argues that under the facts, he was entitled to a jury instruction on his withdrawal defense. ⏺ He limits his argument for the withdrawal instruction to the murder charge. ⏺ However, if this court were to agree with Jackson's argument, it would require us to abrogate the current law regarding the defense of withdrawal.

The State prosecuted Jackson as an aider and abettor to murder. ⏺ Kansas does not recognize the defense of withdrawal from aiding and abetting. ⏺ State v. Kaiser, 260 Kan. 235, 248-49, 918 P.2d 629 (1996). ⏺ Although Jackson asks us to overturn Kaiser, he fails to argue any reason for reversing that decision. ⏺ We have reaffirmed Kaiser in State v. Speed, 265 Kan. 26, 52, 961 P.2d 13 (1998), and State v. Straughter, 261 Kan. 481, 482, 932 P.2d 387 (1997), and find no reason to overturn it now. ⏺ The defense of withdrawal is not available to Jackson as an aider and abettor; thus, the trial court did not err when it refused to instruct the jury on the defense of withdrawal.

Jackson also argues that he was compelled to beat and strangle Williams because he was afraid of Combs. ⏺ The defense of compulsion is defined by K.S.A. 21-3209, which provides: "(1)⏺A person is not guilty of a crime other than murder or voluntary manslaughter by reason of conduct which he performs under the compulsion or threat of the imminent infliction of death or great bodily harm, if he reasonably believes that death or great bodily harm will be inflicted upon him or upon his spouse, parent, child, brother or sister if he does not perform such conduct. "(2)⏺The defense provided by this section is not available to one who willfully or wantonly places himself in a situation in which it is probable that he will be subjected to compulsion or threat."

Although K.S.A. 21-3209(a) precludes the application of compulsion to murder or voluntary manslaughter, Jackson argues the instruction applies to the kidnapping and conspiracy charges and to attempted murder as a lesser included crime of murder. ▢ The defense of compulsion requires coercion or duress to be present, imminent, impending, and continuous. ▢ It may not be invoked when the defendant had a reasonable opportunity to escape or avoid the criminal act without undue exposure to death or serious bodily harm. ▢ State v. Matson, 260 Kan. 366, 385, 921 P.2d 790 (1996).

In State v. Myers, 233 Kan. 611, 615-16, 664 P.2d 834 (1983), this court concluded that compulsion was not available as a defense because the defendant had opportunities to escape from his codefendant and did not contact the authorities to report the crimes. We can apply the same analysis to this case. ▢ Jackson had two opportunities to escape from Combs, once when Jackson and Clanton drove Williams' cousin home and again when Jackson went to the convenience store alone for soda and cigarettes. ▢ Jackson did not use either of these opportunities to flee from Combs. ▢ In addition, Jackson did not alert law enforcement at any time. ▢ Because Jackson had a reasonable opportunity to escape and avoid any criminal acts with Combs and Clanton and to summon law enforcement, he cannot invoke the compulsion defense. ▢ The trial court did not erroneously deny Jackson's request for the instruction.

Aiding and Abetting Instruction

Jackson argues the trial court erroneously expanded on the PIK Crim.3d 54.05 and 54.06 instructions for aiding and abetting, see K.S.A. 21-3205, by adding language to read as follows:

"Instruction No. 9: "A person who, either before or during its commission, intentionally aids, abets, advises, hires, counsels, or procures another to commit a crime with intent to promote or assist in its commission is criminally responsible for the crime committed regardless of the extent of the defendant's participation, if any, in the actual commission of the crime.

"In addition, a person is also liable for any other crime committed in pursuance of the intended crime if reasonably foreseeable by such person as a probable consequence of committing or attempting to commit the crime intended.

"All participants in a crime are equally guilty without regard to the extent of their participation. ▢ However, mere association with the principals who actually commit the crime or mere presence in the vicinity of the crime is insufficient to establish guilt as an aider or abettor. ▢ To be guilty of aiding and abetting in the commission of a crime the defendant must willfully and knowingly associate himself with the unlawful venture and willfully participate in it as he would in something he wishes to bring about or to make succeed." (Emphasis added.)

An appellate court must consider all of the instructions together, read as a whole. "If the instructions properly and fairly state the law as applied to the facts of the case and a jury could not reasonably have been misled by them, the instructions do not constitute reversible error even if they are in some way erroneous. [Citation omitted.]" State v. Cordray, 277 Kan. 43, 48, 82 P.3d 503 (2004). Trial courts should use the pattern jury instruction unless the facts of a particular case are unique and require modifying the pattern instruction. If the facts are unique, the court should not hesitate to add language or otherwise modify the pattern instruction. State v. Walker, 276 Kan. 939, Syl. ¶ 7, 80 P.3d 1132 (2003).

Jackson admits that the facts in this case are unique and the instruction did fairly and properly state the law. But, he argues that there was no evidence to support a finding of mere presence or mere association. He further argues the instruction misled the jury toward conviction because it precluded the jury from considering his dissociation from Clanton and Combs.

We find no merit in Jackson's argument. Withdrawal was not available as a defense to Jackson. Because Jackson's withdrawal theory was invalid, the court did not err in the language of the instruction.

Kansas Jurisdiction

Next, Jackson asserts the trial court improperly instructed the jury regarding the jurisdiction of Kansas to prosecute him. The trial court gave the following instructions for Kansas jurisdiction:

"Instruction No. 19: The place where the conspiracy was formed is immaterial if at least one of the overt acts alleged and proved took place within the State where the defendant is tried."

"Instruction No. 20: A person is subject to prosecution and punishment under the law of this state if he commits a crime wholly or partly within this state. An offense is committed partly within this state if either an act which is a constituent and material element of the offense, or the proximate result of such act, occurs within the state. If the body of a homicide victim is found within the state, the death is presumed to have occurred within the state. It is not a defense that the defendant's conduct is also a crime under the laws of another state or of the United States or of another country."

Jackson's argument as to these instructions is the same argument he raised earlier when he claimed that Kansas did not have jurisdiction to prosecute him because he did not enter into or commit any acts in Kansas. Jurisdiction is a question of law to be decided by the court, not the jury. See

State v. James, 276 Kan. 737, 744-45, 79 P.3d 169 (2003). We have already resolved the issue of jurisdiction against Jackson. We find no merit in his argument that the jury instructions misled the jury regarding the criminal jurisdiction of Kansas under K.S.A. 21-3104.

Felony-Murder Instruction

Finally, Jackson argues the trial court should have instructed the jury on felony murder and attempted murder as lesser included offenses to first-degree, premeditated murder. Jackson requested the instructions, so we must analyze this issue in a light most favorable to Jackson. See Scott, 250 Kan. at 358, 827 P.2d 733.

"A criminal defendant has a right to an instruction on all lesser included offenses supported by the evidence at trial so long as (1) the evidence, when viewed in the light most favorable to the defendant's theory, would justify a jury verdict in accord with the defendant's theory and (2) the evidence at trial did not exclude a theory of guilt on the lesser offense. [Citation omitted.]" State v. Williams, 268 Kan. 1, 15, 988 P.2d 722 (1999).

K.S.A.2003 Supp. 21-3107(2) defines a lesser included offense as "(a) A lesser degree of the same crime; "(b) a crime where all elements of the lesser crime are identical to some of the elements of the crime charged; "(c) an attempt to commit the crime charged; or "(d) an attempt to commit a crime defined under subsection (2)(a) or (2)(b)."

Felony murder and first-degree premeditated murder are both defined by K.S.A. 21-3401. Proof of felony murder requires proof of all of the same elements as premeditated murder, so it is not a lesser included offense pursuant to K.S.A.2003 Supp. 21-3107(2)(b). See State v. Young, 277 Kan. 588, 593-94, 87 P.3d 308 (2004) (noting that felony murder and premeditated murder define the same crime of first-degree murder).

Jackson argues that felony murder is a lesser included offense because it carries less mandatory prison time than premeditated murder. However, the statute does not define lesser included offenses by the sentence imposed. Because felony murder is not a lesser included offense of first-degree premeditated murder, the trial court did not err when it denied Jackson's request for a felony-murder instruction.

Conversely, attempted murder is a lesser included offense pursuant to K.S.A.2003 Supp. 21-3107(2)(c), so the trial court was required to give that instruction if there was evidence to support it. See State v. Reneeson, 261 Kan. 865, 883, 934 P.2d 38 (1997). Jackson does not dispute that Williams died in Kansas after being run over by Combs and Clanton. Rather, he argues that he did not participate in the killing because he withdrew prior to the actual murder. As previously stated, Jackson cannot use the defense of withdrawal because he was tried under an aiding or abetting theory. ⏹ Therefore, this issue is without merit. ⏹ There is no evidence to support a finding that Jackson, Combs, and Clanton attempted but were unsuccessful in murdering Williams. ⏹ The trial court did not err when it refused to give an instruction on attempted murder.

ADMISSION OF EVIDENCE

Jackson raises three issues regarding the admission of evidence. ⏹ First, Jackson argues the trial court erroneously admitted gruesome photographs. ⏹ Next, Jackson argues the trial court erroneously admitted hearsay statements made by Combs. ⏹ Finally, Jackson argues the trial court erroneously admitted his confession.

Gruesome Photographs

Jackson claims the trial court erroneously admitted gruesome photographs and a videotape of the crime scene. ⏹ Jackson argues he did not dispute Williams' death or the manner in which Combs and Clanton killed her, so the visual images were irrelevant. The trial court has wide discretion for admitting photographs in a murder case. ⏹ The trial court's decision to admit gruesome photographs will not be reversed on appeal unless the defendant demonstrates that the trial court abused its discretion. ⏹State v. Pennington, 276 Kan. 841, 848, 80 P.3d 44 (2003). Relevant evidence is any "evidence having any tendency in reason to prove any material fact." ⏹K.S.A. 60-401(b). ⏹ Relevancy is determined as a matter of logic and experience rather than as a matter of law, but there must be some material or logical connection between collateral facts and the inference or result they are supposed to establish. ⏹ 276 Kan. at 847, 80 P.3d 44.

Jackson's argument overlooks the State's theory that Jackson was guilty as an aider and abettor rather than as a principal in Williams' murder. ⏹ Because the State proceeded under an aiding and abetting theory, it was essential to its burden of proof that it establish the actions of the principals, Combs and Clanton. ⏹ The photographs were relevant to establish the nature of the injuries inflicted on Williams and to explain the cause of her death. ⏹ Accordingly, the trial court did not err by admitting the photographs and the crime scene videotape into evidence.

Hearsay Statements

Next, Jackson claims the trial court improperly admitted hearsay statements from Combs. ⏹ Although Combs did not testify, Clanton testified she overheard Combs talking to Jackson on the telephone. ⏹ Although she could not hear what Jackson was saying, she testified, over Jackson's objection, that Combs asked Jackson "what he would do or how would he go about killing somebody." ⏹ Clanton admitted Combs told her he was talking to

209

Jackson, but she could not be certain who was on the other end of the conversation because she did not hear the other person.

Jackson requests a de novo standard of review, citing State v. Deines, 268 Kan. 432, 434, 997 P.2d 705 (2000). ⬜ However, Deines does not address the admissibility of hearsay or any other evidence and does not properly state the standard of review for this issue.

We have recently clarified our standard of review in State v. Elnicki, 279 Kan. 47, 51, 105 P.3d 1222 (2005), and State v. Carter, 278 Kan. 74, 77, 91 P.3d 1162 (2004). ⬜ In Carter, we said: "An appellate court's first consideration when examining a challenge to a district court's admission of evidence is relevance. ⬜ Once relevance is established, evidentiary rules governing admission and exclusion may be applied either as a matter of law or in the exercise of the district judge's discretion, depending on the contours of the rule in question." ⬜278 Kan. 74, Syl. ¶ 1, 91 P.3d 1162.

Jackson does not contest the relevance of Combs' statements. ⬜ We thus proceed to the application of the evidentiary rules. The State argues that Combs' statements are admissible pursuant to K.S.A.2003 Supp. 60-460, which provides in pertinent part: "Evidence of a statement which is made other than by a witness while testifying at the hearing, offered to prove the truth of the matter stated, is hearsay evidence and inadmissible except: "(i)⬜Vicarious admissions. ⬜ As against a party, a statement which would be admissible if made by the declarant at the hearing if . (2) the party and the declarant were participating in a plan to commit a crime or a civil wrong and the statement was relevant to the plan or its subject matter and was made while the plan was in existence and before its complete execution or other termination."

Jackson raises two arguments regarding the admission of Combs' statements. ⬜ First, Jackson contends the conspiracy exception does not apply because Combs' statements were made before Jackson entered into the conspiracy. ⬜ Combs' question about how to kill someone was a general question rather than a specific request for Jackson to join him in killing Williams. ⬜ Second, Jackson argues that Clanton's testimony lacked sufficient indicia of reliability.

Jackson's argument that the conspiracy or coconspirator exception does not apply is not supported by the evidence. ⬜ Clanton's testimony supports the conclusion that Jackson was involved in the conspiracy during the telephone call with Combs. ⬜ A conspiracy may be inferred from sufficiently significant circumstances. ⬜ See State v. Swafford, 257 Kan. 1023, 1039-40, 897 P.2d 1027 (1995), modified on other grounds 257 Kan. 1099, 913 P.2d 196 (1996). ⬜ Clanton testified that Jackson had a small bottle with a white substance and a syringe already prepared when they arrived at Jackson's apartment a few hours after the phone call. According to Clanton, Jackson told Combs that all he had to do was to "stick her with [the syringe], just stick her with it and she will-once it gets in her system she will-eventually it will eventually eat up her system and she will pass out or she will die." The preparation of the substance and the syringe and the reference to "she" in Jackson's directions infer that Jackson was already part of the plan to kill Williams before Combs and Clanton arrived to pick him up. Jackson's prior involvement can also be inferred by Combs' assumption that Jackson was going with him and Clanton. According to Clanton, Combs asked Jackson, "[Y]ou're not going with us?" Jackson responded, "I'm in for the night, you know, you all waited too late." Jackson's response indicates that he had planned to go with Combs and Clanton but changed his mind because it was late at night. If Combs' question about how to kill someone had been generic, Jackson would not have prepared a syringe, referred to the victim as a "she," or planned to go with Combs and Clanton until it became too late. The record supports the inference that Jackson was part of the conspiracy when Combs asked the question about how to kill someone. The conspiracy or coconspirator exception to the hearsay rule applies.

For his second argument, Jackson asserts that Clanton's testimony lacks adequate indicia of reliability as required by the Confrontation Clause of the Sixth Amendment to the United States Constitution. In Crawford v. Washington, 541 U.S. 36, 124 S.Ct. 1354, 158 L.Ed.2d 177 (2004), the United States Supreme Court established a new analysis for Confrontation Clause claims, reevaluating the reliability analysis set forth in Ohio v. Roberts, 448 U.S. 56, 100 S.Ct. 2531, 65 L.Ed.2d 597 (1980). The first step in the Crawford analysis is to determine whether a statement is testimonial. Testimonial statements include, at a minimum, "prior testimony at a preliminary hearing, before a grand jury, or at a former trial . and to police interrogations." 541 U.S. at 68, 124 S.Ct. at 1374, 158 L.Ed.2d at 203. If the statement is testimonial, it may only be admitted if the declarant is unavailable and the defendant has had a prior opportunity to cross-examine the declarant. 541 U.S. at 68, 124 S.Ct. at 1374, 158 L.Ed.2d at 203. If the statement is not testimonial, the Crawford Court stated that it is wholly consistent with the Confrontation Clause to analyze the issue based on the applicable hearsay law. 541 U.S. at 68, , 124 S.Ct. at 1374, 158 L.Ed.2d at 203.

The Crawford Court specifically noted that statements by coconspirators are not testimonial. 541 U.S. at 55-56, 124 S.Ct. at 1366-67, 158 L.Ed.2d at 195-96. Therefore, the proper Confrontation Clause analysis requires us to apply Kansas hearsay law. In Swafford, this court considered whether a coconspirator's statement bore sufficient indicia of reliability. ⏺ The Swafford court concluded that the coconspirator exception to the hearsay rule found in 60-460(i)(2) is a firmly rooted hearsay exception that infers reliability without requiring further proof. ⏺257 Kan. at 1039-40, 897 P.2d 1027. ⏺ The Crawford Court did not overturn the firmly rooted hearsay exception analysis for nontestimonial statements. ⏺ See 541 U.S. at 68-69, 124 S.Ct. at 1374, 158 L.Ed.2d at 203. ⏺ Because of this, Swafford is controlling. ⏺ Combs' statement fits within the coconspirator exception to the hearsay rule. ⏺ This is a firmly rooted exception. ⏺ There is no need to establish further indicia of reliability. ⏺ The trial court did not err by admitting Combs' statement.

Jackson's Confession

Jackson argues his confession was not voluntary because he was suffering from heroin withdrawal and could not resist the coercive interrogation tactics used by police. An appellate court reviews the district court's decision regarding the suppression of a confession using a dual standard. ⏺ The factual findings are reviewed using a substantial competent evidence standard. ⏺ An appellate court will not reweigh the evidence but will give deference to the trial court's factual findings. ⏺ The ultimate legal conclusion drawn from the trial court's factual findings is a question of law which is reviewed de novo. ⏺State v. White, 275 Kan. 580, 596-97, 67 P.3d 138 (2003). ⏺ An appellate court accepts as true the evidence and all inferences drawn therefrom that support the trial court's findings. ⏺State v. Speed, 265 Kan. 26, 36-37, 961 P.2d 13 (1998). ⏺ To determine whether a confession is voluntary, a court must look at the totality of the circumstances in considering the following factors: the duration and manner of the interrogation; the ability of the accused to communicate on request with the outside world; the age, intellect, and background of the accused; and the fairness of the officers in conducting the investigation. ⏺ The key inquiry is whether the statement is a product of the accused's free and independent will. ⏺White, 275 Kan. at 597, 67 P.3d 138. ⏺ Coercion in obtaining a confession can be mental or physical.

Duration and manner of the interrogation

Jackson's interrogation began at approximately 9:30 a.m. A Kansas City, Missouri, police officer began by asking Jackson some biographical information and gave Jackson the Miranda warnings at about 9:45 a.m. At 11:28 a.m., Jackson accompanied officers to a different room to videotape his statement, which was completed at 12:13 p.m.

Jackson's interrogation occurred at the Kansas City, Missouri, Police Department in its standard interview rooms. ⏺ Jackson was not handcuffed during the interrogation. ⏺ The officers interrogating Jackson gave him a cigarette and allowed him to use the bathroom during the interrogation. ⃞ Jackson did not request any food or drinks.

An examination of the videotape shows the interview was conducted in a calm, orderly manner. ⃞ The voices of the officers were not raised. ⃞ The questions and tactics used were not intimidating. ⃞ There is no support for the conclusion that the duration and manner of Jackson's interrogation were coercive.

Jackson also argues that the court must find his confession involuntary because the police only recorded a portion of his interrogation. ⃞ He fails to cite any case law requiring police to videotape every minute of an accused's interrogation. ⃞ We decline to make such a holding in this case. ⃞ The testimony from Jackson and the officer who interrogated Jackson provided a sufficient record for evaluating the duration and manner of Jackson's interrogation. ⃞ None of this testimony supports the conclusion that the duration and manner of Jackson's questioning coerced Jackson to confess.

Jackson's ability to communicate on request with the outside world

Jackson did not request to speak to an attorney or anyone else during his interrogation. ⃞ The record does not support a finding that Jackson's confession was coerced because he was denied contact with anyone outside the interrogation room.

Jackson's age, intellect, and background

Jackson was 42 years old at the time of his interrogation. ⃞ He had four prior convictions, three for burglary and one for driving while intoxicated. ⃞ Jackson argues his confession was coerced because he was suffering from heroin withdrawal during his interrogation. ⃞ Jackson testified he had consumed a substantial quantity of heroin 5 days before his interrogation and that he suffered from withdrawal symptoms if he did not consume heroin every 2 days. ⃞ According to Jackson, the symptoms of heroin withdrawal include cold chills, excessive sleep, and lack of appetite. ⃞ Although Jackson testified he was tired, cold, and nervous during the interrogation, he repeatedly testified he "was not out of it" during his interrogation.

The police officer conducting Jackson's interrogation testified Jackson did not appear to be under the influence of any drugs or alcohol and that Jackson's responses were appropriate. ⃞ Although Jackson's hair was unkempt, there was no physical indication that he was suffering from heroin withdrawal. ⃞ Jackson admitted he did not remember informing the police officers that he was suffering from heroin withdrawal.

The record does not support Jackson's claim that his confession was involuntary because he was suffering from heroin withdrawal. ⃞ The trial court's decision to admit Jackson's confession implies its finding that Jackson was not influenced by his withdrawal symptoms. ⬚ This implied finding is supported by the evidence in the record and will not be overturned on appeal. ⬚ See Hill v. Farm Bur. Mut. Ins. Co., 263 Kan. 703, 706, 952 P.2d 1286 (1998). ⬚ There is no merit to this contention.

Fairness of the officers in conducting the investigation

Jackson argues that the officers pressured him into confessing and told him what to say. ⬚ Jackson testified the officers "just kept pushing me, pushing me and forcing me to say-say it this way." Initially, Jackson denied any involvement in Williams' death. ⬚ However, after the officer conducting the investigation implied that Combs and Clanton had blamed Jackson for the murder, Jackson's story changed. ⬚ The officer told Jackson he did not believe it was Jackson's idea to murder Williams and encouraged Jackson to further explain his involvement in Williams' death. ⬚ The officer admitted the detectives questioning Jackson suggested how the homicide occurred based on the physical evidence at the scene. ⬚ Jackson testified the officers "were saying that all-all of it was coming on me. ⬚ I was facing the murder rap by myself and in order for me to clear myself, that I-that I have to tell them the truth. "

In State v. Kornstett, 62 Kan. 221, 61 Pac. 805 (1900), the police told the defendant that he would feel better if he told the truth. ⬚ This court stated that "mere advice or admonition to the defendant to speak the truth, which does not import either a threat or benefit, will not make a following confession incompetent." ⬚62 Kan. at 227, 61 P. 805. ⬚ In State v. Harris, 279 Kan. 163, 171-72, 105 P.3d 1258 (2005), we upheld the admission of the defendant's confession even though the police told the defendant their theory of the homicide and suggested options for how the murder occurred. ⬚ Jackson cannot distinguish the police interrogation techniques in this case from those used in Kornstett and Harris. ⬚ Furthermore, Jackson has failed to cite any case law that forbids law enforcement officers from suggesting how the crime occurred based on other evidence within their knowledge. ⬚ This factor does not weigh in favor of excluding Jackson's confession.

When the totality of the circumstances is considered in light of the four White factors, there is no support for Jackson's claim that his confession was coerced based on the failure to videotape all of his interrogation, the effects of his drug withdrawal symptoms, or the police officers' suggestions regarding the manner of Williams' death and their encouragement to tell the truth. ⬚ The trial court did not err when it admitted Jackson's confession into evidence.

SUFFICIENCY OF THE EVIDENCE

When the sufficiency of the evidence is challenged in a criminal case, the standard of review is whether, after review of all the evidence, viewed in the light most favorable to the prosecution, the appellate court is convinced that a rational factfinder could have found the defendant guilty beyond a reasonable doubt. ⏎State v. Hanson, 277 Kan. 855, 856-57, 89 P.3d 544 (2004).

Jackson raises five arguments in support of his claim that there is insufficient evidence to support his convictions. ⏎ First, he argues that Clanton's testimony lacks credibility. ⏎ The jury is responsible for weighing the evidence and passing on the credibility of witnesses. ⏎ An appellate court does not invade the province of the jury by reweighing the evidence or determining the credibility of the witnesses. ⏎ See State v. James, 276 Kan. 737, 753, 79 P.3d 169 (2003). ⏎ This argument is without merit.

For his other four arguments, Jackson reiterates arguments previously raised in this appeal. ⏎ He argues there is insufficient evidence to show his intent to murder Williams because he acted from compulsion and withdrew before she was murdered. ⏎ Jackson asserts there is no evidence he entered Kansas or participated in the final act that ended Williams' life. ⏎ Jackson claims there is insufficient evidence to convict him of kidnapping Williams because he did not help put her in the back of the U-Haul truck and it was not reasonably foreseeable that Combs and Clanton would drive to Kansas with Williams. ⏎ Each of these arguments have been previously resolved against Jackson. ⏎ There is no merit to his claim that his convictions are supported by insufficient evidence.

We find no trial errors. ⏎ We affirm Jackson's convictions for first-degree premeditated murder, kidnapping, and conspiracy to commit murder. ⏎ With these conclusions reached, we proceed to the sentencing issues.

HARD 50 SENTENCING SCHEME

Jackson argues that the hard 50 sentencing scheme, K.S.A. 21-4635 et seq., is unconstitutional because it increases the sentencing range by adding 25 years to the defendant's parole ineligibility. ⏎ The constitutionality of a statute is a question of law over which this court has unlimited review. ⏎ State v. Beard, 274 Kan. 181, 185, 49 P.3d 492 (2002).

Jackson's argument has been previously considered and rejected by this court. ⏎ See, e.g., State v. Hebert, 277 Kan. 61, Syl. ¶ 14, 82 P.3d 470 (2004); State v. Washington, 275 Kan. 644, 680, 68 P.3d 134 (2003); State v. Boldridge, 274 Kan. 795, 812, 57 P.3d 8 (2002), cert. denied 538 U.S. 950, 123 S.Ct. 1629, 155 L.Ed.2d 494 (2003); State v. Douglas, 274 Kan. 96, 111, 49 P.3d 446 (2002), cert. denied 537 U.S. 1198, 123 S.Ct. 1268, 154 L.Ed.2d 1037 (2003); State v. Conley, 270 Kan. 18, Syl. ¶ 3, 11 P.3d 1147 (2000), cert. denied

532 U.S. 932, 121 S.Ct. 1383, 149 L.Ed.2d 308 (2001) (upholding the hard 40 sentencing statute).

Jackson asks this court to overturn Conley and its progeny but fails to cite any additional authority to support the reversal of this court's position. An issue raised but unsupported by any argument or authority has no persuasive effect. Conley and its progeny are controlling. The hard 50 sentencing provisions are constitutional.

SUFFICIENCY OF THE EVIDENCE TO SUPPORT A HARD 50 SENTENCE

Jackson claims there is insufficient evidence to support the imposition of the hard 50 sentence against him. He raises three arguments to support this claim. First, Jackson argues the trial court relied on acts committed by his codefendants rather than himself and that such reliance violates K.S.A.2003 Supp. 21-4636(f). Second, Jackson argues his conduct was not especially heinous, atrocious, or cruel. Third, Jackson argues the court relied on inherently unreliable evidence to support its finding that the murder was committed for the purpose of receiving money or any other thing of monetary value.

To address Jackson's first argument, we interpret K.S.A.2003 Supp. 21-4636(f). The interpretation of a statute is a question of law over which this court has unlimited review. State v. Maass, 275 Kan. 328, 330, 64 P.3d 382 (2003). K.S.A.2003 Supp. 21-4636 provides in pertinent part: "Aggravating circumstances shall be limited to the following: "(f)The defendant committed the crime in an especially heinous, atrocious or cruel manner. A finding that the victim was aware of such victim's fate or had conscious pain and suffering as a result of the physical trauma that resulted in the victim's death is not necessary to find that the manner in which the defendant killed the victim was especially heinous, atrocious or cruel. In making a determination that the crime was committed in an especially heinous, atrocious or cruel manner, any of the following conduct by the defendant may be considered sufficient: (3) infliction of mental anguish or physical abuse before the victim's death; (5) continuous acts of violence begun before or continuing after the killing."
Jackson admits Williams' murder was especially heinous, atrocious, or cruel but claims that all of the especially heinous, atrocious, or cruel actions were committed by his codefendants rather than himself. He argues that K.S.A.2003 Supp. 21-4636(f) requires the especially heinous, atrocious, or cruel actions be committed by him rather than his codefendants for the aggravating factor to apply. This argument overlooks the evidence in the record.

Clanton testified that Jackson planned to inject Williams with a poison that would "eat up her system." Jackson hit Williams in the head with a

216

mallet so he could inject her with the poison. When Williams screamed, Jackson jumped on top of her and tried to strangle her. Williams struggled with Jackson, and the two fell on the floor. Jackson then fought with Williams for several minutes on the floor, leaving Williams' blood splattered across her bed, her floor, her walls, and other articles in her room. After quieting Williams, Jackson sat on top of her and told Combs to get the syringe with the poison. When Jackson broke the syringe, he and Combs started looking for an extension cord to use to strangle Williams. Combs found an extension cord and handed it to Jackson, but Jackson broke the extension cord before he could strangle Williams to death. At that point, Combs suggested that Jackson stab Williams. Jackson told Combs to stab her himself because he was tired.

All of Jackson's actions in beating, strangling, and fighting with Williams prior to her death inflicted mental anguish or physical abuse and constituted continuous acts of violence begun before the victim's death as articulated by K.S.A.2003 Supp. 21-4636(f)(3) and (5). Jackson's argument that the trial court improperly applied the statute to him based on the actions of his codefendants is without merit.

Likewise, Jackson's argument that his actions were not especially heinous, atrocious, or cruel is without merit. When reviewing a challenge to the sufficiency of the evidence for establishing the existence of an aggravating circumstance in a hard 50 sentencing proceeding, the court must determine " 'whether, after a review of all the evidence, viewed in the light most favorable to the prosecution, a rational factfinder could have found the existence of the aggravating circumstance by a preponderance of the evidence.' [Citations omitted.]" Boldridge, 274 Kan. at 808, 57 P.3d 8.

Jackson argues that he tried to help Williams. The only evidence that Jackson attempted to help Williams came from his own statement. Jackson said that he told Williams to play like she was dead and that he would call the ambulance. However, Jackson never called an ambulance or alerted police.

In reviewing the evidence as required by Boldridge, Clanton's testimony supports the finding that Jackson's actions inflicted both mental anguish and physical abuse constituting continuous acts of violence against Williams. Jackson was directly responsible for leaving her in a condition that made it easier for Combs and Clanton to run over her with the U-Haul. Jackson's actions clearly fall within the definition of especially heinous, atrocious, or cruel found in K.S.A.2003 Supp. 21-4636(f)(3) and (5).

Jackson's argument that the trial court relied on inherently unreliable evidence for its finding that the murder was committed for the purpose of receiving money or any other thing of monetary value also fails. This is another attempt to discredit Clanton's testimony. ⊠ However, the jury's verdict demonstrates it found Clanton to be a credible witness. ⊠ We do not reweigh the evidence or pass on the credibility of witnesses. ⊠State v. Moore, 269 Kan. 27, 30, 4 P.3d 1141 (2000).

Jackson's argument also overlooks the standard of review set forth previously. ⊠ Clanton testified that Jackson helped load Williams' property into the U-Haul and took a small television with him when he returned to his apartment. ⊠ This evidence supports the trial court's finding that Jackson committed the crime for the purpose of receiving money or other things of monetary value.

The trial court's findings regarding the aggravating circumstances are supported by the record. ⊠ Jackson does not argue that the district court improperly weighed these factors against the mitigating factors. ⊠K.S.A.2003 Supp. 21-4635(c) requires the district court to impose a hard 50 sentence if it concludes that the aggravated circumstances outweigh any mitigating circumstances. ⊠ The trial court did not err when it sentenced Jackson to a hard 50 life sentence.

We have considered all of the arguments and find no error. ⊠ The convictions and sentences are affirmed. The opinion of the court was delivered by LARSON, J.:

Back to the story:

Years later, after the Kansas cases were finally resolved, the two men still had the outstanding Missouri cases pending and they had to be dealt with. Four years later, after the men had already been convicted and lost their appeals of their 50 year sentence, the men were sent back to Missouri to face charges. Even though they were looking at half a century of prison time, the Missouri cases had to be resolved. LeVota was encouraged by some fellow prosecutors to just dismiss the cases since it was overkill but he felt it was important that the state of Missouri resolve their cases. More importantly, he had promised Delisha Williams's family that the men would face Missouri justice also.

On his Missouri case, in exchange to agree to testify in any Missouri cases, Bovi Combs would plead guilty to his cases and was sentenced to 10 years in prison to run concurrent with the Kansas case. Andrew Jackson did not want to plead guilty and wanted a Missouri trial. So LeVota worked his case up for trial and pre-trialed his 20 witnesses for trial. However, the week before trial, Andrew decided to plead guilty to his Missouri charges and he was also sentenced to 10 years. Bovi Combs and Andrew Jackson are in the Kansas Department of Corrections and are eligible for parole in 2051.

4

Auntie Ruth's Neighborhood

While growing up, everyone had that one house in the neighborhood where the friendly, elderly people lived that everybody loved. Maybe it was an older couple or a sweet, elderly woman, but there was that someplace that people were always welcome and where the kids could always find a snack or a safe place to stay. In a Kansas City neighborhood in 2002, that house was the one that Dorothy Hayes and her sister Ruth Hayes lived in.

Ruth was the older sister and had outlived her husband of 40 years. Even when her husband shared the happy home with her, they had a great roommate and companion in Ruth's younger sister, Dorothy. It had been over ten years since Ruth's husband passed so most people just knew the ladies as "Auntie Ruth" and "Dorothy." Ruth gained the nickname "Auntie Ruth" over the years because of her kindness and her nurturing nature. Ruth would always stop whatever she was doing for a visitor to offer them something to eat or drink or even to loan them money or to just talk.

Some people are just more "people oriented" folks and that was Ruth while Dorothy was more introverted. Not to say that once you got Dorothy talking she wasn't the most caring and sweet individual you ever met, but it was usually Auntie Ruth that was the welcoming aspect of the home. But once you got in, it was Dorothy that would talk your ear off. The house was always full of neighbors stopping by to talk or to borrow a cup of milk or even just to sit on the porch. Many times you would find neighborhood mothers hollering for their kids only to find them on the front porch of Auntie Ruth's sipping on some Kool-Aid on a hot summer day. Parents loved the women because the streets weren't always a safe place for kids and they loved that Ruth and Dorothy loved playing neighborhood surrogate parents for all the kids on the block.

On the afternoon of February 27, 2001, Dorothy Hayes was home alone when James Anthony Hill knocked on the door. Dorothy yelled, *"Come on in."* as they always did because they never locked their door. James Hill actually went by his middle name of "Anthony" and he stepped in and asked Miss Dorothy if Auntie Ruth was home. Dorothy told him that Ruth was out with her niece picking up prescriptions at the drugstore but would be back shortly. Anthony didn't seem to want to talk too much to Dorothy because he knew she was a much harder sell for things than Ruth was. But before he turned to leave, Anthony attempted to borrow five dollars from Dorothy, but she said she didn't have any money. He then asked for a cigarette and she reluctantly gave him one. Anthony was disappointed because he knew that Auntie Ruth would have given him ten dollars and a whole pack of cigarettes if he asked. The two chatted while they smoked a cigarette but Anthony didn't wait around for Ruth.

Later, Dorothy heard a car pull up and heard Ruth's and their niece's voices. Trina Rice and her boyfriend Billy Francis carried in Ruth's purse and groceries while Ruth made her way into her house slowly but surely with her walker. Ruth used the walker effectively while holding a small, white bag she got from the pharmacy that held her prescriptions she just picked up. Ruth knew her niece and her boyfriend would be leaving soon so she just placed the groceries and her purse down and worried about putting them away later as she wanted to talk with the youngsters before they left. Trina was a caring relative that knew her two

222

aunts couldn't get around and that she was one of their only ways to get to the store or pharmacy. Trina and Billy had a busy life but took time out to make a weekly trip to take Ruth to the store. They always offered to take Dorothy with them but Dorothy would always jokingly respond, "Why do you have to drag two old ladies to the store?"

Dorothy got up to hug Trina and Billy and again thank them for their time. It meant so much to Ruth and Dorothy because the women were once young and active and the ladies knew it was an inconvenience for the kids to do it but it was so helpful to them. Ruth then hugged the two as they started to leave and thanked them again. As they got in the car, Trina put her hand in her coat pocket and found a five dollar bill that Aunt Ruth had secretly stashed in there as she had done so many time before. Trina was so surprised that a woman in her seventies was always able to stash some money in her pocket, her car, or somewhere without her knowing. Trina and Billy had lots of other things to do that day, but Trina smiled as they drove away knowing that it was important to visit with and help her aunts.

Ruth Taylor did not like cold weather and the winters in Kansas City. She always said they were too long and inflexible. She often complained the cold made her weak and caused her bones to ache. She really came to understand why people moved to warmer climates after they retired, but unfortunately for her, moving south on her small, fixed income was not a legitimate consideration. Instead, she bundled up to keep warm and relied upon the miracles from modern medicine to ease her discomfort.

Ruth's house was located on 5091 Wabash Avenue and had an angled roof that had a cozy curbside appeal. The house was unique to other homes on the street as it had an unpainted, wooden porch that wrapped around the front. All the houses on Wabash were very close together, but large trees framed the north side of Ruth's house and allowed her some seclusion as well as shade in the summers. The white house had an L-shaped yard which was wide open to two cross streets. Too close to the street was the dangling, metal mailbox that had met with too many car's mirrors that left it damaged. At seventy-eight, her house was plenty big enough for her and her sister and still small enough for them to maintain. However, to Ruth she could swear that those steps from the front door to the mailbox seemed to increase every year as she got older.

On the front door was a double lock encased in a single gold rectangular frame. From the outside, one key unlocked both locks but from the inside, Ruth had to unlock each lock individually. She couldn't lock it from the outside because she had long lost her key and she never even thought to lock her doors. She had lived in the neighborhood for over 25 years and she could tell you all about the changes but she would always say it was "her neighborhood" and regardless of any crime or being rundown, she wasn't ever moving. Some would assume that two seniors living in the area might feel unsafe based solely on its appearance. Nevertheless, Ruth felt that it was safe enough for her. She knew and liked her neighbors and they knew and liked her as well.

Later that day, Ruth was feeling the influences of the winter as she sat at the dining room table and talked with her neighbor, Sabrina Thomas. She was properly dressed for the season and wore a long-sleeved, blue and white, striped, button-down shirt and a black cotton jacket that zipped up the front with matching sweatpants. She hated the cold but loved when that door opened and someone was visiting. When the cold ripped in through that door, Dorothy would yell to close the door but Ruth did not complain as her door opened and closed many times throughout the day.

But Ruth did feel her hands and knees aching as heat spilled from her home and cold air crept in. At the table visiting with her neighbor, Ruth practiced some at-home physical therapy exercises to relieve some of the discomfort of her arthritis due to the cold. She also cradled her hot coffee mug to embrace the heat from it.

Ruth had known her friend and neighbor Sabrina since Sabrina was a child. Ruth was probably about thirty years her senior. Ruth had even babysat Sabrina when she was a little girl and when Sabrina grew up; Ruth later babysat Sabrina's two children also. As they talked, Sabrina strummed her fingers on the green tablecloth as they drank black coffee in Ruth's kitchen. A large glass fruit bowl was the only thing between her and her guest as she listened to Sabrina talk about her health and money problems.

Ruth played with a gold locket dangling from a roped chain around her neck as her and Sabrina spent the day talking and she offered her coffee, cookies, and the wise words of an older woman. As the two conversed, there were multiple interruptions by an assortment of neighbors coming by but one neighbor, Anthony Hill, made more than one appearance. It didn't surprise Sabrina or Ruth because at Auntie Ruth's house, all are welcome and there is a clear open-door policy.

James Anthony Hill was a middle aged man and certainly not one of the kids in the neighborhood. Both Ruth and Sabrina knew him only through his Aunt Alma, who lived across the street. Anthony had moved in with his Aunt Alma several weeks ago after he had been released from prison. Ruth Taylor was not one to judge whether someone had been in prison or not and Anthony was as welcome as anyone else in her home. Hill's appearance was normal for the men that lived in that area as well as those who visited her home and nothing was out of the ordinary. He wore a ball cap and dark jeans but what he wanted out of his visit at Ruth's that day was not at all ordinary. He had already been at the house earlier in the day and asked Dorothy for money and a cigarette.

Hill had been to Auntie Ruth's house enough times to know the routine and as he entered the residence for the second time that day, he wiped his feet on the bristly rug near the front door. With his hands tucked in the sides of his coat, he entered the dining room and said hello to Ruth and Sabrina and asked to use the restroom. It was not uncommon for people to stop by just to use the restroom because many people who were walking didn't have a place to use the bathroom. Ruth told Hill that it was fine and pointed to the hallway to the left of the dining room.

An archway separated the living room and the kitchen area. Before he headed to use the facilities, Hill stood there for several minutes. Hill made unsolicited small talk to the two women and just as he had asked her sister earlier that day, he asked Ruth for five dollars for cigarettes and a soda. Ruth sweetly told him she didn't have any dollars but she had a dish full of change and he was welcome to take $2.00 in quarters out of it. Hill didn't want the change, so now after his second rejection for five dollars in the same day, he made his way to the restroom, used it, stopped back by to say thank you and then left.

Dorothy had been in the other room watching TV and she then walked into where the women were and joined her sister in the kitchen. Dorothy warmed up some chicken and cornbread for lunch and ate it as the women talked. Twenty minutes later, Sabrina mentioned that she had to go in a little bit but before she left, Dorothy told Ruth that she was going to her bedroom to take a nap. Dorothy went to her bedroom but she never talked about Hill asking both of them for money or that there were two separate incidents of money requests.

Within the hour, Hill was back on Auntie Ruth's porch. This time he didn't knock but just came in the Taylor home for the third time that day. Sabrina and Ruth remained seated when he

226

reentered the kitchen with a second request to use the bathroom. Hill lingered in the kitchen for a few minutes and without explanation at all, he sat down at the table with the ladies. He didn't say much but seemed lost in thought as the women continued talking.

It seemed that Hill had an agenda on his third time to the house and it wasn't to use Ruth's home as his personal bathroom. Ruth was too trusting and sweet to realize it. What Ruth didn't know was that Hill had a history of violence and theft. His chief method of operation was forcefully robbing women. In 1991, Hill was convicted for grabbing a woman's purse then throwing and knocking her to the ground. In 1994, he accosted a female in an apartment building, forcibly took her money, and bit her. In 1995, he attempted to rob a dry cleaning store being attended by a female clerk. Hill was a career criminal and he preyed upon females. Hill felt them to be weak and easy targets and was a coward of the worst kind.

Hill was frustrated on his second visit to Ruth's house because he did not factor other people being around in his equation. His third visit proved frustrating as well when he found Sabrina still there with no immediate intentions of leaving. Hill made up a story about locking himself out of his Aunt Alma's house and asked to use her restroom again. Ruth never suspected a thing and didn't think to check out his story.

But Hill didn't go to the restroom but made himself at home and joined in their conversation. Sabrina never saw Hill go into the bathroom and she decided she needed to get home. Before she walked out the door and left Ruth alone with Hill, she never gave Ruth's safety a second thought. When Sabrina left, Hill was still sitting at the kitchen table with Auntie Ruth, the community's favorite and sweetest neighbor.

After Sabrina left, Ruth told Hill he was welcome to stay as long as he needed. It was cold out there and Alma would be home soon. Ruth excused herself and started her late afternoon ritual. She stopped by the thermostat and turned up the heat and then went to her bedroom to exchange her day clothes for her light housecoat.

Hill waited until he heard Ruth shut her bedroom door before he got up and quietly made his way into the living room. He went straight for the front door but didn't open it. Instead he turned the deadbolt on the door to lock the door but did it ever so slowly that he was the only one who heard the tiny click as it locked out the outside world. As he tiptoed his way towards the bathroom, he could hear Ruth opening and closing her dresser drawers. His decision to follow through with his bathroom request was not so much out of need as it was to catch his target off guard and once inside, with his ear pressed up to the door, he waited and listened.

Ruth made her way back out to the kitchen and took the last piece of cornbread out of the cast iron skillet on the stove. She put it in a paper towel, crumbled it, and stood at the back door. This was another one of Ruth's routines and even before she opened the door, several birds gathered at the door as if they were expecting it. As soon as the door opened, cold air ripped through Ruth's cotton duster and she felt her bones stiffen but she smiled as her birds were chirping up a storm. She opened and closed her hand to loosen her ridged fingers before she threw some cornbread out into her back yard. As she stood exposed to the cold, she shivered and talked to the birds. Ruth knew it would take hours to warm up her chilled bones, but enjoyed watching the birds devour their supper.

Ruth walked back into the living room and heard her guest exit the bathroom. As she entered the kitchen, she turned around to see Hill right in front of her. The first thing she noticed was his unzipped pants and as a polite way to attempt to advise him of his forgetfulness, she cleared her throat and pointed. However,

Ruth had no time to say a word as Hill grabbed her arm and twisted it. He said, *"Don't say a word, Auntie Ruth or I'll kill you."*

Hill pushed and backed Ruth up quickly towards the table and Ruth thought her legs would snap as he forced her to move faster than she could manage. One can only imagine the fear that Ruth was feeling. Ruth called out for her sister, but Hill didn't tolerate her disobedience and punched her in the face and wrapped his hands around her throat. Ruth couldn't yell for help and she couldn't breathe. He choked her against the table and then forced her down onto her dining room floor. Ruth had no idea what was happening but realized that Hill was going to kill her.

Although she was frail and weak, Ruth didn't forget her attacker's primary area of weakness. She was now in a "fight for your life" mode that few people ever are faced with. In her fight on her way being forced to the ground, Ruth grabbed at Hill to defend herself. She managed to grab ahold of his groin area and actually got both of his testicles in her hand. Her hands were ridged and inflexible and the grip she had on her assailant was only slight and hurt him but not very much. It only made him mad. Hill instinctively and angrily released her and threw her to the ground but unfortunately not long enough for her to get away.

He grabbed his groin and grunted in pain. He then realized that Ruth's chain was stuck to his hand and he shook his hand several times before the piece of jewelry flew off. He was mad. This sweet old lady was just supposed to be an easy victim but she had spunk and she fought back. His anger grew and he looked around the room for a weapon. He was going to make her pay for fighting back.

The same heavy glass bowl had sat on Ruth Taylor's table for decades. Sometimes it held candy, other times it was a fruit bowl, and on even other occasions, it was full of nuts. On this day, it was empty and Hill saw it not as a utensil that held refreshments for visitors but he saw it as a weapon. Flinching in pain, he grabbed the glass bowl and raised it high above Ruth's head.

As he brought the bowl down and struck Ruth's head, the force of the blow shattered the bowl over Ruth's skull. The energy behind the blow forced her to fall backward on the hard floor. The many pieces of the bowl fell around Ruth's body. Hill wasn't sure if he had knocked her out so he looked for another weapon. Hill then grabbed a piece of the broken glass and made a long cut across her throat. Even though she put up no fight, Hill kicked and punched Ruth in her face and body until she was completely still and silent.

Ruth was sprawled out, bloody, and vulnerable on the cold linoleum floor of her kitchen. The ruckus had not alerted Dorothy and Ruth was barely conscious. But Hill was not done and his next plan was to take his victim's dignity also. Hill ripped open the front of Ruth's tan housecoat, grabbed the wing of her bra, and pulled it over her left shoulder. Ruth's head hit the floor and slightly bounced as he maneuvered it over her head, letting it drop onto her opposite shoulder. With her breasts uncovered, he worked her nightgown above her waist and then raped the unconscious 78 year old woman.

After he had violently assaulted her, he stood up, pulled his pants up and tried to clean himself off. His demeanor was one of someone who had just performed some casual task and not one of someone who just violently assaulted and raped the neighborhood matriarch. Hill immediately turned to Ruth's purse and took all of her money out and jammed it into his pockets. He then turned off the kitchen light, stepped over her body, and left her for dead in a puddle of her own blood and urine. Ironically, Hill left through the same back door that Ruth stood at earlier while she fed the birds sustenance that would sustain their life.

The sun had already set when Trina and Billy stopped back by to give Ruth a grocery bag that she had left in the car from the afternoon. Trina knew immediately that something wasn't right when she tried to open the front door and found it locked. She was even more alarmed when there was no answer after her knocking. Trina knocked hard several more times and when no one answered, she put her ear up to the door and listened for activity inside the home. She heard faint groans from within and then moved from the door to the window. Trina cupped her hand around her eyes, peered inside, and saw the frame of the open backdoor illuminated by the outside streetlight.

Trina and Billy ran around back and went in through the open back door. The door opened into the kitchen-dining room combo and as they stepped in they heard moaning as Trina frantically ran her hands across the wall in search of the light switch. Trina found the switch and when she hit it, the white light stung their eyes as it filled the dark room. The red blood they saw that covered the dining room filled their bodies with panic. As they moved around the table, they found Ruth lying on the hard floor with her breasts exposed, her bra unhinged and draped across her neck, and covered in blood. Ruth, barely alive, mumbled the name of her assailant to Trina. Trina yelled to Billy to call 911 for an ambulance and told him to stay with Ruth while Trina ran to Sabrina's house for additional help.

It was only after Trina returned from Sabrina's that she went to find her Aunt Dorothy. Fearing for the worst, she was relieved to find Dorothy in a hard sleep and unaware of anything that had happened. Soon after, the fire department, police department, and the ambulance were at the home within minutes. Several of the officers knew Ruth and took a very personal interest in getting the paramedics in the house to Ruth and getting her out to the awaiting ambulance all the while protecting the crime scene.

The crowd outside of Auntie Ruth's house numbered well over forty people as she was pulled out on the stretcher. It was deathly silent as all were saddened by their friend being hurt. Some thought maybe it was a heart attack but no one dreamed that someone in their own neighborhood would have harmed their sweet neighbor.

Police officers had already secured the home by the time detectives Williams and Wiggins responded to a reported crime scene involving a robbery and assault on Wabash Avenue. They noticed the large crowd of people and were surprised that they were all out there in such cold weather. Williams and Wiggins ducked underneath the yellow police tape and gave their badge numbers to the officer who was standing outside the doorway.

Upon entering the residence, the familiar odors of blood and urine confronted them. These were two smells that were always a precursor to tragedy and ugliness. Knowing the history of the odors; however, allowed them to predetermine the seriousness of the crime even before they entered. The broken glass strewn about the interior and the large amount of blood told the detectives they were correct in their initial assumptions and that someone had committed a terrible crime against another. From the police already on the scene, the detectives received the name of the victim and a list of possible witnesses. The detectives knew that if they didn't document the small details timely, they were often forgotten. So while crime scene technicians combed the house for evidence, Williams and Wiggins canvassed the area for witnesses.

Sabrina's small yellow-sided home was just two doors down from Ruth's and when the detectives ascended her dark steps, they found her standing against the side of her porch. Sabrina sat looking at the commotion going on just two houses down and smoked a cigarette. Despite the freezing temperatures, the three remained outside while Sabrina gave her statement. A combination of adrenaline and a puffy white coat protected Sabrina from feeling the bitter cold as she told the men what she remembered. She answered their questions respectively in chronological order and showered them with the chain of the day's events as well as the name and description of the male that visited Ruth's house several times that day. However, she barely looked at them during their conversation and kept her focus on the activity outside her friend's home.

With the exception of when she pointed to a house nearby, indicating where the suspect lived, Sabrina kept her arms crossed against her chest and her hands tucked under her arms. She watched police officers come and go as she told them about the guest's odd requests to use the bathroom. As the blood dried on the floor of her neighbor's home, Sabrina supplied elaborate details that helped the detectives form a link between Ruth's guest and the crime at 5901 Wabash.

Immediately after they interviewed Sabrina, the detectives made their way across the street to 5910 Wabash Avenue which was the suspected residence of Anthony Hill, who they now knew was actually James Anthony Hill. The detectives completed a short interview with Alma Alamgar. Alma denied that Hill lived with her but indicated they may be able to find him at a residence off Park Avenue. She told them that he was there earlier in the day but that she hadn't seen him since. Detective Wiggins jotted the notes down just as Alma reported them; however, he had a suspicion that Alma wasn't being completely truthful.

A large piece of glass appeared to have been at least one of the weapons used to injure Ruth Taylor. Crime Scene Technician, Charles Johnson found additional thick glass fragments strewn about the home. Some were small and hard to

233

detect but some were large with bloodstains obvious to the naked eye. Nevertheless, he knew some of the most important evidence was not always visible to the naked eye and was never surprised at how far glass travelled when broken. Johnson searched all the adjacent rooms and their floors for additional pieces and other evidence.

Bits of human tissue clung to some of the glass. With tweezers and careful not to smudge any latent or invisible prints, Johnson removed the evidence and put it in tubes with specific color-coded lids. He photographed and collected a blue baseball cap and hair and fiber fragments and sealed them all in brown paper bags. When he returned to the crime lab, he would send them to the Latent Print Section for examination and evaluation.

When Williams and Wiggins arrived at Ruth's niece Trina's residence, they already had the name of their suspect but securing the maximum amount of useful information was always the goal. She expected that the police would be by to talk to her and she answered the door on the first knock. Wearing the same gray hooded sweatshirt and jeans she had on when she found Ruth nearly dead and bleeding on the kitchen floor, the forty-three-year-old motioned them towards the sofa.

The detectives declined and remained near the front door while they asked her a string of questions. They took notes as she nervously blurted out details of what she observed. She told them that it was cold and completely dark outside when she arrived, but with the exception of the locked door, she saw nothing unusual. She started to cry in the midst of the questioning and both detectives were silent as they waited for her to compose herself.

Trina grabbed a tissue from a small table near the door, wiped her nose, and wadded it up tightly in her right hand before she continued. Trina added she could hear moaning but thought it was the TV or Ruth's sister. She described how when no one answered and she couldn't get in, she peeked through the front window and saw the back door wide open. Trina emphatically described Ruth as brave and told them how, despite her condition, she managed to tell them her attacker's name. The detectives noticed blood on the sleeve of Trina's sweatshirt and had no reason to suspect her involvement; however, they confiscated her shirt for evidence nonetheless.

The police first secured statements from all the available witnesses in the neighborhood before Williams and Wiggins drove a few miles northwest to St. Luke's Hospital. They wanted to talk to Ruth; however, the attending physician had different ideas about the detectives' ambitious goals. The doctor itemized a long list of Ruth's injuries, informed them that she was still unconscious, and then refused them admittance.

The emergency room had concluded that Ruth had sustained bleeding to her brain, fractures to her face, and her eyes were swollen shut. The phrase most often used around the ER about Ruth Taylor was that "she is lucky to be alive."

Williams and Wiggins were again at St. Luke's the next morning in another attempt to visit the critically ill woman, but just like the night before they couldn't show Ruth the photospread they had created as she was still unconscious. One doctor told the robbery detectives that he was afraid that they might be handing the case off to the homicide detectives as Ruth's diagnosis wasn't good.

Williams and Wiggins shifted gears and headed to meet with Sabrina Thomas to show her the same photo line-up they wanted to show Ruth. James Anthony Hill's picture was in the number four position along with five other black males with similar characteristics. They showed the photospread to Sabrina and asked her to take her time. Sabrina looked at the six males in the picture and pointed at Hill's picture and identified him as the same man she saw in her neighbor's house. The detectives asked her to initial and date the photo and Sabrina did so and Williams took it to be placed in the file back at the Violent Crimes Division.

Almost a week passed before Ruth Taylor regained consciousness and then another day before she was able to do any talking. Due to her advanced age, her badly beaten body healed slowly and the detectives had no choice but to wait patiently to get her statement. On March 4, they sat on either side of Ruth's hospital bed with a recorder running and pencil and paper in hand. They documented her visible injuries during the interview.

White bandages were still attached to her wounds and the discolorations from bruising were still obvious on her shiny brown skin. Detective Williams talked while Detective Wiggins took notes as Ruth held onto the right bed railing of the hospital bed obviously in excruciating pain. In a weakened voice, Ruth gave them the details they had been waiting for and from an identical photo spread, they had carried a week prior, she identified James Anthony Hill as her attacker.

On that same day, Williams received a call from the latent prints division and told him they had completed the comparison of latent lifts collected from broken pieces of a glass bowl and fingerprints on a 1987 fingerprint card of James Anthony Hill. The examiner's conclusion was that the prints from the broken bowl were Hill's fingerprints. An arrest warrant for James Anthony Hill was requested and signed on March 12.

The offender had been identified and an arrest warrant had been issued. The police were actively looking for Hill but somewhere in the investigation or treatment of Ruth Taylor there was an error. For the reason that she was unconscious for so long or maybe the sheer disbelief that someone would rape a 78 year old woman, there was a bypass of protocol to investigate if a rape had occurred because there were signs of a sexual assault.

Key witnesses indicated that when they found Ruth on the ground, her breasts were exposed, her bra was partially removed, and it hung loose around her neck. But it wasn't until over a week later when Ruth complained of a burning sensation when she urinated that a rape kit was considered.

The suspicion of sexual assault required a signature from Ruth to agree to further medical exams to rule out or include forensic evidence of rape. Ruth was hesitant to authorize it as she was barely recovering from her injuries. However she did agree and when the rape protocol was followed and she was dragged through a series of embarrassing tests and procedures including a pelvic exam and a comb through of her pubic hair. The nurse examined Ruth and found external injuries near her vaginal area. Ruth had severe bruising and abrasions on her inner thighs and abrasions inside her vagina walls. All of these injuries appeared consistent with signs of a sexual assault.

As Ruth recuperated in the hospital, her residence of 5901 Wabash was a busy place. Police were in and out at random times and neighbors came to offer support. Some visitors were helpful and some were nosy, but the home remained blocked off by police tape until the police finished collecting evidence. However, despite all that was collected and all the support offered, the investigation and evidence collection left Ruth's home in worse condition than when they arrived. Unfortunately, no one told Dorothy that there were professional agencies that would clean her home and bill her insurance company. Dorothy didn't know what else to do but to clean her house and she bought Clorox and cleaning supplies and worked to put her home back to its pre-crime condition.

Detective Williams felt sick in his stomach when Ruth's attending nurse called him to tell him that Ruth may have been sexually assaulted. Both Detectives responded back to the hospital for a second interview with the victim. Ruth moved around easier than she did the last time they visited and she nervously flipped through TV channels with the remote control as they asked sensitive but necessary questions. It was hard for the detectives to keep Ruth on task and she talked to the detectives about random things. She asked them about their jobs, the weather outside, and continued to change the subject at hand. However, Ruth finally described her symptoms for them but denied any knowledge of a sexual attack. She was truthful when they asked her when last time she had sexual intercourse and told them she had sex with a gentleman friend of hers back in January.

Immediately after the notification of a possible sexual assault, Williams contacted CST Johnson and informed him of the new information received and requested he return to the victim's residence for a supplementary examination of the crime scene. Johnson contacted Dorothy and responded back to the crime scene the same day. She met him at the front door and informed Johnson that she had cleaned the home with soap and bleach. Nevertheless, he examined the home, but his inspection for male bodily fluids was negative.

Criminals often return to the scene of the crime and that's possibly what Anthony Hill sort of did when he learned Ruth Taylor was not dead. On March 7, a nurse in Ruth's room answered the phone as it rang in her room. The nurse spoke to a male who did not identify himself but claimed to be Ruth's godson. The caller asked the nurse if Ruth was able to remember what happened to her and if so, was she able to identify her attacker? The only problem was that Ruth didn't have a godson.

The nurse explained to the man that she was not able to provide any information about Ruth; nonetheless, the man continued to ask questions about her mental and physical status before he abruptly hung up. The nurse knew something wasn't right about the phone call and she notified hospital security and the KCPD of the telephone call. For her protection, the hospital assigned Ruth to another room and listed her under a fake name. Ruth was placed on a "No Information" status.

Anthony Hill was not located until several months after the issuance of his warrant but both detectives were present on June 12 when the KCPD brought Hill into the Jackson County Detention Center and booked him on four counts. They were first-degree assault, first-degree robbery, armed criminal action, and forcible rape. Hill was advised of his rights before the detectives interrogated him; however, it didn't take long for the interview between Anthony Hill and the two detectives to end.

Anthony Hill did not remain calm when they questioned him concerning his knowledge and possible involvement in the robbery and assault that occurred against Ruth Taylor. Hill defended himself against their accusations because he said he only robbed white people and then refused to answer additional questions. The detectives returned him to the custody of the Jackson County Deputies within an hour after the start of the interview. Detective Williams was frustrated because he was hoping for at least some sort of statement from Hill. There was no eyewitness and he knew Ruth would be a timid witness if the case ever went to trial. He needed more evidence for the prosecution

On June 13, Detective Williams typed up a search warrant to collect physical evidence from the body of Anthony Hill. The detectives presented it to an assistant prosecutor who reviewed it and signed off on it. After one more stop by the judge's office for his signature, the cops were on their way back to the jail to get Hill. Both detectives transported Hill to Baptist Medical Center where head hair, pubic hair, and blood were recovered from the suspect and retained for analysis. They transported Hill back to the Jackson County Detention Center.

Hill was steadfast in his innocence and remained in the Jackson County Jail until his trial in 2004. Hill's attempt was

239

obvious and although he was not successful in killing his prey, he was successful in raping and beating her, almost to the point of non-recognition. Several eyewitnesses placed Anthony Hill at the scene, as well did a baseball cap found in the bathroom of the Taylor residence. However, there was no DNA evidence of the crime of sexual assault. Hill's victim was reluctant to testify, and her injuries alone did not make Hill a robber/rapist beyond a reasonable doubt. Hill pleaded not guilty and left it up to a jury of his peers to decide his guilt or innocence.

The prosecution was represented by prosecutors Phil LeVota and Renee Sinclair. The case would be an interesting one and Sinclair, who was a relatively new prosecutor, had all the makings of an outstanding trial attorney to handle this unique case with LeVota. Sinclair had a sharp mind and was quick to grasp the evidence of the case in relation to the presentation to the jury that often times trial attorneys with decades of experience never grasp.

LeVota and Sinclair made a great trial team as Sinclair was a soft spoken, rule following, quietly assertive attorney and it complimented LeVota's brash, direct, envelope pushing, and aggressively passionate pursuit of justice in representing the people of the state of Missouri against violent crime. As her senior attorney, LeVota chose Sinclair as his second chair as often as he could because she was a great trial attorney and she exemplified the traits of an ethical prosecutor. Sinclair and LeVota shared the same prosecutorial ethic of fairness in each case and truly believing it is not about the conviction but about justice. In each case, they "lived with" with all of the problems involved in a criminal case but all the while sharing everything with defense counsel.

The job of a prosecutor is to take the case to trial and play by the rules even if sharing a piece of evidence with the defense

240

would hurt your case. It is about doing the right thing. And in practicing this theory of prosecution, LeVota and Sinclair were perfect in obtaining guilty verdicts against their defendants. The two attorneys had a great demeanor and never a trial went by that jokingly LeVota didn't inform someone in the courtroom that in addition to being a great attorney, Sinclair had also been a cheerleader for the Kansas City Chiefs.

In his long career as a prosecutor, LeVota never tried a sexual assault case or a child victim case and that was by design. Of the hundreds of homicide cases he was involved with, LeVota always had adult victims and he was able to separate the case from real life and he never took those pressures of the cases home with him. He saw how the specialized prosecutors who worked in the sex crime unit and the domestic violence unit were dedicated to their causes but also how it took its toll on them. He was proud of his colleagues in those specialized prosecutions but he shied away from those cases. But for now he was getting ready to try a rape case and as he got to know the victim, he would realize just how invested he would become in fighting for her.

LeVota received a crash course in many aspects of sexual assault and sex crime prosecution. He even obtained a detailed lesson in internal injuries that an elderly woman would face in a rape by a doctor at St. Luke's. However, what LeVota lacked in sex crime prosecution, he more than made up for it in trial presentation to a jury. He knew that if he could learn what the evidence meant in a short period of time, he would be able to explain and present it to a jury because the jurors also did not have the specialized knowledge. This was just another lesson in how to explain a case to a jury so the prosecution dream team's lack of sex crime prosecution didn't phase LeVota or Sinclair. They knew how to try a case.

In trying a case one of the most important issues is pre-trialing your witnesses and especially your victim. The prosecutors found Ruth to be exactly as all the reports read. A sweet, non-assuming, senior lady that would much rather talk to you about the weather than the terrible things that happened to her. When LeVota sent one of his investigators to pick up Ruth Taylor to bring her to the courthouse, he was not sure what to expect. When he met her, he immediately knew why everyone called her Auntie Ruth.

Ruth had an immediate way of making whoever she spoke with feel comfortable and was eager to please. However, LeVota found it difficult to keep her on task about the facts of the case and quickly found that she was just too embarrassed to talk about it. And why wouldn't she be? Any woman would be uncomfortable talking about any sexual issues with friends let alone talking about a violent assault and rape with strangers and then being told she would have to tell the story in open court.

When pressed about some if the issues, Ruth would tear up quickly and could not follow through. Ruth would then mutter excuses about maybe the police should just let him go or that she might be too ill to testify. LeVota decided not to push her and just got the commitment from Ruth that she would be ready next week when the investigator would pick her up for trial. LeVota promised her that when she would be on the stand, it would be just like her and he talking and no one else. LeVota assured her that no one was going to make her feel bad. He knew he only had one shot at getting Ruth to open up and he would save that for her trial testimony. He didn't want to traumatize her so much at the pre-trial that he would lose her altogether in front of the jury. As they said goodbye, Ruth left LeVota's office with the investigator for her ride home.

LeVota looked at his second chair and shook his head. Sinclair nodded back acknowledging as she realized that this was going to be hard for Ruth and hard for them. However, before they could speak, Ruth turned around and walked back in. "I *almost forgot about these,"* she said to LeVota as she pulled a Ziploc bag of cookies out of her purse. LeVota immediately remembered when he spoke to her on the phone to set up the interview that Ruth said she was baking peanut butter cookies and LeVota told her he loved them. Ruth stepped back into LeVota's office and she laid the bag containing six peanut butter cookies on LeVota's desk and said, *"My prosecutor has to keep his strength up."* She turned and walked out the door. LeVota turned and smiled at Sinclair but he didn't share his cookies with her.

Judge Vernon Scoville, a middle-aged man with an impressive resume that included a history as an assistant prosecutor as well as a Missouri State Representative, presided over Hill's trial. Scoville scored high ratings from attorneys on his fairness and understanding of rules and procedure. He was firm with his rulings and fair on his dispositions. However on the day of trial, Scoville seemed unimpressed with defense attorney, Jerry Garrison's request for a continuance on the morning of trial and denied him his request to put this case off once again.

In the State's opening, the prosecution described the defendant as an uncaring and violent man and how he smashed a heavy glass bowl over a frail and elderly woman's head, rendered her unconscious, and then raped and robbed her and left for dead on her dining room floor.

However, the defense painted a different picture in their opening statement. With the unsurmountable evidence that put Hill in Ruth's home, they decided on another strategy other than the *"I didn't do it"* defense. The defense attorney said they didn't dispute that Hill grabbed Ruth and a struggle ensued. But their theory was that in the struggle, Ruth grabbed his client's testicles and twisted them. The defense attorney then added that his client grabbed the bowl in self-defense, hit the victim in the head,

243

and left soon thereafter but not before, he took fifteen dollars from her purse.

With the implication that his client only hurt the victim because she was hurting him, Garrison asked the jury at the end of the trial to find the defendant guilty of assault in the second degree but not guilty of assault in the first degree. He also asked the jury to find his client not guilty of robbery in the first degree, but guilty of stealing. Finally, he said Anthony Hill did not rape Ruth Taylor and the jury should find him not guilty because the rape didn't happen.

For the State, prosecutor Sinclair began evidence presentation with testimony from the responding police officer who arrived first at the crime scene. Paul Thilges, a five-year veteran for the KCPD described how he found the victim on the floor bleeding and surrounded by broken glass. He gave a list of injuries he observed that included cuts on her right eye, right lip, and swelling on her entire face. The thirty-year-old officer added that the victim gave him a description of her attacker and told him where they might find him. Sinclair ended her direct exam with a question about the victim's cognitive state. Thilges stated she seemed dazed but added that she spoke clearly and he was able to understand her.

Defense attorney Garrison cross-examined the officer with only a few questions. He reiterated the list of injuries to the officer and then asked if he noted any injuries that appeared to be a result of forcible rape or if the victim told him she was raped. Thilges stated he did not note any injuries indicative of rape and the victim told him only that a neighbor assaulted her.

Despite the different day, nothing else had changed inside the courtroom when Ruth's neighbor Sabrina Thomas took the stand on the second day. The bailiff had on the same brown deputy sheriff uniform, the staff shuffled through paperwork, and the attorneys wore suits that looked identical to the prior day. The clerk swore in Sabrina and advised her to sit in the witness chair. Just as she did for the detectives when they interviewed her, she identified the defendant as the same person she saw at the victim's residence and the same person she identified in the photo spread. She stated that although she was at her house for a good part of the day, she went home prior to the attack and took a nap. Sabrina continued and said that she learned of the incident when Trina woke her up by knocking on her window. She elaborated and indicated Trina was crying and very upset at the time.

Ruth's niece, Trina Rice testified right after Sabrina. The witness explicitly described Ruth's condition when she and her boyfriend found her. The jury listened intently as Trina indicated the victim had blood all over her body, her breasts were exposed, appeared to have bite marks on them, and her robe was ripped and pushed above her waist. She added that the victim did not have on a bra or panties. Trina continued and stated when she talked to Ruth, she said, *"It was that Anthony, Alma's nephew."* Trina told the jury they called 911, but didn't stay too long after that. Trina indicated and that she didn't remember what happened after the police and ambulance arrived and didn't remember if she gave a statement to the detectives.

Garrison cross-examined both Sabrina and Trina and asked them very similar questions. To Sabrina, he asked if Trina indicated that the victim was raped when she came over to her house to tell what happened. To Trina, he asked if Ruth indicated she was raped but also questioned her about her recollection of talking to the detectives. Both witnesses denied receiving specific information concerning whether or not a sexual assault occurred. In her cross examination, Trina reiterated she could not remember if the detectives interviewed her and that she was on heavy medication since the event.

The police didn't formally interview Trina's boyfriend, Billy Francis but the prosecution added him to their witness list. Billy testified that he and Trina stopped by Ruth's house, found the front door unusually locked and heard moans coming from inside. He elaborated and stated they got inside through the back door and found her on the floor surrounded by blood and glass. LeVota asked the witness to describe the victim's clothing. Billy indicated the victim's nightgown had been partially torn off and pulled up around her hips and added that her bra had been ripped off and her breasts were exposed. The witness went on and stated that out of respect for Ruth, he covered her up and then called for an ambulance.

Public Defender Garrison had been fortunate in his cross examination up to this point because he got all of the witnesses to say that Ruth never said that she had been raped. However, Billy Francis testified to the contrary. Billy told the jury that after Trina left to go get Sabrina, Ruth told him that *"Anthony tried to rape me."* When asked why he had never told anyone that, he said that the police never talked about it and he just assumed that Ruth would have told the police and he didn't want to embarrass her.

The next witness was Ruth's sister Dorothy but it took some time to get Dorothy Hayes to the stand. The elderly witness was waiting on a different floor to testify and needed some assistance. The judge gave the jury a ten-minute break while the court administrator helped get her into the courtroom. Sinclair made sure the Dorothy was secure in the witness chair and close to the microphone before she administered her questions.

Counsel asked the witness to recount the events of the day that led up to her sister being attacked. Dorothy spoke slowly and often had long pauses between sentences but explained that the defendant came over three separate times. He came by in the morning when Ruth was gone picking up her prescriptions with

Trina and Billy. He came by a second time after Ruth came home and was visiting with her neighbor, Sabrina Thomas. And he came by again after Sabrina left.

Dorothy stated she was in and out of her bedroom throughout the day to cook and eat, but eventually went back into her room and took a nap. Sinclair inquired as to when and what awakened her. Dorothy responded that she woke up when she heard her sister calling for help and found her on the floor surrounded by broken glass with her housecoat above her knees.

Sinclair told Dorothy that she needed to remember what she saw when she first came out of her bedroom and first saw her sister in the dining room. Dorothy described Ruth as sitting up, covered in blood, with glass in her hair and around her on the floor. She was then asked if she saw the defendant when she came out to help her sister. Dorothy stated she saw a back of his tennis shoes as he ran out the door but then paused and indicated that the shoes she remembered must have belonged to Trina's boyfriend because they arrived at the same time she found her sister.

Like Officer Thilges and Trina Rice, Dorothy graphically itemized her sister's injuries but added that she noticed a bruise to Ruth's neck in addition to a shoe imprint on her throat. The prosecutor had one last question for her witness before the defense attorney cross-examined her. For affect, she asked her if she remembered how long her sister was in the hospital. Dorothy looked directly at the jury and indicated that the defendant put her sister in the hospital for approximately three weeks.

In Dorothy's testimony, LeVota realized that there was an inconsistency in Dorothy's direct examination. Dorothy said that she was awakened by her sister crying and she got up and found Ruth. However, Trina said that she and her boyfriend found Ruth and then woke Dorothy. LeVota saw that Sinclair also realized the minor contradiction and quickly moved off the irrelevant issue.

Frankly, it had no merit to the guilt or innocence of the defendant and it could be Dorothy misspeaking but Sinclair was correct to move on and not swell on it. But would the defense attorney?

During his cross exam, the defense reviewed a similar format of questions as his opposing counsel did and Dorothy reiterated similar answers. Garrison asked if she thought there was anything abnormal about his client or his behavior and Dorothy indicated his behavior was ordinary. Garrison moved away from the conduct of defendant prior to the attack and again shifted his focus to the appearance of the victim. He asked the witness if she remembered if her sister's breasts were exposed when she found her. Dorothy stated she could not remember if her breasts were exposed. Garrison didn't touch on the "who found Ruth" issue and later confessed to the prosecution that it didn't matter and he didn't want the jury to think he was badgering sweet Dorothy.

LeVota, a veteran trial attorney and prosecutor, normally exhibited the power of smooth and influential dialogue. However he had a very difficult time prior to the trial persuading his most important witnesses to speak up and testify against her perpetrator. However, despite her fears, Ruth took the stand on June 16 and bravely testified against Hill. Her droopy smile caused by an injury from her assailant was obvious as she sat in the witness chair. Ruth acknowledged she knew the defendant and then pointed in the direction of the defense table and identified Hill as the one wearing the green shirt.

Ruth told the jury she remembered it was still daylight and she was visiting and drinking coffee with a neighbor when the defendant stopped by and asked to use her bathroom. She described his clothes and the baseball cap he wore on the day of the attack and told the jury how he came out of the bathroom with his pants unzipped. It was clear that Ruth wanted to tell her story as quickly as she could and get off that stand.

However, her prosecutor wasn't going to let her off that easy because this was now about the jury and how they digested the evidence and her testimony. They would only get one shot at it so LeVota continued to slow Ruth down and back her up in his questions. LeVota directed her to tell her story in chronological order and focused in on questions concerning incidents before the attack. He methodically went through the minutia of the day and each step that would lead up to the attack. LeVota asked his witness if she remembered the defendant asking her for money. Ruth paused for a minute as if to summon the memory but then stated she could not remember that event.

When Ruth said she couldn't remember the defendant asking for money, LeVota knew she was becoming emotional. He apologized for the difficult questions but asked her to continue and tell the jury what happened when the defendant came out of her bathroom.

Ruth composed herself and testified the defendant grabbed and choked her and that she attempted to defend herself by grabbing his testicles. Auntie Ruth said, "*I grabbed at his balls because it was all I could do.*" She added that the defendant choked her so hard that it snapped her necklace. She then described how she fell to the floor as she tried to free herself from his grip and how Hill reached over with his left hand and grabbed her fruit bowl off her table. Ruth used her hands to show how she grabbed the defendant's groin and the size of the bowl he smashed over her head.

LeVota asked the witness if she remembered the defendant attempting to cut her neck with glass from the broken bowl. Ruth admitted that she passed out and there were many things she couldn't recall but stated she did remember seeing a cut on her neck in the hospital bathroom mirror. Ruth elaborated

249

about the injury to her neck and stated it appeared to look like someone had sawed on it. She continued and described all of her injuries, surgeries, and stitches. She was very open describing her head fractures and broken eye sockets,

But when LeVota approached the witness about the abrasions on the inside of her thighs and the pain and injuries to the inside of her vaginal walls, she denied remembering anything except painful urination. This 78 year old sweet woman was so embarrassed she hardly could even speak. These would be difficult questions and LeVota had not asked her these questions in the pre-trial. As they started talking about the topic, Ruth became increasingly anxious.

LeVota knew he was about to make Ruth even more uncomfortable but he had to get these questions and her answers in front of the jury. If he erred on the side of "being polite" to Ruth and not impose on her, the jury would not hear the evidence of the rape. He had to push on regardless of Ruth's apprehension.

LeVota asked if the hospital employees ever completed a rape kit on her. The witness indicated they had but they never gave her the results or told her the injuries were consistent with sexual assault. Ruth reiterated that she didn't remember being sexually assaulted but conceded it was a possibility as she was unconscious during part of her attack. Through her testimony and then introducing graphic photos into evidence, LeVota forced Ruth to relive her nightmare to the jury.

LeVota showed her pictures of herself lying in the hospital bed with her eyes swollen shut and stitches covering her face. These were pictures he had not shown her in her pre-trial. Ruth's eyes welled up with tears as LeVota handed her a box of Kleenex. LeVota showed her the actual necklace that she was wearing the day of the attack that Anthony Hill ripped off her neck. Ruth looked through the pictures of herself and her voice cracked with emotion as she told LeVota she had never seen them before but identified the necklace as the same one she wore when she was attacked. She admitted that she willingly let Hill into her home but added she didn't know he was capable of harming her. Although she told LeVota she had tried to forget the ordeal and get on with her life, she also said she felt sorry for the defendant and his family.

On cross examination, public defender Jeff Garrison handed Ruth another tissue and let the witness compose herself before he started his cross. Garrison focused hard on what Ruth couldn't remember and she admitted that she didn't remember being punched, kicked, slapped, or sexually assaulted. With the tissue, she dabbed at the corners of her eyes and listened as the attorney revisited the condition of the defendant's pants as he exited her bathroom. He asked her if his pants were down, unbuckled, or only unzipped. She indicated they were unzipped but she couldn't remember if they were unbuckled. Garrison continued and asked if the defendant's penis was visible. Ruth's expression became very serious. She firmly answered the attorney's question and told him that it was not visible.

In question form, Garrison reiterated to the witness the statement she gave to police that she didn't remember being raped and then he focused on what she was wearing. LeVota was furious that the defense attorney would even ask a question about what she was wearing in her own home in a rape case and before he could formulate what an objection might be, he looked to his jury.

Before he stood up and made that objection, LeVota looked long and hard at the jury because that is what trials are about. And when he looked at the jury as Garrison finished the question about her attire, he saw several jurors with the same disdainful look on their faces that he had. LeVota knew he didn't need to do a thing. This jury got it. In answering the question,

Ruth described the housecoat, bra, and panties she wore but when asked if she remembered if they were off her body when she regained consciousness, Ruth, once again, admitted she couldn't remember.

Ruth had completed her testimony and her ordeal was done. In the only way to hold this defendant accountable for his crimes, she had to come into open court and be re-victimized again. It was sad and disheartening but Ruth summoned the courage to do it. Ruth collected herself and stood up. She walked slowly from the witness stand to the door as she was released from her trial responsibilities. As amazing as it was, she even had a smile on her face as she left the courtroom.

LeVota started his direct examination of Charles Johnson like all of the other witnesses and asked him to introduce himself. He then asked the veteran crime scene technician to tell the jury how his job compared to what the popular TV show, CSI depicted. Johnson explained that unlike the television program, which implies crime scene technicians interrogate suspects, they actually only take photos and collect evidence.

Johnson testified and gave an itemized list of the photos he took and evidence he collected. LeVota helped support his statements and presented some of the photos that he took including a close up pictures of the ball cap, broken glass recovered at the scene, and the victim's blood. He also presented two sealed bags and asked the witness to identify the contents for the jury. Johnson dug deep in to the bags and retrieved a large piece of sharp glass that was still covered in blood and fingerprint dust, a baseball cap, and fingerprint cards lifted from those items. Johnson named them as the same ones he collected at the crime scene.

Johnson waited in the witness chair while LeVota put additional photos on a large tri-pod to the left of the witness stand. He asked the witness to step down and address them individually. He looked at each of the pictures of the victim in her hospital bed and specifically identified each injury and where they were located on her body. He elaborated and stated he took the pictures the same day of the assault, packaged them, and sent them and all the other evidence to their proper areas. Johnson added that he went back out to the victim's residence a week later to look for evidence of sexual assault but was unable to recover any evidence.

The defense took up where the prosecution left off and re-asked Johnson if he found any evidence of semen at either visit to the crime scene. The witness indicated they did not look for it during the initial visit and did not find any on the subsequent visit. Garrison knew the technician's testimony slanted heavily in his direction and hoped to score extra points with the jury when he asked if he took pictures of the rash or abrasions on the inside of the victim's thighs. Johnson admitted he was not aware or told of any injuries or skin issues to that area on the victim.

The prosecution's next witness, Detective Errol Wiggins gave his version of the events and the jury listened to a story similar to the two prior witnesses. Wiggins described the condition of the victim's home and her injuries as he remembered them from interviewing her in the hospital. He explained that while they interviewed her, they showed her an exact replica of the photo spread they showed Sabrina Thomas and the victim identified the defendant as the suspect.

The prosecutor asked the detective what their role with the victim was after they interviewed her. Wiggins indicated they kept in touch with her to check on her condition but also responded back to the hospital when they obtained information from the nursing staff about the possibility of a sexual assault.

253

Wiggins added they had the hospital perform a rape kit to aid in their investigation.

On cross examination, Garrison's questions to Wiggins were not unlike the ones he asked the prior witness. He asked if when he learned of the alleged assault and the related injuries of swelling and bruising within the victim's vaginal walls, did he see them personally, or did he take any pictures. The detective stated that they did not see or take any pictures of the victim. Garrison also revisited and reviewed the detective's witness statements. Individually, the attorney asked if Ruth Taylor, Sabrina Thomas, or Trina Rice had told him anything about a. Wiggins indicated there was no mention of sexual assault by any of those witnesses.

For better or for worse, Ruth Taylor forgot many of the horrible things the defendant did to her. However, it was the State's job to prove their case despite all those misplaced details and with statements taken from the victim. By the State's next witness, Detective Williams, LeVota tried to fill in many of the open gaps, despite many objections from opposing counsel.

LeVota asked the witness to read specific parts off the hand-written papers. As directed, the detective read word for word specific questions he had asked the victim and the answers she gave. During the interviews that were taken inside her hospital room, Ruth was able to recall that the defendant asked her for money and that he cut her neck. Through the review of her in-hospital interview, the jury heard what Ruth remembered back then and not what possibly her embarrassment and months of time had made her forget.

Garrison's cross examination was short as he asked to refer to the part of the interview where the detective asked whether she remembered being touched in her pelvic area. He read the specific section, which indicated the victim did not recall being touched in that area. Garrison was still fighting for the *"there was no rape"* defense and not worrying about the evidence of the assault or theft because he defended the assault as self-defense for Ruth grabbing his clients groin and the defense had already stipulated to the theft.

Gathering enough good evidence and presenting a solid case to a jury is less complicated when the suspect is careless and leaves good fingerprints and DNA at the scene. Kathleen Hentges, an expert fingerprint examiner for the KCPD, testified that fingerprints found on a large piece of glass and a piece of jewelry found at the crime scene matched Anthony Hill's fingerprints.

Another interesting piece of evidence was presented by Senior Criminalist, DarVene Duvenci. She testified that a single dandruff flake found inside a baseball cap was forwarded for her analysis and she used genetic profiling (DNA) from both Anthony Hill and Ruth Taylor as comparison. Remarkably, the piece of dandruff tested 99.7% positive as that of Anthony Hill. However, she also indicated that she found no sexual assault evidence from the rape kit submitted to her but added that finding a positive test for semen or detecting sperm cells after twelve hours was rare and most likely impossible after 6 or 7 days.

Garrison didn't touch the DNA conclusion of the dandruff because it was probably one of the main reasons the defense used the strategy they did of admitting to everything but the rape. There was way too much evidence that Anthony Hill was in that house and attacked Ruth. But Garrison did reiterate to the jury on cross examination that the DNA expert did not find any of Anthony Hill's DNA in the rape kit.

Next up for the prosecution was Patricia Lohe, the primary care nurse, who testified to the victim's condition on the night the ambulance brought her to St. Luke's Hospital. She indicated the linear bruising to her neck was consistent with the victim's statement that she was choked and the extensive bleeding and bruising was consistent with someone who was severely beaten.

To explain to the jury about the process of sexual assault investigation and kits, LeVota called Connie Brogan, a sexual assault nurse manager to the stand. Ms. Brogan testified and detailed the steps of a sexual assault kit and then specifically the sexual assault exam she completed on Ruth on her sixth day in the hospital. She explained that in every sexual assault kit she takes blood and hair samples, performs a pelvic exam, and swabs for DNA. She stated she did all of those with Ruth.

She described that during the process Ruth was pleasant and agreeable but also indicated that Ruth often changed the subject when she tried to get her to talk about the alleged sexual assault. Brogan indicated that at first, she was hesitant to do the exam on Ruth because most foreign DNA is gone after seventy-two hours; however, she noted that the victim had friction burns on the inside of her thighs and tearing and bruising within her vaginal vault. Brogan elaborated and indicated that the friction burns were indicative of something rough being rubbed back and forth between her legs and the tears inside her vagina were consistent with something being put inside her and moved back and forth and it was way too violent to be consistent with consensual intercourse.

Any real direct evidence surrounding Anthony Hill's forcible rape was weak and Garrison wanted to broadcast that and make it crystal clear to the jury. When he crossed Duvenci, he asked if she found his client's DNA in the vaginal swab. Duvenci indicated that she did a presumptive test on the swab under a microscope, which did not indicate the presence of semen so she didn't send it for DNA testing. When he cross examined Patricia Lohe, Garrison addressed Augmentin, a medicine Ruth was on in the hospital and asked her if she realized that a side effect of that medication was rashes. Lohe admitted that one of the side effects was a rash but it normally presented itself all over the body and not just in between the thighs. Garrison followed up her answer and asked if it was possible for the rash to be localized. The witness responded that it was possible.

Garrison's last opportunity to impress the jury on cross examination was with Connie Brogan. Using a list of closed-ended questions and her report to refresh her memory, he set the nurse up to fill the jury with impressionable doubt about the guilt of his client. Through the nurse, he verified the victim was on Augmentin. Garrison then asked if the victim indicated if her attacker used any weapons or foreign objects. Brogan studied her report stated the victim indicated she did not know if they were used.

The defense continued and inquired if Ruth had told her if she remembered if penetration or ejaculation occurred. Brogan again referred back to her report and replied that the victim stated she was unsure of both. Garrison had just two more questions before the judge released the last witness. He asked if the victim agreed to the sexual assault exam and if she ever indicated that she was sexually assaulted. Brogan stated that the exam was voluntary but she never stated she was sexually assaulted. That was the last question of the last witness in the trial of *The State of Missouri v. James Anthony Hill*.

In their closing arguments, Prosecuting Attorneys LeVota and Sinclair indicated they wanted nothing but justice for their seventy-eight-year-old victim of unspeakable crimes. Sinclair told the jury that James Hill planned the brutal robbery and rape that placed Ruth Taylor in the intensive care unit for a very long time. She reviewed the long list of injuries the defendant caused before he left her for dead on her own dining room floor. She told them how he rendered his victim unconscious and then raped her. Sinclair then closed her half of closing argument by urging the jury not to give the defendant credit for beating Ruth so terribly that she couldn't remember him raping her.

The defense closed its case without the testimony of the accused but stressed the physical evidence was not indicative of rape. Garrison pointed out that no one in the hospital staff observed any signs that would cause them to suspect sexual assault and all of the witnesses were consistent in their statements in that Ruth Taylor never said she was raped. He advised the jury that his client was right handed and the evidence indicated he used his left hand to grab the bowl. Garrison elaborated and clarified that his client hit Ruth with the bowl out of reflex because she had a hold of his testicles. Garrison declared his client didn't intend to seriously harm her and that he just wanted her to let go. He asserted the defendant acted recklessly and did not intend to harm or rob her with the bowl.

LeVota got the last word in the prosecution's last half of closing argument. It would be the last thing the jury would hear from the attorneys. LeVota meticulously explained the charges against Hill and the elements that must be proven for the jury to find him guilty of each. He talked about the difference between assault in the first degree and assault in the second degree. LeVota insisted that the jurors heard the evidence and that they knew that Hill didn't act recklessly in harming Ruth. He talked about the difference between robbery and theft and he sarcastically implored the jury not to buy the defense's "I only hit her because she grabbed my balls" defense! The defendant smashed her in the head with a heavy glass bowl and then he kicked and punched her in the face with his feet and hands. As Ruth succumbed to the brutal beating, she fell and then he raped her.

LeVota told the jury that Anthony Hill came out of that bathroom with his pants undone fully intending to rape and assault the woman the whole neighborhood called Auntie Ruth.

LeVota wrapped up his closing argument with, *"You must return the only verdict that the evidence proves and justice demands. A guilty verdict on all counts. The State of Missouri awaits your verdict."*

Ruth Taylor had been at the trial every day but waited upstairs in the prosecutor's office until the end of each day where she got her update. She could have been in the courtroom after her testimony but she didn't want to but did want to be in the building. After the closing arguments, LeVota walked into his office where Ruth was sitting. LeVota explained the process and what the defense strategy was to try to get just a second degree assault and a theft and no rape. LeVota told Ruth he was confident that the jury would come back with the first degree assault and armed criminal action as well as the robbery but he wasn't as confident with the rape.

The last thing LeVota wanted to do is to explain that the main reason that they might not find him guilty of the rape was that she just didn't remember. And as if Auntie Ruth was reading LeVota's mind she said to Phil, *"You know I'm not worried about the rape part but he needs to go to prison for a while for what he did to me."* Before LeVota could even respond, Auntie Ruth pulled out a Tupperware container with some of her homemade stew that she had made for what she called her "prosecution angels." LeVota doesn't remember much about the rest of the day because the judge sent the jury home to come back and deliberate the next day but he did remember that it was the best stew he had ever had. Also, he didn't share any of it.

Twelve jurors did their job and listened to four days of testimony and they took their time deliberating the case. The prosecution knew the jury would come back with at least some sort of guilty verdict. The prosecution believed there was no question that Hill raped Ruth but the evidence was not as great as it could have been. While the jury was out, the defense asked to plea to second degree assault if the state would dismiss the rape charge. LeVota said no deal. The prosecutor was passionate that Hill should be held accountable for all of his actions.

Finally, when the jury returned with their verdicts, they found James Anthony Hill guilty of assault in the first degree, robbery in the first degree, and armed criminal action. However, they found him not guilty of forcible rape and the armed criminal action associated with that rape charge. In speaking with the jurors after, they told LeVota that they all believed that Hill raped Ruth but they were following their oath to find him guilty only if the evidence was beyond a reasonable doubt and they didn't have enough evidence. The jurors knew that the convictions on the other charges would put him away for a while so they were fine with the rape count.

Like she told LeVota, Ruth was ok not getting a conviction on the rape but she wanted him to go away for a long time. On August 9, 2004, as Ruth Taylor sat in the courtroom, Judge Vernon Scoville sentenced Hill to thirty years for each of the three counts. James Anthony Hill would be going away for a long time for what he did to Ruth Taylor. Hill is currently carrying out his sentence in the Jefferson City Correctional Facility.

5

His Name Was Murder

A person's name can be an invaluable gift, albeit an intangible one. Often not easily recognized by its owner, a good name is a precious commodity and possibly a positive contribution to ones' future; however, a poorly chosen name can be a set up for failure. Unfortunately, not all parents are sharp enough to appreciate the power of a name and the influence it can have on one's life opportunities.

One of the first and most important jobs one has as a parent is naming their child. Parents spend months or even years planning on a name. Some mothers have picked out their child's name before they were old enough to even have children. Whether to name your kid after a saint, a celebrity, or something trendy are all questions the new parent must face because that name will identify that child for the rest of their life. Maybe you might name the child after a friend or family member, but whatever the parent does, there is usually some thought to it.

In Kansas City, in the 1980s, a young single mother was about to give birth to her baby boy and she was thinking about a name. As the woman was currently grieving over the loss of her recently murdered brother, it influenced her choice of names. On that wonderful day of birth as the nurse was asking all the pertinent questions, she came to the name. *"And what have you decided to name him?"* The nurse was a little taken aback when the mother said, *"His name is Murder,"* as the mother filled in the spot on the birth certificate.

The mother told the nurse the story about her murdered brother as a reason for the name and the nurse responded that maybe it might be better to just name the boy after his uncle, but mom declined. The nurse knew it was an awful decision but it wasn't her job to fight with mothers about the names of their children so she completed the paperwork and sent it off for the young boy to start his life with his new name of **"Murder Mitchell."**

"Murder" remained his legal first name until the Missouri Department of Social Services intervened when he was nine years old, legally changing his name from "Murder" to "Montea" (pronounced *Mon-tay*) which was the name of his murdered uncle who he was named for in the first place. For the state to get involved in this name change was extreme but there were too many reports of problems with this young boy and having his name be "Murder" seemed to be at the root of them. However, even after his name was changed, Montea Mitchell was never good at adapting to change and regardless of the reason for his name change; he chose a lifestyle pursuant to his former name.

Montea was the oldest of eight kids abandoned by their mother. All eight kids, under the age of seven, were left to be raised alone by their often out-of-work father in a small housing complex in Kansas City, Missouri. The stress, both physically and financially, of taking care of eight children was too much for one parent to bear so Montea and his younger brother Miguel helped take care of their six younger siblings. Huge responsibilities were unfairly placed upon the two oldest boys and, of the two, Montea was the most independent and self-sufficient. Regardless of his tender age, Montea embraced his unfortunate circumstances and took on many of the domestic tasks willingly and without guidance.

The conditions in which the nine Mitchells lived were severe. Their section-eight apartment located on 57th Street in Jackson County, Missouri was tiny for the amount of people that lived there. With the large family it was tight and depending on how much work the father was able to find, the apartment was often without heat or power on any given month.

Public housing seems to always be neglected by the rest of the city and it is one of the causes that crime rates spiked and allowed the complex to become a vibrant playground for criminal behavior. Montea and his siblings were often spectators to crimes that most kids only thought existed in movies. Nonetheless, the four-unit building with tan vinyl siding was what the nine family members called home. Yes it was home, until the Missouri Department of Social Services became involved and dissolved their family unit.

Montea's dad never wanted to give up his kids but after multiple calls from his neighbors to the child welfare division, a caseworker told him that the three-bedroom apartment was too small and he needed to find housing that was more adequate. Not able to find affordable and sufficient housing for his family, Montea's dad discussed his options with his caseworker who suggested he leave his kids with DFS until he found a more appropriate place for them to live. Thinking he made an unselfish choice for the welfare of his children, Montea's dad left his kids in the care of Jackson County Children's Division where they placed all eight in the custody of other family members and foster care homes. However, when it came time for Montea's dad to get his children back, he found it a goal he could never attain.

One of the most dangerous zip codes in America is located inside the limits of Kansas City, Missouri. It is a place where drugs and rebellion flourish. This harsh area of Kansas City is lined with small rundown houses and home values so low that

265

disadvantaged, law-abiding citizens cannot pass them up regardless of the constant criminal activity. The atmosphere makes the community appear dismal and dejected regardless of the weather. The unmaintained streets and fractured sidewalks are just another symbol of its brokenness. Like a powerful vacuum, a criminal mentality hovers over this several square mile area and sucks the innocent residents in and spits them back out as killers. This is where Montea "Murder" Mitchell lived and grew up.

Montea spent most of his childhood inside the boundaries of that tainted venue. The area known for its drug and gang related activity was often also known for murders, shootings, and assaults. It was a neighborhood that plagued everyone. For Montea, the combination of dangerous streets and a broken foster care system left the young man with little understanding of how to create a stable life for himself and a diluted idea that only limited options existed. However, despite his early socialization in the criminal atmosphere and his own certainty of restricted opportunities, he was much smarter than he gave himself credit. Unfortunately, Montea often lacked the capacity to see the true nature of a circumstance. Montea's lack of insight was extreme and was the flaw that eventually derailed his life.

Despite all of his troubles, Montea was resourceful. It was a learned behavior as he was alone a great deal from the time after he left the apartment on 57th Street. Social Services placed Montea in multiple foster and group homes over the years, but like most kids removed from their natural environment, he became angry, resistant of change, and rebelled by running away. Montea was on the run more often than not. He rarely knew the luxury of a warm bed or reliable transportation, but one thing he did know was the city's streets. When Montea was not in foster care, he learned the streets of Kansas City while looking for food or an abandoned shelter for which to sleep,

Through all the uncertainty in his life, one thing remained constant about Montea and that was his independence. However, Montea's self-governing personality evolved into constant control battles with authority figures as well as peers and he struggled with getting along with almost everyone. After a few years of being in the system, Montea began to completely rebel and defy authority. He filled his school records with incidents of defiance, fighting, stealing, and threats to classmates and teachers. Montea despised any type of structured setting trying to govern his behavior and truancy became more of a lifestyle than an occasional act of mischief.

Regardless of their honorable objectives, the social organizations in which Montea was placed under deprived him of the natural family support to which many other people are entitled. But Montea also deprived himself of those same entitlements by his choice to ignore those institutions. Nevertheless, without a support system, Montea sought out his necessary physical and emotional requirements on the city's streets and unfortunately became reliant on unnatural and devastating substitutes of bad friends, bad habits, and bad decisions.

These stand-ins did nothing good for Montea's character and in effect expanded upon his already rebellious nature. Montea would quietly feel sorry for himself and blame others for his problems but truth be told, many young men are born to the same circumstances and work to better themselves to be productive members of society and do not get into trouble. Montea may have had a hard life, but a tough childhood in a bad area does not excuse later criminal activity.

Montea thought living on the streets and depending on himself was considerably better than living in an unfamiliar and controlling environment but one thing he didn't like about the streets was the cold. Warmer temperatures made it easier for him to sleep as well as walk to the places he needed to go. Montea eventually associated summers with freedom and comfort. However, as he grew older he drew pleasure from other things. Montea's definition of "freedom and comfort" became not only applicable to warm weather and easier foot travel but he discovered cigarettes were good time passers.

Later, he found that alcohol and drugs worked like a warm blanket on the cold hard floors where he often had to sleep. School and a place to call home are building blocks for one's future but by the spring of 2000, Montea had been in too many foster homes and kicked out of too many schools to count. His bad reputation for opposition and defiance limited his future options and reduced his character building opportunities even further. For Montea, it was too-little-too-late to mitigate life's damages to the already hardened juvenile.

A sad statistic is that 25% percent of foster kids not adopted by the time they turn eighteen end up in jail within two years or at least that's what Montea's social worker told him. However, Montea did not care about statistics or the social worker that provided him with that data. Drugs and thievery had found their way into Montea's complicated life. Despite his defiant history, his involvement in those things had been relatively minor. Nevertheless, his choice set in motion a vehicle which was paramount to his future housing options and eventually led him to become one of the sample subjects by which those foster care statistics were gauged. However, it was not until the summer of Montea's seventeenth birthday that his offenses evolved and went from infrequent and small to serious and reoccurring. In a relatively small period of time, Montea became involved in serious crime and misbehaving that went way outside the norm of adolescent mischief.

The summer of 2000 was a mirror image of summers-gone-by in Kansas City. Kids and teens anticipated the getting out of school for months and the freedom of staying up late and sleeping in but no sooner than their vacation began, they complain of boredom. Parents tried to satisfy their children's complaints with swimming pools and water parks as a way to keep their children busy and out of trouble. The water and sun has a history of magically satisfying both kids and adults alike and parents took advantage of that rarely occurring phenomenon most every summer.

Montea's ritual of walking had always been a habit of necessity and not a chosen behavior. He seldom had any money to ride the bus. The extreme heat that summer was almost too much for even him so the outdoor swimming pool at a local community center became his favorite location. Almost daily, he walked in the scorching heat and humidity to the packed facility and hung out by the door. He would look for an inattentive parent paying for a group of kids and blend his way onto the pool grounds.

Montea was up to no good when he was there and so were DonMarr and Albert. Seventeen-year-old DonMarr Reneeson and seventeen-year-old Albert Allen were cousins but they did not even know that until the end of their first year of high school. They had lived in the same dangerous neighborhood since grade school but the news that they were family gave them a connection and a reason to hang out together. The two became friends, alliances, and deviant business entrepreneurs the very year they met.

At the pool all three had a common goal of earning a paycheck, but it wasn't as a lifeguard. They would steal their wages. DonMarr and Albert were two drug dealers-in-training and had attempted to avoid trespassing on other dealer's turf. The young men tried out their skills as freelance sellers at the

269

crowded water center when they met Montea in his self-employment endeavors as a common thief. DonMarr and Albert recognized Montea from a fight he had recently been involved in and knew of his aggressive history. In an effort to sidestep any issues, DonMarr convinced Montea that a partnership was the best way to do their business. Montea had no skills at selling drugs but as luck would have it, drug selling required minimal talent.

Group selling was not a normal practice but the three felt their union was a good way to protect their territory and since their objective was the same, it seemed it would be a fortunate venture. That particular business adventure was just one of the many missions the three young men would undertake during the next few months. However, it was the last time that Montea would allow DonMarr to be the organizer of any other plans. From that point, Montea was the mastermind of all their schemes.

Without transportation, the packed pool grounds offered the young men an advantage of doing business in a single venue. It became their pot of gold. Not every paying pool customer was a paying customer of theirs, but many of people who gathered there certainly made it a one-stop shopping arena for the trio. When people weren't looking, the three black teens rummaged through bags that weren't theirs. They were rookie criminals that summer and they specialized in marijuana, crack, and theft.

One of their most successful tactics was while one was preoccupying a buyer with the illegal exchange of drugs, the other two would pilfer through the unsupervised pool bags of the very same client. Unfortunately, the drug buyers were not the trio's only targets that summer. They also took advantage of all the unsuspecting patrons and their unguarded gear as well as unlocked cars. The exploits at the community center were successful for the entire summer but when school restarted, Montea's business relationship with DonMarr and Albert, as well as his source of income, came to a screeching halt.

The swimming pool gig worked well in keeping the youth occupied but by the time the Labor Day Weekend celebration was over and the pools closed, most of the city's young had traded their swimming suits for new school clothes and backpacks.

Skipping school and stupidity generally go hand in hand and Montea had little to motivate him to attend class. Living in his precarious neighborhood, Montea had known his share of shifty people and he had seen first-hand an unfortunate amount of criminal activity. For some, those occurrences would prove to be a lifestyle one would choose not to partake in; however, the beginning of the school term, he used those experiences as training tools. Fine tuning his criminal activity was his new "class" time trying to rebuild a similar business that went so well in the summer. The ill-advised teen did not see his decision to skip school as brainless choice but more as a smart business decision. The small taste of the summer's revenue planted a seed of delusion in Montea's mind.

The promise of easy cash from the sale of crack and stolen goods sounded much more lucrative to Montea than any legitimate job he could find. Not surprisingly though, his call to blow off school did not pay off as he had planned and, despite his rebellious efforts, his ill-gotten gains were minimal.

Montea found that getting to his destinations of dishonesty was problematic and did not want to steal from his own neighborhood but found walking was time consuming and limiting. As many people often do, he placed the blame of his failures on two things; his lack of transportation and lack of good help in his crimes. He never blamed his failures on his own bad choices. Unfortunately, Montea's lack of accountability was another personality flaw that helped drive him toward a deadly pattern of bad decision-making.

Montea saw the unfairness of this cycle and he took it personally. His solution was to handle the unjust life event just as he had been handling most other things and act out unlawfully. To Montea, crime was a way of making retribution to the world that had been unfair to him. Montea's constant rebellion towards social institutions allowed him to make no concessions in the current direction of his life or the tradition of school.

By the last week of summer, the upcoming exchange of seasons replaced Kansas City's green lawns with blankets of leaves and only a mere taste of the green foliage was left. Montea knew his warm days were numbered and he dreaded the discomfort of the approaching weather. A near obsession to increase his income combined with the anxiety of the impending winter instigated an idea in Montea's greedy mind. Exercising his right to crime's versatility, his thoughts ventured outside the narrow world of crimes of which he was already familiar. A plan simmered in his head and it was a plan he thought would surely maximize his income and decrease the time and energy he used to produce it.

Montea, like most criminals, could not ignore a moneymaking opportunity and on the morning of September 21, 2000, he expanded his felonious resume to include car theft. His history of being a savvy businessman was less than dazzling but he believed his idea would lead him down a money making path. He had a scheme and he had partners in crime so now he just had to put it all into motion.

DonMarr and Albert were not the most educationally inclined students, but they attended class on most days. Central Senior High School was located directly across the street from a pristine Christian church. It had an almost prestigious boarding school appearance with a two-story, stone frame, and green manicured lawn. Any unknowing passerby could easily be deceived into thinking just that by its well-kept perimeters.

However, the inside was much less than that of a snobby preparatory school.

The inside, just like the outside, was just as deceiving. Security guards and metal detectors blocked the entrance into the cold gray hallways and all who entered the building were first subject to inspection. However, the security measures set in place did little to control the students, including DonMarr and Albert as they roamed the unsupervised hallways, smoked cigarettes, and sold drugs in the bathrooms.

Montea anxiously killed time on that warm and sunny day by waiting for DonMarr and Albert outside the school. In his head, he worked on his plan as he sat on a stone fence located directly across the street. Regardless of the amount of disorder inside, he knew Central High did not tolerate loitering on the school grounds so to avoid any type of interruption of his plan, he waited on the much more forgiving church property instead.

When the last school bell rang, Montea met DonMarr and Albert as they walked off the school grounds. It took some convincing but as the men walked South on Cleveland towards Montea's home, he explained his business proposal and the persuasion of one evolved into the evil intentions of three. Montea was the sole proprietor of the idea but DonMarr helped facilitate Montea's plan. DonMarr contributed to the design by diverting them in the direction of his friend's home on Montgall Avenue. It was not as much of a diversion as it was a schedule change for DonMarr and Albert, as they already had plans at the residence on Montgall.

Thursday was the day the two friends replenished their product for the next week's market. The teens walked and talked the idea down the deteriorating streets, stopping once to buy cigarettes from a small convenience store before they arrived at their destination. The men had travelled a mere ten blocks but by

273

the time they arrived at 4144 Montgall, Montea's bad idea had turned into a life-threatening scheme.

Daylight Savings Time was several weeks away and several hours of daylight were still ahead of them when they knocked on the door at 4:30 in the afternoon. From the outside, the residence looked maintained and clean, unlike many of the homes in that area. The house was old but the lawn was green and flawlessly edged. White wooden pillars framed a swept and clutter-free porch of the same color. A brown and tan stone-wall wrapped the bottom half of the house and a red porch swing gave accent to the exterior's earthy colors. But the inviting exterior was far from the standard in that area.

Countless other homes in that vicinity were in disrepair and neglected and the worst of those were often targets of the police for suspected drug activity. However, this house appeared immune from that epidemic and while the owner's plan to aim the light of investigation in someone else's direction might have fooled some, the misleading exterior did not deceive DonMarr and Albert. They had been there before.

A young black male who DonMarr and Albert only knew as "Smoke" met them at the door dressed in a sleeveless, white ribbed t-shirt and jeans. The shades were drawn and the inside was dark. It took some time for their eyes adjust but even in the shaded room, there was a distinct, sweet smell of recently cooked crack and the herb-like odor of marijuana. Montea figured out quickly why they called him "Smoke" when they followed him from the front door through a hallway with sticky, smoke stained walls and into the kitchen. Smoke opened a handle-less, brown cabinet door and pulled out a red coffee can. The container resembled an unopened can of Folgers coffee but was actually a 'can safe' full of pre-packaged crack. Smoke had no questions for DonMarr and handed him a bundle of bags of crack in exchange for fistful of cash. Smoke stuffed the cash inside the canister, replaced it, and closed the cabinet door. Smoke then grabbed a cheap bottle of rum, opened the bottle, and handed to DonMarr. DonMarr pushed the drugs down into his jeans pocket with one hand and accepted the bottle with the other. The four passed the bottle around until it was empty.

The fact that the house was set up as a drug distribution site did not shock Montea; however, the elaborate arrangement in the small room did surprise him. Multiple cabinets housed scales, bulks of plastic bags, and chemicals for packaging and cooking. A large safe about the size of a refrigerator slid into an area that appeared to be an old pantry with the shelves and the door removed. The safe was flush with the walls and was stained like the old flowered wallpaper that was peeling around it. The four of them spent only a small amount of time in the kitchen before going into the main living area but the information Montea gathered from those few moments told a very detailed story.

A brown particle board coffee table covered with plastic baggies, empty soda cups, and ashtrays full of cigarette butts sat in front of an old L-shaped, black sectional. They made small talk as Smoke motioned for them to sit down and the four men spaced themselves between exposed springs on the torn leather. With a quick swipe of his arm, Smoke moved the majority of the debris onto the floor and replaced it with a plastic, red Budweiser tray he pulled from underneath the couch. Displayed neatly on the tray was a purple Crown Royal bag filled with marijuana and related paraphernalia. Montea, DonMarr, and Albert watched as Smoke spread green sticky clumps out on the table before crumbling one and packing some of it inside the silver bowl of a glass water pipe.

Buying drugs from Smoke was a weekly routine for DonMarr and Albert but that day it was not the only thing on DonMarr's agenda. The four passed the bong back and forth while DonMarr discussed getting some items he had left there for Smoke to look after almost a year earlier. It was an easy request and without getting up or asking any questions, Smoke pulled a black canvas duffle bag from underneath the couch.

DonMarr retrieved a long rifle from the bag, checked its safety, and handed it to Montea to examine. DonMarr and Albert gathered a handful of bags and methodically packaged their rocks for individual sales. They watched Montea study the 12-gauge shotgun in awe. Montea was never one to admit his flaws or limitations but it was clear to everyone else that he was inexperienced in the safety of gun handling. He held the smooth brown stock up to his right shoulder and placed both hands on either side of the black barrel. He never thought to ask if the gun was loaded but DonMarr and Smoke knew it was. He pointed the gun straight out and let his right ring finger slide down the barrel and to the trigger and as his body pivoted slowly to the right and then back.

DonMarr, Albert, and Smoke all ducked for safety from the inexperienced gunman. All three yelled obscenities at Montea and Smoke jumped up and took the weapon from him. With a cigarette dangling from his mouth, Smoke stood in front of him and tried to give him a brief tutorial on proper gun handling. Montea's pride was much larger than his concern for safety and he refused Smoke's expert advice insisting that he knew what he was doing. Smoke took the gun and leaned the loaded weapon up against the end of the sofa.

The three stayed at the drug house until after dark. When they arrived that Thursday afternoon at the residence on Montgall, they were three young teenagers who had made some extremely bad choices but yet still had time to redeem themselves. However, when they left late that evening, they were armed and dangerous and at a point of no return.

At nine o'clock p.m., the men drunkenly walked north to DonMarr's house on South Benton carrying illegal drugs and a black bag. They were high and intoxicated but not prepared to stop partying. They left the bag at DonMarr's, walked down the street to a friend's house, and reconvened their partying. The large amount of inebriating substances depleted any inhibitions they may have had about their plan. After several more hours of partying, Montea convinced DonMarr and Albert it was time to leave. They made one final stop at DonMarr's house to collect one of the items they had left behind earlier that evening. They needed the shotgun and Montea slid the shotgun down the inside of his dark grey sweatpants. His oversized, black long-sleeved t-shirt helped cover it well. Unsure how the scheme would exactly play out, Albert grabbed a green handled, flathead screwdriver and shoved it in the back pocket of his jeans. At approximately midnight, the three set out to put their plan into action.

Debra Goodard had a history of picking the wrong type of men. Two times divorced, Debra found herself alone raising the children she had from each marriage. Each failed marriage started with a cheating husband and ended with a mandated order for child support; however, as her luck would have it, she rarely received her child support payments and struggled hard to raise her kids on one income. In 1999, when she was 45, the attractive black female was nursing the wounds of yet another failed relationship when she met Garland Hicks. Garland, or "Sonny" as he preferred, was a new employee at the same well-known cellular phone company as Debra and the two started dating immediately. She thought her days of bad guys and bad dating were forever behind her. Sonny seemed to be the perfect man.

Sonny was once an athlete. In high school, he excelled in basketball and football. Sonny even held multiple records in track and field. After high school, he played college football in Ohio and graduated with a B.A. in Social Services. But, sometime, between his record breaking sprints in high school and his job at Sprint in his mid-forties, his goals became distorted and way off track.

On September 22, 2000, the one-time Dallas Cowboy draft pick was far from where the talented athlete should have been when he drove his girlfriend's car down a deadly street in Jackson County. A whole host of bad decisions had led the talented football player away from his once very promising future and into the hopeless world of drug addiction. Fortunately, his decision to take a drive down Wabash Avenue was one of the last bad decisions Sonny would ever make.

At approximately one o'clock in the morning, the white economy car Sonny was driving traveled down Wabash Avenue, a street of which the driver was very familiar. Sonny drove slowly down the diseased section of the city and he was confident that there was someone waiting up ahead who wanted what he had in his wallet. He had made this drive many times and he knew just being on the street at this time meant he was a customer for those wanting to sell.

Even though it was after midnight, it was common for police to patrol the notorious neighborhood for suspicious activity. Not wanting to draw attention, Montea, DonMarr and Albert sat in an empty field on the west side of Wabash waiting for customers. The three were willing to sell what they had to any wanting customer; however, that evening they were waiting for a very specific type of customer. The wanted a customer with a car.

DonMarr and Albert knew that this open field that was located directly across the street from a string of houses always saw a lot of drug traffic. The men had been there and sold drugs there before. Thick bushes lined a small portion of the field and made it easy for the dealers to hide and watch for clientele and the buyers always knew where to stop and shop. The three black males were all purposely dressed in dark clothes and were hard to see on that last night of summer. And even harder to spot was the black and brown 12-gauge pump shotgun lying on a bed of leaves between Montea and Albert. The still drunk trio sat with their backs up against the bushes, passed a joint back and forth, and smoked cigarettes while they waited for their customers.

Albert and DonMarr were the most experienced in the drug-selling arena and they thought it was easy to spot crack addicts by their often-debilitated physical appearance and ragged clothes. Therefore, they were easy marks and easy sales. However, in the dark, these noticeable characteristics were hard to see but they were confident that only certain people would be out in the area this late at night. They remained behind the bushes exiting only to make a deal with those in serious need of their product.

DonMarr heard the vehicle before he actually saw the Topaz creep slowly towards them. Its slow speed was a clear sign that the driver was looking for something and DonMarr did not think it was directions. The writing on DonMarr's dark blue t-shirt casted a reflection from the headlights and helped Sonny see the black male as he came from behind the bushes and stood in the street. DonMarr made no gestures towards the oncoming vehicle but Sonny knew there was a deal to be made even before he stopped his car.

When DonMarr saw Sonny's car coming towards them, there was no way to tell for sure if he was an addict but DonMarr took his chances and stepped out to greet his potential client.

Sonny pulled over and stopped his car on the west side of the street facing south. DonMarr lured Sonny out of the car and into the field by a threat of a possible police drive by. Sonny knew it was best to remove his keys from his car and so with his keys and money in hand, he left the driver's door open and followed DonMarr out of the street and into the field.

In the dark, it can be difficult to see flaws in someone's skin but DonMarr was spot-on with his assumptions about Sonny. He had nothing on but a pair of faded black sweat pants. His hands were soot stained and callused from the repetitive lighting of crack pipes. His lips were burned and blistered from smoking the addictive chemicals. True to DonMarr and Albert's beliefs, Sonny had nearly every flaw of an addict.

Even in the thick of the night, Sonny could see Montea rise from his sitting position and come towards him. At first, Sonny thought he was the delivery guy and he was very ready for the exchange of merchandise. Sonny counted out his money. DonMarr slowly traded places with Montea. With the baggy of goods in the palm of his open hand, Montea walked towards Sonny. He looked directly into the eyes of the man and turned his hand over and let the crack fall to the ground. Sonny bent over and with his empty hand and picked up the bag not yet fully realizing what was going on. The translucent packaging and white rocks were easy to spot even at night. But just as his hand closed around the package, Montea jumped Sonny and forced him to the ground.

With Montea on top of him, Sonny's fists remained tightly clinched around his possessions. He was on the ground and flat on his stomach. Even in the best of his football days, Sonny had always hated that powerless position and begged his assailant to let him up. Nevertheless, his priorities were hopelessly out of place and while Montea gained the upper hand almost effortlessly.

Sonny remained determined and tried desperately to keep tight control of his drugs, money, and keys. Montea grabbed Sonny's right outstretched arm and forced it down and behind his back. Sonny cried out in pain as he pried his fingers open and dragged his uncut fingernails across his palm and ripped Sonny's keys and cash out of his hands. The now shirtless, middle-aged man had no chance against the strength of the healthy young man and Sonny's personal belongings were gone in seconds.

Montea pushed himself up off Sonny and, satisfied with his accomplishment, left his victim on the ground and went back to where he was once sitting with his friends. Sonny tried to get up but his bare feet slipped out from under him and he stumbled. The struggle had took something out of him and he fell with a thud back onto his stomach. However, he quickly regained his composure and his traction and jumped up. Sonny took off running at top speed, but not away. Sonny took aim at Montea.

Sonny put his professional skills to the test and successfully tackled Montea to the ground. Montea did not see it coming and before he realized it, he too found himself forced onto the ground. The two wrestled in the field, but only for a short time. Before Sonny had any chance to get his things back, a loud blast rang out into the night. It was a sound not unfamiliar to that part of the city.

Sonny's old sweats had clearly misplaced themselves from his waist to his mid-thighs as he and Montea rolled around on the ground. Although DonMarr appreciated the amusing behavior of the two, he nonetheless thought it was a waste of time. Wanting to avoid unwanted attention from the police, DonMarr fired the shotgun once in the air to stop the men from fighting. His intention to bring the wrestling match to an end and expedite their plan was successful. Sonny instinctually pulled up his pants as he and his enemy found their way back up and on their feet. Montea was fully aware of the gun's existence but nonetheless stared at DonMarr with a stunned expression. Sonny, however, had no knowledge of the gun until he locked eyes with DonMarr. Sonny knew that the situation had just escalated from a playground fist fight to a strong arm robbery, and within seconds, Sonny took off running but this time not towards anyone but away from the trouble.

Like a relay race that Sonny was once very familiar with, Montea handed the keys off to DonMarr and DonMarr took off running towards Sonny's car. Sonny was searching for safe cover and ran from the field and towards his car. Unfortunately, Sonny was not as fast as he once was and DonMarr beat him to the car. Sonny had no idea what the men's final intentions were but he diverted his path and headed north away from them and away from the gun.

Sonny never even saw Albert. Albert was not sitting behind the bushes when Sonny headed back toward them because Albert had left to go buy cigarettes a few blocks north from where the evening's festivities were playing out. He had only walked a few hundred feet when he heard the gunshot and as if his two friends were providing him with the evening's entertainment, Albert climbed atop a concrete wall leftover from a house that had burned down years earlier and watched and listened as Montea and DonMarr dealt with the helpless Sonny.

DonMarr now had the car keys to the Mercury Topaz that Sonny had driven that evening to Wabash. Montea now had the shotgun taken from Montgall earlier. DonMarr and Montea had traded the two items as thoughtlessly as two children would trade toys. Montea's plan to steal a car had come to fruition and DonMarr waited for Montea and Albert to join him inside Sonny's car.

DonMarr sat and waited for his friends longer than he anticipated. He wondered where Albert was as he watched Montea track Sonny up the street. As he waited, he sat sideways with the door open and his feet outside the car while his elbows rested on his thighs and his open palms cradled his face. He was ready to get out of there with the car because every minute they stayed meant more chances to get caught.

Carrying the shotgun as he chased Sonny provided Montea with an abundance of adrenaline and an overwhelming sense of power. With those feelings, he took an inexperienced aim and fired his first shot at Sonny as he ran from him. "Boom," the shot rang through the night air. Montea shot but missed his target. Sonny's body stiffened instinctively at the sound of the gunshot. Nevertheless, he kept running. Sonny couldn't see what was going on behind him and didn't know if the shot was aimed at him or just up in the air again, but he wasted no time in trying to find out and took cover at the first place he could find.

Sonny prayed the darkness would protect him as he searched for shelter. In his attempt to conceal himself, the panicked college graduate made yet another bad decision and tried to hide behind a light pole. Sonny's efforts were fruitless and unrewarding. With his back and head pressed firmly against the wooden pole, his hands were down and to his sides and he naively thought it would provide him with some additional protection. In fear for his life, Sonny squeezed his eyes tightly shut as well. Sonny could only take partial refuge behind the light pole. Sadly, neither the pole nor his shut eyes provided him any shelter as Montea clearly saw him and brazenly stalked towards him.

Sonny heard the movement behind him and he hoped it was just leaves rustling in the wind, but he suspected it was something much more dangerous. Not wanting to be heard, he tried to control the sounds of his breathing as it powerfully tried to push its way out of his lungs. Sonny turned his head to the right to steal a look and bravely opened his eyes. Unfortunately, just as he had presumed it was not leaves he heard. He saw the teenager he had just fought with only about 25 yards away slowly walking towards him with the shotgun pointed in his direction. The pole he had hid behind to protect him had a light on the top that shone directly down and spotlighted him.

It did not look good to Sonny as he looked at Montea and then up at the tattling streetlight. It became clear to Sonny that he had never been hiding from anyone and he shook his head at his own lack of common sense. What Sonny did not understand was why the man had it out for him. The guys had his keys and money. Why was this guy hunting him down like an animal? Sonny had no idea what he had done to piss off this man. The truth that Sonny would never find out was he had done nothing to make Montea angry. Montea "Murder" Mitchell was always angry.

Sonny thought about his options and decided he had no other choice but to run for it or get to Montea and get the gun away from him. With his back still to the gunman, he tried to throw Montea off by means of surprise. Sonny stepped out to the left, made a complete 180 degree turn, and ran directly towards Montea. That was the last bad decision Sonny would make before coming, literally, to a dead stop right in front of Montea.

The two men stood face-to-face. Highlights and lowlights of Sonny's life flashed through his mind. He analyzed and, sadly, recognized his own blame in the choices he had made that had put him in his current life or death situation. Similarly, Montea's life played through his mind as well. Several events and several faces flickered through his mind like a bad movie. This reflection gave Montea a tiny intermission from his current criminal conduct and for a very brief second, a small amount of consideration evoked for the man standing in front of him. It also allowed him to make a decision on what he could do. They did have Sonny's keys and money. Why was he chasing him? His answer was because Sonny disrespected him and fought him and for that he needed to die.

The rise of memories and harbored resentment towards people in his past overpowered any kind idea concerning his victim.

Montea made the decision he could never come back from but he made it after deliberating about it. Like always, Montea did not take any blame for his current circumstances. His inner monologue never gave him another chance to debate his decision and Montea was convinced that more harm in his life had been done than good and he could find no reason to act kindly. For no other reason than selfish fulfillment, he pointed the shotgun at Sonny and, as he looked in his victim's eyes, he pulled the trigger and he fired the gun and shot Sonny point-blank in the chest.

Sonny dropped to his knees and fell face down on the sidewalk. It was the second time that evening Montea had caused him to drop but this time Sonny wasn't getting up but he wasn't dead. With a shortness of breath, Sonny begged for help from the man who had just shot him just seconds earlier. Montea bent down and hovered over Sonny's back. Sonny thought his shooter was going to help him and he turned his face towards him. Montea never intended to help Sonny and instead he tore the bag of crack out of the dying man's hand and he turned back towards his cohorts. Montea left Sonny laying in front of 3825 Wabash Avenue alive and still clinging to life.

The house in front of where Sonny was laying showed no indication of anyone being home. Sonny was very aware of the large amount of blood leaving his body and pulled himself up to his knees and looked at the houses on the street for any signs of activity that he could get help. As he tried to catch his breath, he noticed a house about three doors down with a light on and a car in the driveway. The weakened man with a shotgun blast to his chest could not muster the strength to stand so he crawled on all fours toward the light. He was light-headed and in shock but used the glow from the lit house to guide him as he crawled, hopefully, towards help.

While leaving a highly visible trail of blood behind him, Sonny made slow progress down the hard pockmarked sidewalks. The determination Sonny had to reach his final destination was significant, but it would be the last goal of Sonny's season. Sonny finally made it to the house with the light and felt somewhat satisfied that he had made it. However, he never got anyone's attention.

As he neared the doorstep of the lighted home and he stopped and laid down on the lawn which was blanketed with freshly fallen leaves. Sonny rested his body on his stomach in that yard and he died in front of 3833 Wabash. On September 22, 2000 and in the thick of the last days of summer's humidity, the one-time healthy athlete died on the front lawn in an unhealthy neighborhood.

Albert never got the cigarettes he went in search for as he stopped and was preoccupied with the antics of his friends. But after he heard the second shot, he jumped off the stone slab and ran back to where he had left his friends. The taillights from Sonny's car flashed several times as he approached the field where he was once sitting and he knew that was a signal meant for him. The street lamp lit the area well and as he travelled further up the street and he had no problem seeing DonMarr as he watched from the waiting car.

Albert had heard the gunshots but missed seeing the action. However as he walked quickly towards the getaway car, he saw the blood from the product of the gunfire trailing down the street. Albert slowed only long enough to pull the screwdriver out of his pants and place it on the side of a green truck bed. Albert wanted any and all evidence to be off of him and he just thought he ought to get rid of the screwdriver. He paid no attention to Montea who was standing on the opposite side of the truck and set his sights on the white car ahead of him.

As Montea hunted down and killed Sonny Hicks with a 12-gauge shotgun for no reason at all, DonMarr claimed the victim's car and started it in preparation for departure. But DonMarr knew he would not be the getaway driver because he did not know how to drive. He was still sitting in the driver's seat with his feet planted firmly on the ground when Albert breathlessly stuck his head in and told him to move into the passenger's seat. Albert left the driver's side door open and they looked at each other with disbelief that Montea had just shot the dude. The plan was to rob someone with a car so they had transportation. No one said anything about killing anyone. The two said nothing but sat and waited for Montea to return.

Still parked in the very place Sonny had left it, Montea ran towards the white Mercury Topaz. He told Albert to get into the back and slid the gun into the front seat and onto DonMarr's lap. Montea drove several blocks north on Wabash.   However, Montea was a terrible driver and kept almost crashing the car so after constant complaints from his two passengers, he pulled over and switched places with Albert. Montea, DonMarr and Albert drove right back past Sonny lying on the ground bleeding and begging for help while they fled down the street.

Albert saw they were low on gas and drove to nearest convenience store.   Montea's blood-soaked shirt stuck to his chest while he sat in the back seat and rummaged through his victim's belongings. The car's upholstery was a red vinyl and the empty fast food bags explained the sticky seats. He found a moneyless blue, plastic wallet that appeared to him to belong to a young boy. But when he opened it up he found a driver's license in it. Montea saw that it clearly belonged to the man he left bleeding in the street. He continued rummaging and found

287

nothing of value but wanted to be rid of all possible evidence. He gathered up all the items and put them in one of the empty food bags. Montea could smell the blood on his shirt and decided to kill two birds with one stone. Montea took off his shirt and stuffed it in the same bag with Sonny's things. As they pulled into the QuikTrip on Main Street to get gas, Montea decided he would just jump out and dump the trash and in the trashcan in between two gas pumps as Albert gassed up the car.

Albert did not know much about cars or pumping gas but of the three, he was the most experienced. It was almost 6:00 am on Friday morning and daylight was fast approaching. On their way to work many cars were pulling in and out for gas and coffee at the popular convenience store. Albert pulled under the large silver and red canopy and drove laps through the maze of gas pumps several times before finding an open spot.

Albert turned off the ignition, got out of the car, and scoped out the parking to make sure no one was watching him. He chose his gas, removed the nozzle from its holder, walked it towards the back of the car, and then realized he had foolishly pulled up to the wrong side of the pump for the car. While listening to his passengers ridicule him for his mistake, he pulled the stolen car forward and turned it into the next aisle.

Guilt pushed him towards paranoia and it appeared to Albert that everyone was watching him. As he attempted to put gas in the stolen vehicle, he found that without a credit card he would have to go inside and pre-pay the attendant for the gas. Upset that he was spending more time at the busy store, he angrily asked Montea for money to pay for the gas. Montea laughed at Albert's nervous behavior and pulled the money he had stolen from Sonny out of his jeans pocket. Montea handed it to Albert and told him to buy cigarettes first then put the rest of the money towards gas. Montea jumped out to dump the sacks of Sonny's things and his bloody shirt and then got back in the car.

Inside the store, it was brightly lit and was full of people dressed and ready for an honest day's work which was something Albert and his friends had never known. In an odd feeling after this night of murder, Albert felt envious of a less complicated life that some of the people in the store may have had. Albert paid the cashier for the gas but the salesclerk refused to sell him cigarettes without identification. He started to panic but took a deep breath and just said he didn't need the cigs.

They could have purchased cigarettes at a less law-abiding store but when Albert was turned down for cigarettes he put all the money towards gas. The money Sonny had provided them was gone and the trio decided that having a car without money or cigarettes was not fun. With that they decided it was time to use the car for the main purpose they wanted to get it for and that was to "make money."

To Albert, the fifteen-minute stint at QuikTrip seemed more like hours and he was glad to be gone from the intimidating store chain. Albert drove only about ten minutes and into Kansas when Montea told him to stop at a Hy-Vee grocery store located near 76th Street. In the short drive from QuikTrip to Hy-Vee, Montea, DonMarr and Albert wisely decided it would be a mistake to keep driving around in a stolen car. But fortunately, Montea had a plan. The new plan was to rid themselves of the car which was evidence that would connect them to the shooting and armed robbery of who they now knew as Garland Hicks and replace it with another.

A nurse at a local hospital was already dressed and ready for work as she exited the Hy-Vee store. Her white t-shirt peeked through the V-necked opening of the blue scrubs she was wearing, but the gold cross she wore every day dangled out of sight on its solid gold chain underneath her layered clothes. In one hand, she carried a plastic grocery bag and with her other, she unlocked her car door with its remote key and made her way to her car. She had made an unscheduled stop at the store to buy donuts for a co-workers birthday.

The well-known Hy-Vee grocery store had a well-lit parking lot and a modern architectural design. The large windows followed the storefront from end to end and from the inside their huge lot and the many other businesses surrounding it were largely visible to its patrons. From the outside, amber lighting glowed through the large brick encased windows and presented like a fireplace offering its customers an illusion of warmth and safety. In addition, the oversized panes of glass gave the customers a clear view of the sparkling clean interior and the wealth of merchandise on display.

The major difference between the Hy-Vee Grocery store and the QuikTrip was that there were lots of people at the gas station and hardly anyone at the grocery store. Regardless of the safety measures that Hy-Vee had put in place, the multiple street lamps shining down onto the empty parking lot did nothing to help Martha McGrew. Safety comes in numbers and Martha was alone when she walked out a mere thirty minutes before sunrise and into the empty parking lot and towards her car.

Martha unlocked her black Honda Civic and threw her purse towards the passenger's seat. The strap of the purse caught on the 5-speed gearshift mounted on the center console causing the purse to swing around and land in the passenger's floorboard with the strap still around the gear lever. Martha bent over into her car, placed the bag in the passenger's sea, and sat down. As she closed her door, she saw the white Mercury Topaz as it drove diagonally toward her from across the far end of the parking lot.

Martha, instinctively, got into her car quickly and locked her doors. The other car pulled up parallel to Martha's Civic but in the opposite direction, with Montea's rear passenger's door even with Martha's driver's window. When he rolled down his window and motioned for her to roll hers down, Martha should have driven away. But she didn't and she rolled down her window and listened as Montea asked for directions to Wornall Road.

In answering his request for directions, Martha pointed Montea east towards Wornall. And as she continued to explain, he leaned over the front seat of Sonny's car. Martha assumed he was attempting to get something on which to write directions, but Martha was wrong. In a matter of seconds, Montea was out of the Mercury followed by DonMarr and through Martha's open window, Montea shoved the 12 gauge shotgun into Martha's forehead. He reached in to unlock her door from the inside and he had her door open that quick.

Martha screamed a quick short scream before Montea slapped his hand to her mouth to quiet her. Montea ordered Martha out of her car and into her own back seat. Martha said nothing but did as she was told and watched the gun as it followed her. Montea kicked her door shut and sat down confidently in the driver's seat. Certain that he would do better at driving this time, Montea handed the shotgun off to DonMarr and he climbed into the front passenger's seat. DonMarr immediately turned around in his seat and pointed the gun at Martha. Montea saw the keys were already in the ignition and attempted to start the car but the car only jumped forward and died. Realizing it was a stick shift with a manual transmission, Montea screamed and hit the steering wheel hard with his fists.

Martha sat very still behind the driver's seat and listened without saying a word as Montea and DonMarr made murderous threats to her. She had never been as terrified in all of her life but purposely focused on the blue, cardboard, Jesus air freshener dangling from her rearview mirror. Occasionally and almost unwillingly, without moving her head, her eyes diverted to the gun barrel just inches away from her face.

DonMarr was reckless with the gun as he argued with Montea about the car. From time to time, Martha could feel coldness emanating from the steel tip of the weapon on her cheek. She could also smell the unique smell of burnt gunpowder. With that smell, she realized the gun must have been recently fired and she was even more terrified.

Like Sonny, Martha had no idea what her carjackers' objectives were, but for a fleeting second, she hoped that their lack of ability to drive a stick might be the end of their use for her and her car. She was very wrong. The gun never left its position and DonMarr suggested that she should get back in front and drive. Without hesitation, Montea got out of the driver's seat, opened the back door, and grabbed Martha by her arm. Martha still had the gun to her face so she was obedient to their forceful demands. Montea pulled her out of her seat and pushed her back into the front seat.

Other than the first initial eye contact with Montea and DonMarr, Martha purposely avoided looking at her assailants and most of the time she kept her eyes focused straight ahead. As Montea manhandled her back into the front seat, she noted that the white car that Montea and DonMarr drove up in was still running. Through her peripheral vision, she saw that someone was in the driver's seat but she did not know what part he would play in what was going on with her.

Martha never got a good look at Albert and her eyes remained focused on things in front of her. She pretended not to notice the accomplice in the other car as Albert watched on. For the second time in only a few hours, Albert did nothing as he watched Montea and DonMarr commit a brutal crime against an innocent person.

Montea ordered her to start the car, walked around the front of the vehicle, and opened DonMarr's door. Montea took the gun from DonMarr, got into the back seat behind Martha, and rested the gun upon the back of her headrest. The ridged texture of the leather held the smooth steel in place nicely. Martha's head was shoved slightly forward as the barrel was pushed against the back of her head.

Like a robot, Martha showed no external emotion and methodically turned the key in the ignition   as DonMarr threateningly explained to her how they had already shot and killed somebody already that evening.   DonMarr told her that they weren't afraid to do it again. Montea said *"Fuck yeah!"* as he gave the gun a quick thrust, which propelled Martha's head forward and then back against the cold butt of the gun. He backed the gun away from direct contact with his hostage and Martha felt a moment of senseless relief but quickly reconnected with the seriousness of her situation and finally pleaded with her kidnappers to spare her life. Montea had no empathy for the single mother who was just inches away from his weapon. This time as a trigger man, Montea was satisfied to know that should he decide to shoot her, he would surely hit his target on the first try.

It didn't take long for daylight to spread and as the sun rose over the Kansas parking lot, all the street lamps went out and the neighborhood became visible. The red and blue flag was all Montea needed to see before ordering his hostage to drive up to the Bank of America ATM located in the same parking lot as the grocery store and about two hundred yards away. Montea asked Martha is she had an ATM and she said yes. Montea smiled at DonMarr.

DonMarr dumped the contents of Martha's purse onto the floorboard and thrust her wallet towards her face. Martha unfolded it and ran her fingers through the layers of cards

293

organized inside the tiny plastic pockets before locating her ATM card and sliding it from its protective jacket. Even under this pressure, Martha was good at multi-tasking as she put the card in her left hand, switched gears, and drove with her right. Through her rearview mirror, she watched Albert in the other car as he followed close behind them.

Martha was not a Bank of America customer but she assumed the machine would work just like her ATM and clumsily, she went through the routine steps of withdrawing money. Martha was scared and nervous, but she was able to answer the questions and orders Montea and DonMarr were yelling at her. Although it took her several attempts, she successfully withdrew several hundred dollars from the unfamiliar machine.

Martha rolled up her window and answered their questions. She explained that she did not have a cell phone because she could not afford one and she had no other way to get them more money. She handed over the money and ATM card. DonMarr commanded her to give him her PIN and she complied and wrote down her PIN on the back of the bank receipt.

During the hours when most people were sleeping, Montea and his friends were wide-awake from the adrenaline that pumped through their veins. They had not thought about sleeping and continued carrying out their dastardly deeds without concern for time. However, as the night evolved into full-blown morning and the streets became congested with traffic, Montea finally became concerned with the damaging effects that daylight could have on people committing crimes in being seen.

Without explaining details to DonMarr, Montea jumped out of the car and tapped on Martha's window with the butt of the gun. Afraid for her life, she hesitated to roll down the window but knowing the results could be the same with or without the window being down, she pushed the remote button on the door and watched her kidnapper's head find its way inside her car. The still shirtless Montea ordered Martha to take off her uniform top and Martha assumed something worse than murder was about to happen to her.

She prayed silently as she lifted the shirt over her head and wadded it up between her hands on her lap while she waited for orders for additional items of clothes to come off. Martha looked straight ahead, only glancing once through her rearview mirror to confirm that the white car was still behind. Martha let out a little scream as Montea reached in with his left hand and grabbed the shirt from her hands. She hadn't realized how tightly she was holding on to it until she felt the rough material burn her fingertips as he ripped it out of her hands. Martha silently released the deep breath she was holding as she watched Montea pull her shirt over his own head.

Martha stared blankly out the front windshield concentrating heavily on her relief that Montea just wanted her shirt to wear and she was momentarily and mentally transported away from the reality that danger still existed and was seated in the seat to her right. DonMarr, with his open hand, slapped Martha on the back of her head and reeled her back into the nightmarish journey. Martha watched DonMarr's hands work hard as he pulled her driver's license out of the tight clear pocket in her wallet. He waved it in her face and said he knew where she lived. Although he had no idea if she had a family, DonMarr threatened both her and her children's lives. DonMarr made her swear she would not tell the police or anyone about any of this that just happened. Martha nodded her head in agreement and at the same time verbally promised the young man that she would not tell anyone or say anything.

Martha's car was actually useless to them as none of them could drive it. DonMarr got out of the black car and he and Montea jumped back into their respective seats of the dead man's car. They left Martha still alive at the Bank of America ATM.

Martha heard the tires squeal but did not bother to look which way the men went but instead, she pulled the necklace from underneath her shirt and rubbed the cross between her fingers. With the necklace still in her hands, Martha remained parked beside the ATM for several more minutes staring at the dangling air freshener.

Some might say that Martha did not abide by her promise not to tell. Some would say a promise made to a person with a gun at your head is not one you have to abide by anyway. Understandably, Martha did not keep her word to DonMarr. She drove home, checked on her kids, and then did exactly what she swore she wouldn't do. She grabbed the home phone and called 911. The Prairie Village, Kansas Police Department responded to her home and Martha gave them all the information about her attackers. The Kansas police, in turn, conveyed the information to the Kansas City, Missouri Police Department. Now, at least, the three men were on law enforcement's radar.

In less time than it takes a person to get a full night's rest, Montea, DonMarr, and Albert had committed a series of crimes that would likely cause a normal person years of sleepless nights. However, the three men weren't phased and they were not interested in resting at all. With all of them still hyped up over a murder, a kidnapping, and armed robbery, it was not hard for Montea to convince his posse that it was time to lay low for a while. They needed a safe place to get out of the public so they drove the tainted vehicle to DonMarr's house and parked the car in the back yard.

As the men were pulling into DonMarr's house, sunlight had arrived on Wabash Avenue and a homeowner had stepped out of his house and found Sonny's body. The man immediately called 911. The street was soon blanketed with police officers and crime scene technicians going up and down the street collecting evidence. As the homicide detectives arrived, they observed Sonny's body.

The posture of a dead body always tells a story and Sonny's body told the detectives that the victim was not shot where he fell and the bruising and cuts on his upper torso led them to believe there may have been a scuffle before he was shot. The way the blood flowed from the 2-inch hole in his chest, down past his feet and into a puddle on the street, indicated the body was on slight incline and the detectives supposed the victim used his last remaining energy climbing the small hill.

The steps leading towards a front door were just three feet from his outstretched arms and it told the homicide detectives the person was attempting to get help for his injury before he died. Additionally, the trail of blood the victim left behind told the detectives that he was still alive when his killer left the scene. After the thorough investigation, Sonny had nothing on his body to help the Kansas City Police Department identify him. Their team of detectives and crime scene technicians took Sonny's fingerprints and collected evidence found at the scene to identify their victim and to connect the criminals with their crime. But on that morning, KCPD only had a "John Doe" homicide victim with no identity or no clues to the suspect.

Montea felt that the white car parked at DonMarr's house on South Benton was his salvation and he thought he had literally gotten away with murder. As they were getting out of the car, DonMarr's brother, Donald and Montea's brother, Miguel walked up to the car. Montea bragged of their evil adventures, while he attempted to clean the evidence out of the car. Without the faintest show of remorse, the men ate, slept, and partied for almost two days before they saw a story about a carjacking on the television news.

The news was showing a video tape from the Hy-Vee parking lot as well as pictures taken at the Bank of America ATM. Seeing themselves on the Saturday evening news made all of them immediately silent. They all realized that the idea of staying at the same place where Sonny's car was parked, and so close to where they had actually killed Sonny, no longer sounded like the safest hideout for the now wanted suspects. Donald convinced his brother that the three should still stay out of sight and that he would dispose of the car and destroy the murder weapon. With that guarantee from DonMarr's brother, the three outlaws contemplated their next course of action.

But Donald did not do what he had promised his brother. He did not destroy the weapon but as a quick fix, he merely returned the shot gun back where DonMarr had told him he had gotten it. He took it back to Smoke on Montgall Avenue. Also, he did not get rid of the car because he was happy to have a free car, so he and two friends took it out for a joy ride the very next day.

While they were driving, they were spotted by two homicide detectives in an unmarked police car who just so happened to be looking for the very car they were in. The police arrested all three boys and took them in for questioning. The boys told the police all about how they got the car from Montea, Albert, and DonMarr. Within minutes, the KCPD issued pickup orders for Montea, DonMarr and Albert.

Montea, Albert, and DonMarr did not know that the boys had gotten stopped with the car as they were already working on their next move. They thought that the boys had destroyed the items connecting them with the murder of Sonny Hicks, so they only took the black duffle bag that had once contained the murder weapon. They destroyed Martha's ATM card and used some of the money to purchase three bus passes and a room at a local hotel to hide out in for a while.

At the time of Martha's robbery, the immature criminals saw nothing but dollar signs when the bank machine kindly and obediently spit out twenty dollar bills. With one swipe of Martha's debit card, they managed numerous bank transactions and several hundred dollars. With that, Martha's hard-earned salary was gone. However, the state-of-the-art banking system was being more than compliant and as Montea and DonMarr collected their earnings, the high-tech camera installed inside the machine had thoughtfully snapped pictures of them as well as the white car behind them.

To avoid detection, they waited until it was completely dark before leaving DonMarr's house that Saturday evening. They caught the bus at the corner of 39th and Benton and rode it to the Holiday Inn located in Downtown Kansas City. On a normal day, Montea would have been happy to ride the bus, but this time was different. Montea was pissed that he was forced to ride the bus when just hours before he had solid transportation readily available. However, he realized how easy it was and he knew there were more cars to be had and his inconvenience was only temporary.

Sonny had to give up his life for them to take his car and Martha's withdrawals paid for the Holiday Inn room where the men holed themselves up. Nevertheless, both of those things were only temporary. Montea wanted a more permanent solution to all his problems, including his most recent problem of now being wanted by the police. The men sat on one of the two beds at the hotel and used the other to empty out the remaining contents of the duffel bag. Then they discussed their options.

The 12-gauge shotgun that killed Sonny was not the only weapon inside the black bag when they had picked it up but now it was gone. Montea ran his fingers down a sleek 22-caliber rifle and he slowly handed the weapon over to Albert as if to inspire him. Albert took the gun and did just what Montea had done just two nights earlier. He fumbled with the gun and put the butt of the gun against his shoulder and pretended to aim it. Montea easily convinced his sidekicks that the rifle was their ticket to freedom and all they needed was some ammunition.

Montea, DonMarr and Albert remained mostly in their room until after dark Sunday evening. The men made detailed plans to buy bullets, steal another car, and then head to St. Louis to stay with DonMarr's relatives. They laid low and were careful not to draw attention to themselves. The three never exited the room at the same time and took turns leaving for food and cigarettes. Montea knew that summer was officially over when the temperature dropped thirty degrees from Friday to Sunday. In a quick change, clouds and rain came in and darkened the city. It was dreary but it was time to go. Montea, DonMarr, and Albert left the hotel room and took the bus to the closest place they could buy bullets about 10 miles away.

When they got off the bus, it was still raining. Lights from streetlamps and the giant letters attached above the storefront reflected off the numerous water puddles covering the pavement. The oil left behind from the thousands of cars that had once parked there, coexisted peacefully on top of those puddles and enhanced the already sparkling atmosphere. Just like the Hy-Vee grocery store, multiple security measures were in place at the Wal-Mart Supercenter, a popular superstore in Kansas City, Missouri. In order to protect its venue and its customers, cameras monitored both the outside and inside. At night multiple forms of lighting hit the area so that the entire vicinity was visible to all. However, there were three customers on a specific Sunday evening that did not need protecting and they were precisely the type of people the lighting and cameras were put there to detect. Yet, the highlighted parking lot failed to shine the light of detection on the three as they zigzagged through the rows of cars carrying a rifle encased in a black bag.

The Second Amendment allows for American's right to bear arms and in one of its plainest examples, someone can buy bullets at any time night or day. It was surprising that no store employees paid attention to the three as they went straight to the sporting goods section and then pulled out a rifle to figure out what bullets would fit. Neither the management, the sporting goods staff nor the cashier paid much attention to the rifle brought inside their store. In the middle of the sporting goods department, Montea opened boxes of bullets and tried to load the gun several times before he found the correct ammunition. As he placed the gun back into the bag, he considered stealing the bullets but he was aware of the security cameras placed around the store. He begrudgingly closed up the open box of bullets and headed to the front of the store to pay for his items.

After selecting the correct ammo to support their next spree of violence, they hurried to the front of the store but not before stopping at the costume section and choosing three Halloween masks. They decided on three identical masks but not the plastic masks that were attached to an elastic string they had as children, but instead they chose hooded, cloth masks that covered both their faces and necks and completely concealed their identity. To match the ruthless intentions, they picked out the scariest ones they could find. The best description of the masks are that they were the ones used in the movie "Scream" and had white misshapen faces like a ghost or ghoul or skeleton covered by a black hood.

Montea scoped out the selection of cashiers before he picked a line. To a normal law-abiding citizen, the young cashier Montea chose did not stand out above any other employee aside from maybe his red hair. His assigned uniform consisted of only a blue vest and a nametag and was identical to what every other employee was wearing. He wore a black t-shirt underneath and blue jeans. However, to Montea, he did stand out and he was different. This guy was one of his peers. The cashier was

301

approximately the same age and Montea had hopes the teenager shared the same indifference to regulation as he did when he tried to pay for his contraband.

The abnormal combination of items would not necessarily be an assumption of guilt but in reality, the items were a recipe for disaster. Also it was protocol to check all drivers' license to verify the buyer's age when any kind of ammunition was purchased. All three men were under the required age to purchase ammunition but regardless of their age, none of the three had any form of proper identification. However, Montea's intuition was spot on about the cashier. The red-haired, young teen was oblivious to Montea's age and did not follow store procedure so both the irregular purchase and the illegality of it went unnoticed and under the radar of regulation. So with the permission from the cashier, Albert, DonMarr, and Montea walked out of the supercenter with three scary masks and a box of bullets. They were more than prepared to continue their crime spree.

Out in eastern Jackson County, two hours after school had dismissed for the day on September 25, only a few cars remained at the elementary school parking lot. Windows lined the entire front of each of level of the three-story building and every window was indicative of an individual classroom. It was still daylight when 34 year-old Michael Walker peered through the windows and out into the schoolyard as he walked down the long hallway of the first level of the schoolhouse. The windows allowed Michael a full view of the lawn and the traffic on a small portion of 45th Street that ran parallel to the school. Michael analyzed the weather as he walked towards the rear exit.

Michael Walker saw the rain that had started the prior day was still falling and since the temperature had dropped significantly over the weekend, he anticipated it to be cool outside as well. He prepared himself for the elements by slipping on a green nylon jacket he had brought with him that day. Aside from the weather change, the picture he saw from the first level hallway was consistent with what he saw every other day. Michael walked the same route to the back of the building and closest to where his car was parked. Michael was aware of the weather and what was going on in the front of the school, but he was not prepared for what lie outside in the back of the school. Out back lying in wait were Montea, DonMarr and Albert. But they were not as prepared for the weather as Michael was and all three were dressed in jeans and light t-shirts. They shivered in the rainy 50 degree weather as they waited outside for their third victim.

Michael's job as a school counselor was to assist his students in the areas of educational and citizenship development, as well as help with emotional and social development. He took his job seriously and tried very hard to treat all children with the courtesy he believed they needed so when he exited the school building at 5:30 p.m. on Monday and saw two black teenagers, he nodded at them respectfully even though they looked particularly out of place at the kindergarten through fifth-grade campus. Michael knew something was not right about this particular scenario but kept walking towards his car.

He had covered fifteen feet of the thirty-foot walk to his car before he would feel the steel barrel of a rifle against the back of his head. He had only seen two men before and quickly realized the third man with the gun had been hiding from him and had come up behind him. With the rifle pressed hard against his body, Michael stopped and two men walked towards him. However, he could no longer see their faces as they had put on their masks. The muffled voices from behind the masks ordered Michael to lie face down on the grass and Michael did what he was told.

Montea's method of operation was the same as it was with Martha and he held the barrel against Michael's head until Michael gave Montea what he wanted. On the ground, Michael's pants immediately soaked up the moisture from the ground but the water resistant jacket he had put on just minutes prior to coming outside protected his chest. The leaves underneath him were wet but Michael could still feel the sharp edges of the dead leaves scratching the side of his face. As if being held at gunpoint was not enough to keep Michael immobile and compliant, Montea put his foot on Michael's back and pressed the steel harder into his skull.

Facedown and completely helpless, Michael begged for his life as DonMarr and Albert searched his pockets and took all of his cash, his credit cards, his cell phone, and his car keys. The three disregarded all of Michael's pleas until they needed to know which of the few remaining cars on the parking lot was his and it was not until then that they cared about what Michael Walker had to say.

The mask Montea wore protected only his head from the rain but the rest of him remained vulnerable to the cold and because he hated being cold, he made one final demand from his victim. He commanded Michael to take off his jacket and give it to him. Montea's foot did not budge an inch off his back but Michael managed to remove his jacket from his hostage position nonetheless. Still pointing the rifle, Montea grabbed the coat and walked backwards away from his victim until he reached the white Lincoln that belonged to Michael Walker.

Just like Sonny, Michael found himself in the same compromising position. He was face down on the ground and helpless, but unlike Sonny, Montea did not shoot Michael. Fortunately, Michael was able to get through the ordeal virtually unharmed. Trembling from both fear and the weather, Michael gathered himself off the ground and watched Montea put the rifle in the back seat of his car and then put on his jacket. Montea then hollered at Michael that if he raised his head or even a finger that he would shoot him. Michael slumped back down, turned his head away from the men, and dared not move again.

He laid on the wet ground and he heard the familiar sound of his car ignition. He thought for a second that maybe they might try to run over him as he was laying partially on the asphalt. He wondered if he should move but remembered Montea's admonition. As he heard what he thought was the car driving away from him, relief came over his trembling body. Michael lay on the ground for at least 5 more minutes after the car left before he got up and ran back in the school to call the police.

As Albert peeled away as the driver of the newly stolen car, Montea and DonMarr kicked back in the roomy backseat of Michael's well-maintained, older Lincoln Town Car. Montea placed his feet upon the back of the cloth front bench seat and counted out Michael's cash while DonMarr went through an assortment of stolen credit cards. DonMarr told Albert to head east as they headed out of town as the plan was to head to St. Louis. It took less than ten minutes to rob Michael Walker of everything and it took even less time for Albert to drive the two miles down 45th Street and in the direction of freedom on Interstate 70. However, once again, motivated by greed and violence, Montea made an impromptu decision, and by 6:00 p.m., their immediate plan to get out of town had changed directions.

Still headed east on I70, Albert temporarily but reluctantly exited off the interstate after being convinced by Montea that they should rob some more people before they got on the long drive to St. Louis. Both Albert and DonMarr wanted to keep driving and at first objected to the sidetracking decision, but the promise of additional fortune made the time-consuming detour easier to accept. Obeying Montea's command, Albert pulled the older model luxury car off at Lee's Summit Road and took a right.

The men drove through a Home Depot parking lot just a few miles from where they had victimized Michael Walker. Montea directed Albert to drive slowly through the large parking lots while he looked for another get-away vehicle. Home Depot was not productive in finding a new car or anyone to rob so the crew traveled further south on Lee's Summit Road until they reached 40 Highway. After a quick right turn, Montea told Albert to pull into a car wash.

As the three men pulled into the Castle Car Wash, there was still plenty of daylight. The men were just looking for the right person to prey upon when Montea spotted the sporty, blue vehicle and knew he wanted it. He not only liked the looks of car but the car and its owner were the only things at the multi-bay establishment. Or so he thought. Montea told Albert to stop and pull into a wash bay to the side of the blue car. Montea grabbed his mask and his gun. If you are counting, this would be Montea and his crew's fourth victim in their terror of the city.

In the same way parents love and nurture their children, Bradford Thomas babied his vehicle. He devotedly bathed the rectangular piece of sheet metal at the popular castle shaped car wash in Independence, Missouri. With the bright orange cloth he always kept in his glove compartment, the strong 42 year-old made sure to wipe the few remaining water spots off the driver's door of his vintage Monte Carlo. Bradford was careful not to get his shoes wet from the puddles of water that had accumulated on the uneven concrete floor as he walked around the back of his car and to the driver's side door.

The left-handed real estate appraiser had just pulled his keys out of his left jeans pocket when he heard something behind him. Before he could turn he felt something in the middle of his back and the words, *"Don't move, mother fucker!"* Montea had jammed the rifle into his body from behind. Without heeding the command not to move, Thomas instinctively turned around and was face-to-face with Montea wearing the skeleton mask.

With DonMarr by his side, Montea told Thomas to hand over his keys. But due to the mask covering his face, his words were muffled and unclear. Unsure of what the masked gunman said, Thomas did not immediately obey. Before he even had a chance to ask what he said, DonMarr stepped forward, and firmly yelled to give him the keys. Thinking it may have been an early Halloween prank, Thomas made a huge gamble and attempted to get into his car.

Albert sat in the white Lincoln in the bay to the left of Thomas's Chevrolet and with the window rolled down, he listened as Montea and DonMarr did their work. He listened for verbal cues to help prepare and warn him for the appropriate time to escape. However, Albert heard something that his co-conspirators couldn't because of all the yelling. With the masks and all of the yelling to get the car keys, Montea and DonMarr didn't hear the barking and growling dog. It appeared Thomas's car was not the only thing he pampered and his German shepherd sat in the front passenger's seat waiting patiently for his master to finish the car wash. But as he saw these people messing with his master, he became protective and started barking.

Thomas's risk of trying to get in his car quickly did not pay off and Montea's younger reflexes were faster than his victim's reflexes were. As Thomas stepped towards the car, Montea fired the rifle and he shot Thomas in the stomach at close range before he was able to get to his car door. Still alive and in a defensive manner, Thomas put his hands in front of his face and stopped moving. He lowered his hands just in time to watch as Montea shot at him again. The second bullet travelled through his left

307

hand and then into his chest and lodged itself underneath his left shoulder. Thomas's blood sprayed out of his body and onto the brown stalls inside the bay.

Thomas fell down beside his driver's door but managed to find some energy to crawl for cover under his car. He couldn't fit very well under the car but he moved in as far as he could to get away from the gunman and in fear for his life. Unfortunately, his attempting to hide did not stop the evil that evening and Montea wasn't done with him. Montea raced around the car and almost knocked DonMarr over as he went to the other side of the car.

Montea kneeled down and said, *"I told you not to move, mother fucker!"* as he stuck the rifle underneath the car. Montea was now all the way on his stomach as he fired the last shot. The bullet entered Thomas's back and there was no movement from the man who had just been washing his car a few minutes ago.

Blood poured out of multiple holes in Thomas's body and down the water drain beneath his car but he was still alive. Thomas could see the men's feet as they attempted to get into his car and all he could think about was that they would shoot his dog. He also realized that if they pulled off in his car, they would run over him but his concern was for his dog, Roscoe. He could hear Roscoe barking and growling and he held his breath for a gunshot but heard none. He heard several clicks and someone say, *"Aw shit!"* As luck would have it, the rifle jammed and Roscoe was spared. Thomas's blood was splattered on the walls and pouring down the drain and Roscoe fought for his master. In another showing of their cowardice, both Montea and DonMarr ran away leaving the car and angry dog behind. The men got back in the Town Car and Albert sped away. As Thomas lost consciousness, he smiled that his best friend, Roscoe was still alive.

The bloody scene at the carwash did nothing to dissuade Montea from wanting to keep on committing crimes. The instant he and DonMarr were safely back into their car, Montea immediately started talking about finding another car and person. His evil and selfish motives never left room for guilt or remorse and Montea commanded Albert to get back onto the interstate and drive east towards a mall just off the Interstate, near Independence, Missouri.

When the Lincoln pulled in at 7 p.m., the streetlights were already on, but to their disadvantage, Monday nights were not the busiest of shopping days. Only few cars occupied the hundreds of available spaces at the Independence Center shopping mall. As Albert pulled into the huge parking lot that was home to several large retail shops, Montea scanned the premises for another car. Montea was tired from his victims fighting back so he wanted to take his time to find just the right person to rob and the right car. With this large of a parking lot, they would find the right victim.

Penny McGinnis was a doting mother and instinctively told her daughter to wait inside the store while she went out to her car to get some additional money to buy her a blouse she wanted. Leaving her daughter inside, as it turned out, was the best decision she could have made because when she opened her trunk to retrieve her purse, Montea Mitchell grabbed her and put his hand over her mouth and shoved her on to the hood of her own car. Penny was amazingly calm as the men descended upon her and violently ripped her purse from her hands and tore her keys from her. Penny only thought about her ten-year-old daughter waiting inside and she wanted this robbery to be over quickly so as to not involve her daughter.

Penny quickly realized her robbers were young men and she knew just how to handle them when she exercised her expertise as a mother and interacted with them like the immature men they really were. As they started their plan to steal her 1995 Oldsmobile Aurora, she knew that her reaction would be the difference between life and death. She told them they could have anything and everything they wanted and she wouldn't fight. She talked to them sweetly and guided them through their clumsy mishandling of the several sets keys she had on one key ring.

Once again, Albert stayed with the Lincoln and DonMarr and Montea were going to take Penny's car. Montea pointed the rifle at Penny and DonMarr fumbled through the multiple keys but couldn't get the doors unlocked. Penny pleasantly suggested that DonMarr try the remote key to unlock the door and referred to her carjackers as "sweetie" and "honey" as she calmly talked DonMarr through the overly drawn out process of unlocking a car door. DonMarr could not help but give in and pay attention to her nurturing voice. He located the black remote surrounded by the large collection of other keys and with one quick push, all the locks popped up. The men were into the car within seconds. The car fired up and peeled off. They left Penny in the parking lot unharmed.

But in one final example of evil, Montea pointed the gun at her and mouthed the words "Shut Up" to Penny as they drove away. It all happened so very quickly and Penny watched the men race away from her in her car followed by the Lincoln they had all just gotten out of. As they tore out of the parking lot, the reality of what had just happened hit her and she dropped to her knees. Within seconds, the shopping center security was at Penny's side and assisting her, but the assailants were long gone.

The criminals drove the stolen vehicles south on 291 through Lee's Summit, Missouri and turned onto US 50 where they drove for over an hour before stopping at a convenience store near Warrensburg, Missouri. Albert pulled the Lincoln up to a gas pump and Montea pulled the Oldsmobile to the side of the store.

Albert swiped Michael Walker's credit card through the card reader, placed the nozzle in the tank, and locked the lever to the 'on' position on the gas pump letting the automatic pump do all the work. He grabbed Michael Walker's cell phone from the front seat and met Montea and DonMarr inside the store. The three walked the small aisles several times before picking out some junk food and paying for their purchases. With their cigarettes already in their mouths and ready to light before they reached the door, they walked back outside towards freedom.

Albert had no choice but to park his car in the front of the store where the attendants could see him because that's where the gas pumps were located. He walked straight out to his car, replaced the nozzle back into its housing, but watched and waited for his friends to exit from the side. Montea, on the other hand, had parked his stolen car in a place less visible to the store's employees and its patrons. Montea and DonMarr returned to their car and got into their respective seats but they were in no hurry to leave. Montea turned on the radio and the two listened to music while they searched through Penny McGinnis' car and counted their money.

Montea had instructed Albert to keep the Lincoln away from the Oldsmobile until it was time to leave. To pass time, Albert stood outside his car and attempted to make phone calls on the unfamiliar cell phone. Little did the men know that the Johnson County, Missouri Sheriff's Department was responding to calls about two cars reported to be driving erratically down US-50. Erratic driving isn't usually the most exciting of dispatches to send out on the air to deputies; however, the dispatcher that sent the two officers out on that call also informed them the two cars were possibly involved in a homicide and a string of armed robberies. With even more calls to the department, there was information that someone saw the cars at the convenience store and the dispatcher was sending the officers to the exact location where Montea and Albert were parked in the stolen vehicles.

311

Albert was too involved in trying to comprehend the cell phone in his hand to see the sheriff's car pull in the parking lot and behind the Oldsmobile. Montea, however, saw the patrol car and quickly put the car in reverse but the deputy pulled the car quickly behind him so he couldn't pull out. Ken O'Connor and Mike Minner, two patrol deputies from the Johnson County Sheriff's Department drew their service weapons, approached both sides of Aurora, and ordered Montea and DonMarr out of the vehicle. As instructed, both men got out of the vehicle with their hands above their heads and sat on the ground.

The parking lot of the convenient store was as lit up as its interior and as much as Montea thought he was hiding by parking on the far side of the building, the store's outside lights shone down and spotlighted him for the curious customers. He had not been hiding at all. O'Connor handcuffed Montea and Minner cuffed DonMarr. The deputies both read them their Miranda Rights. Just as the deputies ordered, they sat silently on the hard pavement with their hands cuffed behind their back. However Montea's hatred for authority was never silent and his oppositional defiance reared its ugly head. Montea wouldn't be quiet and loudly and repetitively recited lyrics from a song. After Montea sang, "I shoot pigs daily." O'Connor rolled him from his sitting position onto his stomach and placed his police issued boot on his head, squishing the side of his face into the pavement as he patted him down for weapons.

Albert who had now noticed his friends being arrested jumped in the car and peeled out. Deputy Minner got back in his police car and gave chase. O'Connor stayed with Montea and DonMarr and kept his weapon drawn and his two handcuffed suspects on the ground. Albert didn't get too far as Minner pursued. About a mile away, Albert took a curve too fast and lost control and put his car into a ditch and wrecked. Albert was thrown from the car but not injured and Deputy Minner easily took him into custody and placed him back in his vehicle and headed

312

back to the convenience store where the others were. By this time four other deputies were on their way to assist. Two of them were headed to the car Albert had just wrecked to protect the crime scene and the other two were coming to the convenience store to assist O'Connor and Minner with the three suspects.

Montea, DonMarr and Albert were prone on the ground with their hands behind their back while O'Connor and Minner waited for backup. Montea had calmed down and O'Connor removed his foot off his head but during the short wait for additional officers to arrive, he continuously raised his head off the ground and focused on the Aurora. He was not as clever as he thought and O'Connor quickly figured out there was something else in the vehicle that needed police intervention. Minner kept the suspects under control while O'Connor pulled the loaded rifle from behind the front passenger's seat and for everyone's safety and almost mockingly in front of Montea, he dumped the bullets on the ground, and placed it up against the car. Backup arrived and assisted in taking all three to the Johnson County Detention Center in different patrol cars

All three men were transported back to Jackson County, Missouri where they were held on no bonds as the court found them to be a threat to the community and substantial flight risks. In their first court appearance, all pled not guilty. They would not entertain taking any sort of plea offer and forced the state's hand to take the case to a jury trial to resolve the issue. They would reside in the Jackson County Jail for the next year before their case was set for trial.

Montea Mitchell's trial date was October 29, 2001 and Montea's attorney advised him of his right not to testify among many other issues. The public defender also informed his client that it would be in his best interest to get a haircut and wear civilian clothing during the proceedings. Montea had no money so out of his own pocket, the defense attorney purchased a suit for Montea to wear during his trial. Just over a year had passed since Garland Hicks was found dead on the lawn of 3833 Wabash and Montea Mitchell's control issues he had prior to the trial, did not stop after his arrest. Now it was about to spill into the courtroom.

On the first day of jury selection, Montea sat between his two public defender attorneys dressed in his orange jail jumpsuit and not dressed in the suit purchased explicitly for him by his attorney. It was clear that between attorney and client, there was conflict about what Montea was wearing. His attorney made a record with the judge stating that Montea did have civilian clothes to wear and the attorneys were advising him to wear them. When the judge inquired of Montea about the issue before the jury panel had entered the courtroom, Montea said that he was exerting his Fifth Amendment rights and would not respond to the judge when she asked questions directed specifically at him.

Judge Edith Messina had soft gray hair and a friendly face but in her demeanor, the seasoned judge was surprisingly stern. This was an important issue that Montea was being flippant about. Everyone in that courtroom believed that a jury is more likely to be prejudiced against Montea if he is sitting in an orange jail jumpsuit than if he was wearing a suit and tie. Also, his attorney told the court that before Montea entered the courtroom, he informed his attorneys of an issue that he wanted to discuss directly with the judge. Messina addressed the issue specifically to Montea, but when given the opportunity, he ignored her and remained silent. The judge inquired once again. Montea locked eyes with the judge but again, he remained silent. In assurance that everyone in the room could hear her, the judge made all attorneys at the defense and prosecuting tables acknowledge for the record that they could hear her before she offered the defendant a third and final opportunity to speak.

Still looking at the judge with a cold stare, Montea defiantly made three slow back-and-forth movements with his head. The public defender stood up on his client's behalf and explained his client was merely exerting his constitutional rights. Nonetheless, after verifying his head movement as a "no", the judge firmly explained to the defendant that all questions would demand verbal answers so the record could fairly reflect his response and if he did not, the record could not reflect his answers. The judge concluded that Montea would continue in the same behavior and told him that she had given him the opportunity that he told his lawyers he wanted but Montea refused to address it, therefore she was moving on. The judge asked the bailiff to bring in the 60 members of the jury panel to begin jury selection.

Most people do not consider themselves as being biased but ironically when picking a jury, bias is the chief concern. Selecting a jury panel is a deliberate and slow process and is a process based not on selecting jurors, but more of weeding out jurors who might not be the best for that type of case as their biases or past experiences may make it hard for them to be fair and reasonable.

None of the potential jurors know what type of trial they have been called to potentially sit on until they arrived in the courtroom, but quietly most hope for an interesting case. On November 5, the sixty citizens in this panel filled every row of the hard wooden benches in the fifth floor courtroom. Comfort was not initially a priority as they listened to the long list of charges against the defendant. It was a case highly prioritized by the media and many of the Jackson County residents were already familiar with some of the names and details involved in the case, thus making it even more difficult to filter through the biases.

For two days the defense team consisting of public defenders, and the prosecuting team consisting of prosecutors Phil LeVota and Brent Coleman, fine-tuned their questions to the

315

potential jurors before sending forty-six of them home. Late on March 6, a panel of twelve jurors and two alternates were sworn in at Division 12 of the Sixteenth Judicial Circuit Court of Jackson County, Missouri to hear the case of the *State of Missouri v. Montea Mitchell*.

It was after 5:00 PM on November 6 when the fourteen people selected to decide Montea Mitchell's fate left the courthouse. Daylight savings time had ended just one week prior and it was completely dark by the time their fingers touched the exit doors. The ugly details of the case and the time change made it appear much later than it was and the long day bore down on them heavily. After two long days of jury selection, the jurors were anxious to be done for the day and eager to hear the start of testimony the next morning.

The next morning, the jury listened with fresh ears as prosecutor Coleman gave the opening statement for the prosecution. Typical for attorneys whose salaries were paid for by the state, Coleman wore an inexpensive black suit and shoes. However, the young attorney knew, just like the attire of the defendant, whatever he wore would make an impression upon the jury and Coleman wanted his impression to be a good one. The white shirt he wore underneath his jacket was crisp and white. His black shoes were polished and shiny. The deep color of his purple tie popped and accessorized his suit nicely.

The prosecutor walked towards the jury and remained silent for the three trips he made back and forth in front of them. He stopped and faced them and described the case in four short but concise statements telling them the case would be broken down into one murder, five carjacking attempts, three defendants, and three days. He paced back and forth again as he outlined the crimes in chronological order and each of the eight charges that went along with them. He described Montea as the ringleader to all the events. He then detailed the bloody

316

mess left behind at two of the crime scenes and then set the jury's expectations for upcoming witnesses and their testimonies.

The public defender, Trent Pollard, just four years out of law school opened the defense's side with the claim that his client was not guilty of murder and that his friends, DonMarr Reneeson and Albert Allen were actually the ringmasters behind the crimes. The unseasoned but extremely talented Pollard told the jury the evidence would show the venue used to stage the criminal activity was in DonMarr's neighborhood and also pointed out that the vehicle stolen from Garland 'Sonny' Hicks was also found in DonMarr's neighborhood. Like his opposing counsel, Pollard also paced in front of the jury and ended his opening statement with the suggestion that DonMarr and Albert accused Montea as an easy way out of their terrible situation and indicated that he would ask the jury to find his client not guilty.

Family members and curious spectators gathered in the gallery directly behind the defense and prosecution tables. All but the jury faced the front of the courtroom. Sectioned off to the left and against the wall, was an enclosed area specifically for the jury members. The wall-to-wall traditional brown paneling, brown furniture, and tan tile floors offered nothing remarkable to the courtroom. Aside from the flags on either side of the judge's high-backed, leather desk chair, the room was nearly void of color.

Sonny Hick's girlfriend, Debra Goodard was the prosecution's first witness. The tall and thick woman entered the courtroom wearing a tight red, wool jacket and matching skirt and the bailiff swore in the forty-six-year-old before she took her seat. She seemed large in the witness stand and she answered Coleman's questions with confidence but devastated sadness. It was obvious that the mere year that had passed since her boyfriend's death had not been long enough for her to get over her grief.

Between her responses to questions, she took long pauses to help contain her emotions. She sat completely back into the chair but the robust woman's body took up most of the witness box and even though she was already abnormally close to the microphone, her voice was unnaturally soft for her size. Judge Messina instructed Goodard to speak louder into the microphone to assure that everyone in the courtroom could hear. The witness obeyed the judge and spoke directly into it throughout the rest of her testimony.

Prosecutor Coleman's first goal was for Goodard to identify the victim for the jury. The prosecution introduced a picture that displayed her and Sonny smiling and holding hands as a way to identify the murdered victim for the jury but defense attorney Pollard objected to the picture. Outside the jury's hearing, the defense attorney argued that the opposing counsel was only using the photograph to draw sympathy from the jury and it was not relative to the case. Messina overruled the objection and allowed the picture into evidence. When the trial resumed in front of the jury, Goodard positively identified the man in the picture as Garland Hicks and then later identified her white Mercury Topaz in the additional pictures Coleman presented to her.

Public defender Pollard cross-examined Goodard very briefly by asking the still grief-stricken witness if she was aware that Sonny had a substance abuse problem. She refused to allow the attorney to taint the image she still held for her late boyfriend. Goodard defended Sonny and said that he did not have a problem and denied the accusation.

Every witness in a trial is not going to be the "eye witness" or the actual person who proves or disproves guilt, but each witness adds to the totality of the case. The jury did not derive anything fascinating from Goodard's testimony except the assertions from the defense that the victim was a drug addict and the witness's unrelenting denial of that statement.

The next witness was the responding police officer called to the murder scene on the morning they found Hicks' body who laid out the crime scene to the jurors but also did not factor in on the decision of whether Montea was guilty or not. However, it is important for the jury to hear the whole case and the explanation of what the responding officer saw would be important to later testimony. The jury was a little bit less than excited after these first witnesses as it was easy to tell from their body language to get a general feel for their opinion on whether they are bored or not.

Prosecutor Phil LeVota regained the jury's attention when he called his next witness to the stand. Crime Scene Technician, Lori Keller walked to the jury box as she had done many times before. Unlike Goodard, the brown-haired woman took up very little space in the stand but similarly spoke softly and LeVota reminded her to speak clearly and directly into the microphone. The young woman pushed her glasses up and leaned forward and closer to the witness stand microphone. LeVota, dressed in a grey pinstripe suit and blue tie saw the petite witness was still not as close as she needed to be and walked up to the stand and moved the black arm of the appliance down closer to Keller's mouth, showing her that the audio device was adjustable.

LeVota began by asking Keller to explain her job duties as a crime scene technician. Keller spent some time explaining what her responsibilities were on a general basis and then generically at crime scenes. LeVota then asked if she was working on the date in question and to tell the jury about what she found when she arrived at the crime scene on Wabash Avenue. Keller described a large blood trail leading from a light pole that led down a sidewalk and to the body. Keller approximated the blood trail to be about 135 feet. LeVota then asked her to describe the neighborhood and what she observed at the beginning point of the blood trail. Keller illustrated the neighborhood as a typical residential neighborhood but with a small field on the opposite side of the street from where they found the victim. She also noted that several vacant lots were on both the north and south of where the blood trail began.

She then added that near a light pole she observed an older model green pick-up parked on the east side of the street and facing north. She stated she saw blood on both the passenger side door of the truck and on the light pole. Keller stated she also discovered a blood covered bone fragment laying in the street in the distance between the truck and pole. Keller indicated she followed the path of blood down the sidewalk and to 3833 Wabash where it ended at the victim's body.

LeVota asked Keller to describe what she saw upon her observation of the victim's body. She explained to the jury that when she arrived a plastic shroud was covering the body and was being held down by cinder blocks due to the rain and wind. She testified to the clothing Sonny was wearing and to the large amount of blood that had drained from his body and pooled up around his head. Keller also indicated that after initially removing the plastic cover, there were no discernable wounds on Sonny's body. However, after the medical examiner's investigator arrived, they rolled the victim onto his back and the silver-dollar sized hole in his chest became obvious.

LeVota then showed the jury a large blown up marking of a diagram of the crime scene and asked if this was a blow up of the diagram she made in her report. Keller replied yes, and LeVota asked her to step down in front of the diagram and they went through her same testimony again but this time with the diagram as a point of reference to the jury. LeVota then asked Keller to look at twenty 8x11 color photos and asked if she could identify them. Keller said they were enlargements of the pictures she took at the scene.

After introducing them into evidence, LeVota and Keller stood two feet in front of the jurors and went through each picture detailing what was in it and the relevance to Keller's work with the evidence collection. LeVota observed several jurors wince as they got to the four pictures of Sonny Hicks body as it lay in its resting place. The pictures were graphic but were all part of the prosecution's burden of presenting evidence to the jury to try to prove Montea guilty beyond a reasonable doubt.

During the direct examination, LeVota kept CST Keller busy testifying for over two hours and presented over fifty photographs and diagrams of the crime scene. Keller was back and forth from the witness chair and into the gallery several times, as she pointed at and identified specific information to the jury. The jurors listened intently and observed each photograph as they looked at it and passed it to the next juror.

The defense finally got their chance at cross-examining Keller and dove right into the evidence she observed and collected at the scene but also the possible evidence she observed and did not collect. The defense attorney asked her about a screwdriver on the hood of the green truck. Keller confirmed she observed a screwdriver but indicated they did not collect it as evidence. Pollard went through some photographs already presented into evidence and then presented exhibit number 18, a photograph of the green truck, and asked Keller to point to the screwdriver. Seeing that the screwdriver was not in the photo of the truck, Keller stated that she could not remember exactly where on the truck she observed the screwdriver or if she took photographs of the screwdriver at all.

The cross-examination of Keller by Pollard was brief and lasted less than twenty minutes. Keller testified that she and two other crime scene technicians were at the scene that day and they took blood samples, dusted for fingerprints, collected items for evidence, and forwarded them all to the proper units.

In his cross examination, the defense attorney tried to use an old trick of spotlighting irrelevant issues about evidence not being collected in an effort to confuse the jury to the professional job that the KCPD did in the crime scene investigation. Keller just spent over two hours testifying in her direct examination to the evidence collected relating to a man being shot with a shotgun.

LeVota was confident that his jury wouldn't buy into the tactic but just to make sure, he stood up for a brief re-direct. LeVota asked Keller if there was any evidence at all that the green truck had anything to do with the homicide. She said no but she still took pictures of it. LeVota asked if there was any indication or evidence that the victim was stabbed by a screwdriver. Keller said no and offered that the autopsy showed no stab wound at all. LeVota asked if there was any indication that the screwdriver had anything to do with the crime. Keller responded that there was no reason to assume it had anything to do with the crime and certainly if it would have been on the ground by the victim or if it had blood on it or something, that it would have been collected. Keller said that even though it was not involved, she did still make a note in the report about it in case it was ever relevant for some odd reason. After realizing the jury had not fallen for the defense's attempt to confuse, LeVota responded, *"No further questions."*

Prosecutor Coleman called the next witness to the stand. *"The State calls Brian Bell,"* he stated. The mid-thirties, clean cut, detective wearing glasses took the stand. He introduced himself as Brian Bell, a detective for the Kansas City, Missouri Police Department Homicide Unit. Bell testified how he followed the unidentified victim to the morgue, witnessed the autopsy, and did a wound chart of the victim's injuries. Coleman walked away from the witness to the counsel table, picked up a small packet of paper, and asked the detective if he recognized it. Bell pulled off his round wire-framed glasses, looked through the pages, and confirmed it to be a chart he completed on the victim at the morgue. For the jury, Bell described all of Hicks' abrasions and cuts but indicated the major injury was the gunshot wound in the center of his chest.

The prosecutor asked the detective how the KCPD identified the body of Garland Hicks and how they connected the murder with the defendant. Bell indicated they identified Hicks through a fingerprint check. Upon notifying the next of kin, they received information that he had a girlfriend named Debra Goodard. Bell said when they spoke with her about details about the victim she provided the specifics about the Mercury Topaz he was driving before he was killed.

Bell continued and explained the car was located a few days later by officers and they arrested three boys that were in the car. Bell said that he and his partner went back to the area of the murder to look for the Topaz and learned that someone had been pulled over in the car. Coleman asked Bell if any of the three boys in the car were the defendant and he said no. Bell told the jury they could not connect the boys with the homicide, however; the boys did provide the names of DonMarr, Montea, and Albert during their interviews. Bell said that KCPD issued a pick up order for those three that day.

The jury's interest did not waver during Bell's testimony. He told of how the cooperation of another police department in Kansas helped provide him with pictures of the robbery at the ATM and elaborated on interviews with other key witnesses and suspects including his interview with Albert Allen and DonMarr Reneeson.

Bell stated the sheriff apprehended Albert in Johnson County on September 25 and that Bell interviewed Albert on September 27 back in Kansas City. Bell gave details of the interview and said Albert informed him that Montea and DonMarr were directly involved with the murder of Garland Hicks. Albert also told Bell that they were responsible for the robbery and kidnapping in the Hy-Vee parking lot as well. Bell added that

323

from the photographs they obtained from the Kansas robbery, Albert identified Montea as the person in the back seat of Martha McGrew's car and DonMarr as the front passenger.

The defense's cross-examination was dull but informative, and he focused much of the jury's attention to the close proximity of where the murder was committed and where the Topaz was finally located. With Bell, the defense attorney compared both of the locations with the closeness of DonMarr's neighborhood. He presented a large map of the streets where Bell and his partner located Hicks' car and asked the detective to step down and point to the exact location. With permission, Bell walked in front of the judge's bench and to the courtroom easel that held the large exhibit. Bell pointed to all three places on the street map and the jury took notes to their close proximity.

To the defense team, the area map was merely a stage setter for the evidence they would present later; however, it was very revealing to the jury and they took notes to the close proximity of the locations. Bell answered the defense attorney's questions about details surrounding finding Hicks' car and interviews with the suspects that were in the car. The defense got into very minute detail and when Bell could not recall the information, the defense attorney had the transcripts readily available for him to review. Pollard finished his cross examination with the detective by inquiring if during his interview, Albert Allen, implicated himself in any of the crimes. Bell stated that Allen stated he was with the others but he did not include himself as a participator when providing details about the crime.

Redirect examinations came from both sides and Detective Bell stayed on the stand until the court recessed for the evening. Bell also testified that he interviewed DonMarr Reneeson who said that Montea shot Sonny and Montea had the gun throughout the crimes. Bell testified for the state and the defense that during his interview with DonMarr Reneeson, he admitted being involved in the murder but maintained Albert was uninvolved.

At nine o'clock in the morning, on November 8, the jury was back in their respective seats and prepared to listen to the next witness. Martha McGrew's testimony had nothing to do with the Missouri charges against Montea as the crimes he committed against her happened in Kansas. Nevertheless, for the sake of telling the whole story, Martha McGrew relived her nightmare in front of the full courtroom. The prosecution asked specific questions that allowed the jury to hear, in chronological order, the facts of the crime committed against her.

This witness ended her direct examination testimony by telling the jury she gave the police a description of the car and helped them create a composite sketch of the suspects. The details of McGrew's kidnapping and robbery were graphic and sympathetic. Even though, Montea was not on trial for the Kansas crimes against McGrew, the jury incorporated relevant facts for their future deliberation.

The defense attorney started his cross examination exactly where the prosecution left off and inquired about the suspects' description and then led into questions concerning the days following the robbery. He asked McGrew if she ever heard back from the Prairie Village Police after her initial report. McGrew stated they contacted her a few days later and told her they had possibly caught her kidnappers. She added that she later went back down to the station and looked at some pictures to see if she could identify any of them. The defense attorney asked McGrew if she was able to identify any of the men from the pictures. McGrew responded and said she could not positively identify any of the suspects. To the jury, McGrew's answer was significant but, in the end, not case-deciding information, as it did not disconnect Montea from the other crimes for which he was being tried.

The next witness for the state was the forensic doctor who was responsible for overseeing the autopsies of any non-natural deaths in Jackson County, Missouri. Dr. Thomas Young, the medical examiner for Jackson County, Missouri told the jury that his job during an autopsy was to uncover evidence, preserve it, and, in the best-case scenario, accurately determine the cause of death. Young testified that Hick's cause of death was a shotgun wound to the chest. During direct examination, cross examination and redirect examination, Young's additional testimony about shotgun wadding and pellets found in Hick's body, as well as the cocaine found in his blood and heart, was barely interesting to the jury. The only thing that seemed to rouse them during his testimony was the fact that Sonny's chest wound was consistent with being shot at a very close range and the abrasions found on his body were consistent with him being in a struggle before dying.

The next witness the jury heard from was Charles Closson, who was a senior crime scene analyst for the Kansas City Police Department. Closson testified that after the autopsy, he received a vial of blood taken from the victim as well as a small box containing the shell wadding and pellets recovered from Sonny's chest and that he labeled and logged into the proper storage areas.

Next, Detective Benjamin Kenney told the jury that he interviewed Albert Allen after his arrest on November 25. Kenney said Albert Allen told him that the murder weapon was a 12-gauge shotgun. Albert also told Kenney that the shotgun was at a location on Montgall. Kenney then described how they used the SWAT Unit to gain entry and secure the residence for the detectives at 4144 Montgall. Kenney added they found the 12-gauge underneath a couch as well as additional items including several bags of a green leafy substance and a metal crack pipe.

One of the most interesting pieces of testimony in the trial was given by Melissa Thompson, who was a member of the Kansas City Crime Scene Unit and her testimony wasn't something that proved the guilt or innocence of Montea Mitchell but was something that made the jury say "wow." Thompson's testimony was a follow up to her colleague, Kenney, in testifying and elaborating on evidence found at the Montgall residence.

Crime scene technician Thompson went through different things that were collected and then LeVota zeroed her in on the shotgun. When LeVota showed pictures of the gun that she recovered from Montgall that day, those pictures were introduced as evidence and shown to the jury. As the jury reviewed the photos, LeVota continued the questioning and Thompson described and gave specific details about the gun. Thompson testified about its color and its serial number.

LeVota then paused and asked if Thompson knew the brand name of the gun she collected. She said she had analyzed the gun and she did know the maker of the gun and she did know its brand name. In his final question to Thompson, LeVota asked, *What was the brand name of the shotgun?* Thompson responded that the brand name of the gun was "MITCHELL." The gun she collected from the Montgall residence that the prosecution alleged that Montea Mitchell used to murder Sonny Hicks was a **"Mitchell Arms"** shotgun made by the Mitchell Company. *"Interesting."* LeVota said as he finished his examination.

Even though it did not prove guilt or innocence, it was not lost on the jury that the shot gun had the same name as the alleged murderer so the defense attorney was quick to stand up and begin his cross examination. In that cross, Thompson told Pollard that her job was to respond to crime scenes and to search and collect evidence. With that information, Pollard revisited a topic he had discussed with CST Keller the prior day about the

327

non-collection of the screwdriver at the other crime scene. He was looking for Thomson to remind the jury what her coworker had done less than twenty-four hours prior. He reiterated his questions regarding the screwdriver and asked if she or Keller collected the screwdriver and submitted it to the crime lab for analysis. Thompson's answers were the same as her associate and that they had not collected the screwdriver.

LeVota's redirect was again helpful in extinguishing his opposing counsel's motives of trying to confuse the jury concerning the screwdriver when LeVota asked Thompson if she ever collected more evidence than is used. Thompson stated that it was often hard to determine the relevance of items found at a crime scene and indicated that they had originally believed the green truck was involved, but later learned the owner lived right where the truck was parked and that there was no damage to the truck and it was not involved at all. Since the truck was only involved as that Sonny passed by it in his effort to get help after being shot and for no other reason, it seemed most likely that the screwdriver was not involved.

Throughout the remaining day, the jury heard from eight additional witnesses. Kathleen Hentges, a certified latent print examiner for the KCPD who provided testimony that they recovered a partial palm print that belonged to Montea Mitchell in the back seat of the Mercury Topaz. The victim, Michael Walker testified that in addition to his car, cash, and credit cards, the robbers took his green jacket. Walker also stated he was able to identify Albert Allen through a police lineup. Peter Aretakis, a patrol officer for the KCPD, testified he was on duty and took Walker's statement as well as a statement from a witness. He further said he made his report the day the suspects robbed Walker.

Brent Jones, a detective for the Kansas City Robbery Unit testified that he interviewed Albert Allen and made a written report of his statement. Jones stated Albert indicated he was present during the two robberies involving Michael Walker and Penny McGinnis as well as the shooting and attempted robbery of Bradford Thompson. Jones also testified that Albert identified Montea Mitchell as the person holding the gun during the robbery of Michael Walker as well as the shooter of Bradford Thompson at the car wash.

Michael Juhnke, a patrol officer for the KCPD testified that on September 25 he was on duty and dispatched to the Castle Carwash where he observed the victim, Bradford Thompson on his back with apparent gunshot wounds. Juhnke also indicated that he briefly spoke with Thompson at the scene and Thompson advised him that two black males tried to steal his car.

After Officer Juhnke, the jury heard evidence from Bradford Thompson directly who stated the person who shot him had on a skeleton mask and a green jacket. Thompson also added that before the shooting he was left-handed but suffered nerve damage because of his injuries and can no longer use his left hand. The prosecution showed Thompson a mask and he identified it as the same type of mask his shooter wore. Thompson also identified the rifle as the same type used by his shooter.

Greg Van Ryn, a crime scene technician for the KCPD, followed right behind Thompson and told the jury that in addition to blood and clothing samples from the victim, he collected three spent 22 caliber shell casings from the Castle Carwash at approximately 6:45p.m., on September 25. The state presented him with a small package that contained the three casings and Van Ryn verified the shell casings to be the same ones he collected from the crime scene and that they matched the rifle that was recovered from the car in Warrensburg.

On November 8, Penny McGinnis was the last to testify. In vivid detail, she recalled the event for the jury. Penny stated shortly before sunset in Independence, Missouri, three black males

329

were involved and took her champagne colored Oldsmobile Aurora as well as her purse and cell phone against her will. She reported the incident to the Independence police and she received a call from them later that evening advising her they had found her car and asked that she to go to the location and help identify the subjects. She stated it was nearing dark and her carjackers were wearing masks when they stole her car, but she remembered their clothes. Penny drove to Johnson County, Missouri and she was able to recognize them from their attire. Penny, like the other victims that testified, confirmed the mask and gun as the same ones used against her.

By the third day of his trial, Montea Mitchell had exchanged his orange prison jumpsuit for the blue pinstriped suit his lawyer initially suggested he wear. Both Johnson Country Sheriff Deputies O'Connor and Minner testified to the jury and identified Mitchell for the jury and respectively testified their accounts of the capturing and arrests of the defendant and his accomplices. For LeVota, Deputy O'Connor testified the defendant and his accomplice, DonMarr Mitchell were located at a PDX convenience store while they were sitting in the front seats of an Oldsmobile Aurora. He recovered and removed a loaded 22-caliber rifle from the same vehicle, unloaded it, and kept the subjects at bay until his partner apprehended Albert Allen. O'Connor identified the 22-caliber bullets as the same ones he unloaded at the scene.

On cross examination, the defense attorney's goal was to redirect focus away from his client. He spotlighted attention on a cell phone that was involved in the Independence robbery and collected for evidence. Deputy O'Connor told Pollard that he found and took possession of a cell phone from Albert Allen that appeared to belong to Penny McGinnis during a pat down. Pollard ended his cross by having O'Connor reiterate that he took the cell phone from Albert Allen's front pocket not from Montea Mitchell.

Deputy Minner's testimony was similar in that he recounted the event just as O'Connor had but elaborated on the car chase and added the driver wrecked the car and that ultimately ended the pursuit. He also added he found Penny McGinnis' purse in the white Lincoln and held it as well as the cell phone taken from Albert for the Independence Police Department as they both appeared to be involved in the crime that happened in the Independence jurisdiction.

Lori Keller's participation went beyond the murder investigation of Garland Hicks and the KCPD assigned her to work the robbery case of Michael Walker as well. LeVota had called Keller on the stand earlier to talk about the Sonny Hicks crime scene, but to make sure the two crime scenes did not overlap and to avoid confusion, LeVota called CST Keller back to the stand again but this time to talk about her investigation of Michael Walker's Town Car after it was returned from Warrensburg to Kansas City. Keller testified that the KCPD towed Walker's vehicle to their department where she took pictures and processed the vehicle for evidence. She detailed the evidence found inside the vehicle.

The considerable amount of information was presented before lunchtime on that day and it was tiring the jury out. The jury foreman asked the judge for an early break for lunch. The judge told the jury that court would break in 15 minutes, but as Keller started listing the damning evidence, the jury somehow found the necessary patience and all fourteen jurors leaned forward and listened intently to Keller and her record of vital data. Keller told the jury that while looking inside the Lincoln Town Car, she found a green jacket with two boxes of 22-caliber bullets in the pocket, a black skull mask, and Michael Walker's cell phone.

After 15 minutes, the judge asked if the jury still wanted to break early and unanimously they said no. It seems the case and evidence was getting interesting again. LeVota was anxious to get to the next part of the testimony that he described as the "show and tell" of the case. The jury had "heard" of things like a green coat, a cell phone, and others but now it was time to show it to them and introduce them into evidence.

The prosecution had several sealed bags ready for Keller to identify. LeVota handed individual bags to the witness and asked her to tell the jury what was in each bag. To keep the jury's attention, he asked Keller not to remove the items until they were finished identifying the contents of each bag. When she had finished naming each bag, LeVota requested she pull out the evidence. Keller took out and presented for the jury the green jacket, the boxes of bullets, and Michael Walker's cell phone.

To protect his client, the defense attorney's job was to refute or disprove evidence presented and he made a good attempt at that when he asked Keller if the crime lab dusted the boxes of shells for fingerprints. Keller looked at the property report and indicated that the lab did not dust the boxes for fingerprints. He reviewed the same list of evidence with her as she reviewed with LeVota and she highlighted each.

Pollard also revisited the evidence concerning Walker's cell phone and asked her to verify if it was the same phone she pulled from the Lincoln. Keller indicated that it appeared to be the same phone as the packaging had her initials on the attached label used for chain of custody of evidence. The defense attorney then asked her if she sent both Walker's phone and McGinnis' phone to the lab for potential analysis. Keller stated she only sent Walker's phone as she never received McGinnis' phone. The defense finished their cross by restating Keller's answer concerning McGinnis' phone.

Jason Myers, a crime scene technician for the Independence Police Department testified right after Keller. His testimony was brief and he told LeVota that he found and collected two black skull masks from the back seat of the stolen

Aurora. Pollard's cross was brief and to the point as well. He asked Myers if they dusted the masks for prints. Myers stated that actually they did but they recovered no prints from either of the masks collected.

The next witness was interesting to the jury as well. Albert Allen was only eighteen years-old when he entered the courtroom in both hand and leg cuffs. The prosecution knew Albert would be testifying for a considerable amount of time and asked the judge if she could order the restraints removed for the testimonial part of the trial. The court removed the restraints and swore in Albert to testify against Montea.

One of Albert's first questions was if he recognized anyone in the room and Albert pointed to Montea Mitchell at the defense table. For the record, Albert then described Mitchell as the black male with braids wearing the pinstriped suit. He also provided information about how and when he and the defendant met. The prosecutor also asked him if he had ever known the defendant by any other name.   Albert stated he knew the defendant only by the name, Montea Mitchell, but occasionally he had heard others refer to him as "Tay." The defense objected to the State's last question concerning the defendant's name and called it irrelevant. Judge Messina sustained the objection.

For the State, Albert freely narrated the details of the crime spree as the prosecutor kept him on track with specific questions concerning each event. He explained that his friend DonMarr Reneeson and Montea Mitchell and himself went to a friend's house on Montgall. There they bought some drugs and got two guns: a 12-gauge shotgun, and a 22-caliber rifle. Albert added they wanted to steal a car and got the weapons for protection. He went on and stated later that evening, they started the plan to steal a car. All three of them went down to Wabash Street and hid behind some bushes in an area they knew people went to buy drugs. Montea had the 12 gauge shotgun in his hands the whole time. They then just waited for someone who wanted to buy drugs to drive up.

Albert went on to testify that when someone did drive up, DonMarr coaxed the driver out of the car and behind the bushes. Albert further told that Montea attacked the guy and when the guy ran away, Montea went and shot him on the street. When asked what they did after Montea shot the victim. Albert stated they left Sonny there and drove his Mercury Topaz to a gas station, got gas, and decided to rob somebody else. Albert also went on in detail and described his account and involvement in the robbery and kidnapping of Martha McGrew, the robbery of Michael Walker, the attempted robbery and shooting of Bradford Thompson, and robbery of Penny McGinnis.

Albert indicated he talked to many police officers about the crimes. He said that in Warrensburg, the Johnson County Sherriff's Department arrested him, took him to the Warrensburg jail, and interviewed him. Soon after, the Kansas City Police Department, Independence Police as well as the Prairie Village Police all took him to their respective cities individually and interviewed him. Albert said he told each officer the exact same thing as he was telling the jury today.

When asked what he was charged with in this case, he fumbled with all of them. The prosecutor helped him out as Albert listed the charges against him. But Albert added that of all the charges, the police never charged him with the murder of Garland Hicks or the assault of Bradford Thompson. Albert testified that he had accepted a plea agreement with the State that if he testified to the truth he would receive a reduced sentence. Albert admitted he had made a deal to testify in exchange for leniency but he said that didn't change the fact that he was telling the truth.

The defense attorney started his cross examination trying to uncover the witness's true character and general reputation for

334

telling the truth with a small series of questions to set the foundation for Albert's believability. The attorney asked him if he was there to testify against Montea. To that, Albert answered yes. He then asked him if he was there to testify that it was Montea who was holding the gun and Montea who was the mastermind behind the entire crime spree. Albert's answers, in succession, were yes. Pollard then raised the question of whether Albert understood that it was solely the deal to testify that saved him from the murder and assault charges. To that, Albert's answer was also yes.

To Pollard, Albert's extreme charge reduction was related to the credibility of the witness and he wanted to emphasize it to the jury. The defense attorney hoped that Albert's plea agreement would also open the door of doubt for them as well. The defense attorney kept describing Albert's situation as a "deal" and even sarcastically emphasized the word "deal." For the sole benefit of the jury, Pollard used the word "deal" thirty-seven times in his cross examination of Albert.

The next day of trial brought Albert back into the courtroom and just like the first time he entered, the bailiff unlocked his cuffs for the duration of his testimony. Since the defense was so extensive on their cross examination, the scope of the redirect was broad. The prosecutor let Albert retell a full account of the events. Then he dealt with any issues brought up in cross exam. Albert went back to the beginning of his testimony and recalled his statement indicating that after the shooting he got into the Mercury Topaz and left the scene.

The prosecutor then presented Albert a copy of a transcript of a videotaped statement with Eric Dillenkoffer, a Detective for the KCPD, and asked him if he remembered giving the statement and if he could recall what he told the detective what he did immediately following the shooting. Albert stated he did remember giving the statement and that he told the detective he ran away from the scene instead of leaving in the Topaz. Albert stated he lied to the detective because he was afraid and didn't want to put himself in the victim's car. The prosecution also revealed several other inconsistencies in the statements Albert provided for the several police departments of which he had been involved. But most importantly, the prosecutor asked Albert if he had ever changed his stories about who was holding the gun during the homicide of Sonny Hicks and who was holding the gun during the robbery of Michael Walker. Albert stated he originally told the police DonMarr was holding the gun on both crimes but later changed his story to Montea as being the gunman when he actually told the truth. LeVota was trying to show inconsistencies to be able to impeach Albert with his prior statement as a way to show the video to the jury.

In direct examination, the state was unable to show the videotaped interview according to the laws of evidence but after the impeachment of Albert's testimony, it was now allowable to introduce that videotape. The prosecution called KCPD homicide detective Eric Dillenkoffer to the stand. Each juror was presented a copy of the transcript of the videotaped interview between Dillenkoffer and Albert. The video was then broadcast on a large screen television in front of the jury as they got to see the real live, actual interview between detectives and Albert Allen.

The defense attorney tried to cross examine Detective Dillenkoffer and used Albert's conflicting statements to expose the witness's lack of credibility. The veteran detective seemed to have good control over his recollection of the interview he had with the witness more than a year prior. The jury listened as the defense attorney retraced the video statement they had just seen. Dillenkoffer reiterated details of how at first Albert excluded himself of having any contributory participation in the design of the plan to secure weapons and steal a car as well as his denial of knowing what the weapons were going to be used for.

He added that later in the same statement, Albert admitted being at Montgall with Montea and DonMarr when they took the weapons from the house. The defense attorney asked the detective what Albert told him concerning the amount of shots fired while they were at Wabash. Dillenkoffer replied that Albert indicated that three shots were fired. He ended with one last question and asked the detective if, during their investigation at the crime scene, they found any spent 12-gauge shotgun shells. Dillenkoffer stated they did not find any spent shells.

LeVota stood up with one question for the detective. *"Have you found in your experience that the first time you interview a suspect that they are 100% honest?"* Detective Dillenkoffer replied that in most investigations people will lie to avoid responsibility but detectives are trained to keep pushing for answers. The detective said that in an interview, you will see that later a suspect will try to tell part of the truth but also fib on other things trying to keep themselves out of trouble. *"But,"* the detective said, *"to answer your question, most suspects involved in robberies and murders are not completely honest at first or I wouldn't have a job."* The detective also added that his job was to get statements that are relevant to the crime. He knew that it was not that important whether Albert Allen thought there were two shots or three. What was important is that he always said Montea Mitchell was there when Sonny was killed and that Albert said that Montea Mitchell did the shooting.

The state rested their case after Detective Dillenkoffer. The defense called only one witness and that was DonMarr Reneeson. The prosecution had met with DonMarr before the trial and his attorney said DonMarr was not talking at all. So when defense attorney Pollard called DonMarr to the stand in his prison orange and handcuffs, DonMarr only said, *"I refuse to answer and invoke my 5th Amendment Right not to testify."* The defense attorney asked two more questions and got the same answer. The judge inquired of DonMarr if that would be his answer to any questions

337

and DonMarr said yes it would be. The judge excused him from further testimony and the defense rested without Montea Mitchell testifying in his own behalf.

In his closing argument, LeVota told the jury the defendant, Montea Mitchell was aware his conduct against Garland Hicks had a high certainty of causing death and he should take responsibility for his actions. LeVota described the crimes, explained the charges to refresh the jury's understanding, and reviewed the evidence in minute detail to explain exactly why they should find Montea guilty of murder in the first degree. LeVota told the jury Montea's actions were deliberate and premeditated and explained that when Montea took the time to cock the 12-gauge shotgun, that act in itself was premeditation. LeVota told the jury Montea fired the weapon two times on the night Sonny Hicks was murdered on Wabash and three times during the assault of Bradford Thompson at the Castle Car Wash and explained to them that each additional shot was an act of premeditation.

LeVota reminded the jury the police found Montea, two skeleton masks and the 22-caliber rifle used to assault Bradford Thompson in Penny McGinnis' vehicle. He clarified that the Aurora, just like the other vehicles involved in the crime spree, was stolen and there was never any intent to return any of vehicles to their owners. He reminded them about the pictures of Montea at the Kansas ATM as well as the palm print found in the back of the Topaz. His last issue was to remind the jurors that just because the defense attorney focused on a silly issue that no shell casings were found at the murder scene that did not mean Montea Mitchell was innocent of murder. LeVota finished his closing argument by advising the jury that it was their obligation to the victim and to the community to find the defendant guilty.

Defense attorney Pollard told the jury that his client was not guilty of murder and there was no evidence showing he was at the Wabash address on the night of the murder. He said Albert was not believable and he was lying about Montea to lessen his sentence. Pollard pointed out that in a statement given by DonMarr, he stated that Albert was not at Wabash on the night of the murder. He said the inconsistencies in Albert's statements were simply because he was not there. He told the jury the missing shell casings meant only one thing: there was only one shot fired from the shotgun.

He further explained his theory and stated that after the gun was fired, it was never re-cocked and the spent shell was never expelled. Pollard also added that it was not his client that fired the shotgun, but rather DonMarr or Albert who fired it. Pollard then reminded the jury that several other people were inside the Mercury Topaz on the days following the murder and fingerprints were found from some of those people as well. He did what every good defense attorney would do; throw everything at the jury and see what sticks.

A jury must return the verdict as unanimous and that means every person agrees. If only one person would believe some of the defense's irrational theories, it could mean a hung jury and possible mistrial. Montea Mitchell could only be convicted if each and every juror agreed on his guilt. It was a complex case with a complicated timeline and many witnesses. The defense attorney knew he only needed one juror to hang on one of his arguments to derail this prosecution. He hoped he had thrown enough questions at the jury so they might acquit Montea.

Just before Montea's birth, an evil pair of hands killed someone very close to his mother and shortly thereafter, a baby was born into the hands of a thoughtless and drug addicted woman. Montea's mom wrote out the letters that spelled "Murder" on the blameless baby's birth certificate, possibly stealing his innocence and sealing his fate with the very ink that bled from the pen.

It was a fact that this man was born as "Murder Mitchell" as his full given legal name and LeVota knew that he had lived up to that assignment in life. There were several times within the trial where it was possible to introduce that evidence and that issue to the jury. However, LeVota thought it seemed unfair to present that evidence to the jury as he was prosecuting a man for murder who was actually named "Murder. So in an effort to err on the side of fairness and ethical prosecution, the prosecutor did not use the "murder name" issue in their case and did not tell the jury that interesting piece of information.

It would have clearly biased the jury and a prosecutor must live by the oath of only using admissible evidence in a prosecution and no other outside influences in obtaining a conviction. Mark Twain said, *"Always do what is right. It will gratify some people and astonish the rest."* LeVota was confident that keeping Montea's real name out of the case was the right thing to do.

Albert Allen pled guilty and in exchange for his truthful testimony in the case of the *State v. Montea Mitchell* and the *State v. Albert Allen*, he was sentenced to Robbery in the First Degree: 5 years, Robbery in the First Degree: 5 years, and Robbery in the First Degree: 5 years.

DonMarr Reneeson was called as a witness and exerted his 5th Amendment Right and would not speak. However, he later pled guilty and was sentenced to 28 years for Murder in the 2nd degree, 28 years for Armed Criminal Action, 28 years for Robbery in the First Degree, 28 years for Armed Criminal Action: 15 years for Robbery in the First Degree, 15 years for Armed Criminal Action, 28 years for Robbery in the First Degree, and 28 years for Armed Criminal Action..

Montea Mitchell had many counts against him in that courtroom, but it took the twelve jurors only three hours to come back with eight verdicts. Of the most important count, the jury believed that it was Montea who fired the gun that killed "Sonny" Garland Hicks and they recommended a total sentence of eighty years.

In the sentencing phase after the jury had been excused, the defense attorney finally used his client's original given name of "Murder" to draw sympathy from the judge. They also blamed his conviction son his age and poor life consequences. The prosecution argued that the court should follow the recommendation of the jury. Judge Messina considered the arguments as she reviewed what sentence to hand out. On that fateful day for Montea Mitchell, the judge followed the jury's recommendation when she sentenced him to eighty years in prison.   **THE END**

ABOUT THE AUTHOR:

Phil LeVota is a lifelong Missouri resident and has been practicing law for over 20 years with over a decade as a homicide prosecutor in the Jackson County Prosecutor's office hired by now United States Senator Claire McCaskill. LeVota has a long history of political involvement, has been a sought after nationwide public speaker, and was an instructor at the National Advocacy Center in Columbia, South Carolina teaching prosecutors the craft.

Phil is a published columnist for several Midwest publications, has hosted his own award winning radio talk show as well as appearing as a commentator on many television stations. Recently, Phil won an Emmy Award from the National Association of Television Arts & Sciences for his work as a host and producer of the critically acclaimed television program *"The Power of KC"* showcasing outstanding people and places. His first true love is trial work and defending the rights of people which he continues to do to this day.

Twitter: @Phillevota
Facebook: Phil LeVota
E-mail: plevota@yahoo.com
www.PhilLeVota.com

Made in the USA
San Bernardino, CA
07 March 2016